£30

ART AND THE SEAFARER

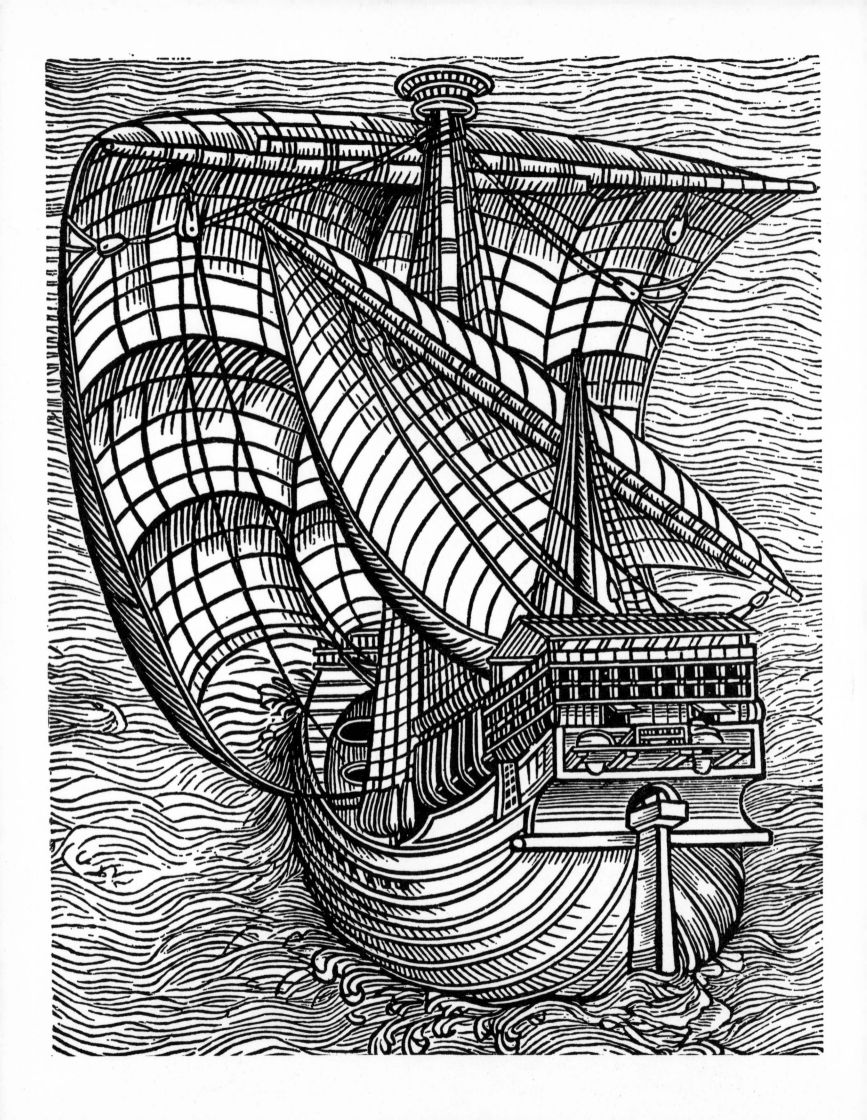

ART AND THE SEAFARER

A Historical Survey of the Arts and Crafts of Sailors and Shipwrights

With contributions by Edward H. H. Archibald, Jules van Beylen, Olle Cederlöf, G. B. Rubin de Cervin, P. Devambez, Henning Henningsen, Marcel B. Keezer, Svein Molaug, C. Nooteboom, Gert Schlechtriem, Hans Soop, Gerhard Timmermann, Arthur L. Tucker, E. Tucker, Jacques Vandier, Alfred E. Weightman and Helen L. Winslow.

General Editor Hans Jürgen Hansen

Translated by James and Inge Moore

FABER AND FABER
24 RUSSELL SQUARE
LONDON

First published in this translation in MCMLXVIII
by Faber and Faber Limited,
24 Russell Square, London W.C.1.

Originally published by
Gerhard Stalling Verlag, Oldenburg and Hamburg, Germany (Federal Republic)
as *Kunstgeschichte der Seefahrt: Kunst und Kunsthandwerk der Seeleute und Schiffbauer*

© Gerhard Stalling Verlag, Oldenburg and Hamburg, Germany (Federal Republic), 1966

This translation © Faber and Faber Limited, London, 1968

Printed in Germany

Bound in Great Britain

Contents

Editor's Acknowledgements

A book like this, which deals with so many different aspects of a subject, could never have been produced by a single author but has called for the co-operation of a large number of experts, each with an intimate knowledge of his particular subject. The editor wishes to thank all those authors who have made contributions and who, by writing them in the necessary form, have made his task of editing the book in a clear and uniform manner so much easier.

The following authors have contributed: Gerhard Timmermann, VDI., STG., formerly head of the maritime section of the Altonaer Museum and head of the technical committee on 'The History of Shipbuilding' of the Schiffbautechnische Gesellschaft in Hamburg, wrote the chapter 'The Architecture of the Ship'; Dr. C. Nooteboom, formerly Director of the Maritiem Museum 'Prins Hendrik' in Rotterdam, wrote the chapter on 'Art in Shipbuilding Outside Western Culture'; G. B. Baron Rubin de Cervin, Director of the Museo Storico Navale in Venice, wrote the chapter on 'Votive Pictures of Ships'; Jules van Beylen, Director of the Nationaal Scheepvaart Museum in Antwerp, was responsible for the chapter 'Glass Paintings of Ships'; Marcel B. Keezer, art dealer and secretary of the Stichting Oude Kunst- en Antikbeurs in Delft, contributed the chapter 'Maritime Objets d'Art and Antiques'. In the chapter 'Art in Early Shipbuilding' the paragraphs on Egyptian shipbuilding were contributed in the main by Jacques Vandier, chief curator of the Département des Antiquités égyptiennes de la Musée du Louvre; those on Graeco-Roman shipbuilding by P. Devambez, chief curator of the Département des Antiquités grecques et romaines of the same museum. They are based on texts by these two authors in the catalogue of the 1965 exhibition 'Trois Millénaires d'Art et de Marine' in Paris, publication of which is by permission of the exhibition committee. The remainder of the chapter was written by the editor. The text of the chapter 'Woodcarving on Ships' was contributed mainly by Alfred E. Weightman, science lecturer on board the training ship *Arethusa* in Rochester, Kent, and was supplemented by a contribution by Arthur L. Tucker of the National Maritime Museum at Greenwich and Mrs. E. Tucker. The passages on ornamentation of Renaissance and Baroque ships especially on the decorations of the *Vasa* and their iconographic and historical background, were written by Hans Soop, curator of the Statens Sjöhistoriska Museum, Wasavarvet, Stockholm, while further information, mainly on Johan Törnström, was provided by Museintendent Olle Cederlöf, Director of the Marinmuseum at Karlskrona. The chapter 'Ship Portraiture' is by the editor, with large parts contributed by other authors: the section on British ship portraits was written by Edward H. H. Archibald, curator of oil paintings at the National Maritime Museum at Greenwich, the passages on Danish portraits by Dr. Henning Henningsen, Director of the Handels- og Söfartsmuseet paa Kronborg in Helsingör, those on Norwegian portraits by Svein Molaug, Director of the Norsk Sjöfartsmuseum in Oslo, and those on German portraits by Gert Schlechtriem, Director of the Morgenstern-Museum in Bremerhaven. Jules van Beylen contributed the information on Henry Mohrmann. The chapter 'Seamen's Crafts' is by Gerhard Timmermann, supplemented by a contribution on Scrimshaw by Helen L. Winslow, publication of which is by permission of the Historical Society at Nantucket, Massachusetts.

In addition to the assistance received from these authors and from the museums and collectors listed elsewhere, the editor has been given valuable hints and recommendations, mainly verbally, and permission to take and reproduce photographs by the following people: Hans Behrens, formerly Director of the Aabenraa Museum at Apenrade; Dr. Friedrich Carstens, Director of the Schiffahrtsmuseum der Oldenburgischen Weserhäfen at Brake; G. A. Cox, Director of the Nederlandsch Historisch Scheepvaart Museum in Amsterdam; Jean Ducros of the Ministère des Armées (Marine) in Paris; Admiral Julio F. Guillen-Tato, Director of the Museo Naval in Madrid; Dr. Klaus Grimm in Hamburg; Dr. Herre Halbertsma, Director of the Fries Scheepvaartmuseum at Sneek; Ralph Hannemann, Director of the Marine Museum of the Seaman's Church Institute in New York; Holger Jacobsen, Director of the Aabenraa Museum at Apenrade; Capitaine de Frégate Javault, Deputy Director of the Musée de la Marine in Paris; Mrs. Jacqueline Kennedy in New York; Dr. W. Kloos, Director of the Focke-Museum in Bremen; Lars-Ake Kvarning, curator of the Statens Sjöhistoriska Museum, Wasavarvet, Stockholm; B. C. W. Lap, curator of the Maritiem Museum 'Prins Hendrik' in Rotterdam; Walter Lüden at Wyk auf Föhr; Dr. Lundström, Director of the Statens Sjöhistoriska Museum in Stockholm; José Maria Martinez-Hidalgo y Téran, Director of the Museo Marítimo in Barcelona; Dr. Herbert Marwitz of the Archaeological Institute at the University of Munich; Hermann Matzen, Director of the Heider Heimatmuseum at Heide; Commander W. E. May, Deputy Director of the National Maritime Museum at Greenwich; Dr. Jürgen Meyer,

Custodian of the Altonaer Museum in Hamburg; Professor Dr. Hans-Wolfgang Müller, Director of the Institute of Egyptology at the University of Munich; Dr. Bredo von Munthe af Morgenstierne, Director of the Orlogsmuseet in Copenhagen; W. Ripley Nelson, V.P., Chairman of the Whaling Museum of the Nantucket Historical Association at Nantucket; Kommendörkapten Stig Notini, Director of the Sjöfartsmuseet in Gothenburg; Kapten Bengt Ohrelius of the Statens Sjöhistoriska Museum, Wasavarvet, Stockholm; J. B. von Overeem, Director of the Maritiem Museum 'Prins Hendrik' in Rotterdam; Philip F. Purrington, curator of the Whaling Museum of the Old Dartmouth Historical Society at New Bedford; Ellen Redlefsen, Director of the Städtische Museum at Flensburg; Bertram Rickmers of the Rickmers Werft in Bremerhaven; Wolfgang Schöningh, formerly Director of the Ostfriesische Landesmuseum at Emden; Dr. Hans Sints, Director of the Schloss- und Heimatmuseum at Jever; S. Arthur Svensson, chief editor of Allhems Forlag, Malmö; Intendent Sundström of the Statens Sjöhistoriska Museum in Stockholm; J. Teensma, curator of the Noordelijk Scheepvaart Museum at Groningen; Dr. Helmuth Thomsen, chief curator of the Museum für Hamburgische Geschichte in Hamburg; Erik Vea, curator of the Norsk Sjöfartsmuseum in Oslo; Pater Vicente Vela-Marqueta, Deputy Director of the Museo Naval in Madrid; Capitaine de Vaisseau Vichot, Director of the Musée de la Marine in Paris; Dr. Steffen Wenig, of the Egyptian section of the Staatlichen Museen, Berlin; Professor Dr. Gerhard Wietek, Director of the Altonaer Museum in Hamburg; Dr. Wirtgen, Director of the Heimatmuseum at Stade; Dr. Rudolf Zöllner, curator of the Städtische Museum at Flensburg.

Thanks are due to the following persons and institutions for photographs and other illustrations for the reproductions in this book (where they have come from published sources these are indicated in brackets and referred to in detail in the bibliography): Allhems Forlag, Malmö (13*, 15, 18, 22, 29, 32, 41, 61, 77, 96a, d, 113, 200, 285, 291); Altonaer Museum, Hamburg (21a, b, 58d, 88); Archaeological Institute, Munich (28a); Bergens Sjöfartsmuseum, Bergen (76); Jules van Beylen, Antwerp (237a, b, 239b–f, 246a–e, 247a–f, 248a–g, 253a, b, 254a–f, 255a–f, 256a, b); Geoffrey Bibby (*The Testimony of the Spade*, 96b, c, 108); M. V. Brewington (*Ship Carvers of North America*, 120b); C. B. Baron Rubin de Cervin, Venice (28d, 159, 168c, d, 287); M. Chuzeville, Paris (28b, 79c, d); Deutsches Museum, Munich (166c, 167d); Ferruzzi, Venice (53c, 56b, 58b, 102a, b, 109a, b, 111a, 112, 113, 134a, b, 135b, 141, 168b, 178a, b, 179a, b, 180a–f, 181, 183, 185a–e, 186a, b, 187a, 188a–f, 189, 194c, 198b, 206a, 226f, 234b, 268c, e, 275b); Antonio Iniesta Garcia, Barcelona (27, 126, 278a); John W. Griffiths (*Marine and Naval Architecture*, 120a, 121,

123); Dr. Klaus Grimm, Hamburg (40 b, d, 47 a, 59 a, b, 153, 154 b, 166 e, k); Hans Jürgen Hansen, München-Gräfelfing (9, 26, 69, 85, 96 e, 143 a, c, d, 197, 198, 199 a–d, 278 b); Heider Heimatmuseum, Heide (156 a); Hirmer-Verlag, Munich (10, 19 a); Historia-Photo, Bad Sachsa (2, 23, 24 b, 293); Jacqueline Kennedy, New York (277 e); Ralph Kleinhempel, Hamburg (53 f); Dr. S. Kooyman, Leiden (176 d, e); August Köster (*Das antike Seewesen*, 77 b, 82, 86 e, f, 86 a–d, 87 a, b, 93, 95, 106, 107); Walter Lüden, Wyk auf Föhr (25 a–d, 29, 30, 31, 33, 34 a–f, 35, 36/37, 38 b, 39, 40 a, c, 45 a, b, 46 b, 47 c, d, 48, 53 a, b, d, e, 54 a–d, 55, 56 a, d, e, 58 c, 59 c, 66, 67, 68 b, c, d, 73, 74, 83, 84 a–c, 97, 98 c, d, 99, 100 a, b, 101, 102 c–f, 103 a–g, i, 104 a–d, 110 b–f, 111 b, c, e, 117 a, b, 118 a–g, 127 a–f, 128 a, b, 135 a, 136, 142 a, b, 144 a–c, 146 a–d, 147 a, d, 148, 154 a, 155 a, b, 156 e–h, 163, 164, 165, 167 c, 173, 187 b, 193, 194 a, b, e, f, 195 a–f, 196 a–d, 198 c, 207 a, b, 208 a–f, 216 a, b, 217 a, b, 220 a, b, 226 a–e, 233 a–d, 234 a, c–e, 236 a, b, 240, 248 h, 257, 258 a–f, 259 a, c, d, 260 a–d, 265 a–j, 266, 267 a, b, 268 a, b, 273 d, e, 274 a–d, 275 a, 276 b, 277 a–d, 279 a–g, 280); Marine Historical Association, Mystic (231 a, b); Marine Museum of the Seaman's Church Institute New York (259 e); Marine Research Society, Salem (42, 43); Marinmuseet och Modellkammaren, Karlskrona (147 b, c); Morgenstern-Museum, Bremerhaven (245); Musée de Beyrouth, Beirut (28 c); Musée de la Marine, Paris (46 d, 56 c, 57, 58 e, f, 143 b, 273 a); Museum voor Land- en Volkenkunde, Rotterdam (168 a, 174 a–c, 175 a, 176 a); Nantucket Historical Association (Nantucket), (206 b, 276 a, 277 d, f); Nationaal Scheepvaart Museum, Antwerp (171, 166 i, 167 j); National Maritime Museum, Greenwich (38 a, 47 d, 60, 115 a, b, 116 a, b, 214 a–c, 215, 218 a–h, 219 a, b); Old Dartmouth Historical Society, Whaling Museum, New Bedford (20, 145 c, d, 166 g, l, 192, 201, 225, 227, 228 a, f, 261, 238 b, 273 b, c); Rickmers Werft, Bremerhaven (205, 213, 235); Rijksmuseum, Amsterdam (268 d); Rijksmuseum voor Volkenkunde, Leiden (175 b, c, 176 b, c, 177); Hannes Rosenberg, München-Gräfelfing (19 b, 239 a, 259 b); Schloss- und Heimatmuseum, Jever (103 h); Town Archives, Stade (172, 183, 194 d, 223, 238 a, 271, 272); Statens Sjöhistoriska Museum, Wasavarvet, Stockholm (89, 90 a, b, 91 a–c, 92, 98 a, b, 110 a, 111 d, 113, 119); Ullstein-Bilderdienst, Berlin (289); United States Naval Academy, Annapolis (46 a, 58 a); Universitets Oldtidsamling, Oslo (65, 68 a, b); Heimatmuseum Vegesack, Bremen (228 e). The picture on p. 2 is an enlarged detail of a woodcut by Erhard Reuwich from Breydenbach's *Peregrinatus in Terram Sanctam*, Mainz 1486.

Left: Model of a Nile boat from the tomb of Tutankhamen, about 1350 B. C., Ca.

Introduction

The ship is the oldest means of transport known to man, and the history of shipbuilding goes back very nearly as far as the history of domestic architecture, which began with the building of the first primitive hut. Water-borne craft existed before man learnt how to tame beasts of burden and by riding on their backs make faster and more extensive journeys than his own muscles would allow, and long before the wheel and the cart were invented. At first they were rafts made of reeds or brushwood, or floating tree-trunks on which men sat astride, using primitive paddles to drive them along. Subsequent development led to hollowing out the tree-trunks so that they could sit inside and cross stretches of water without so much as getting their feet wet.

Technically, then, shipbuilding was a woodworking process right from its earliest beginnings, and it remained so until iron began to take over in the 19th century. We can say that 'naval architecture' was architecture in wood, and like every type of architecture it had technical and constructional aspects as well as artistic and aesthetic ones. This suggests the use of the term 'naval architecture' in a sense similar to that of such accepted terms as 'temple architecture' or 'palace architecture'. Consequently, when the terms 'naval architecture' or 'shipbuilding' are used in the context of this book their meaning is parallel to the other two, stressing the artistic rather than the purely constructional aspects.

So far, except in a few isolated instances, the general study of the arts, numerous as its specialized branches may be, has hardly acknowledged the ship as an object worthy of investigation. It is impossible to say exactly why this should be so, but the main reason may simply be the lack of visual material, of objects for study. Ships have never grown old. Few of them have ever survived one or two generations, and much more often they have been shipwrecked long before that. If wood is constantly exposed to water it quickly rots, even if it is carefully looked after.

Danzig Cog, 1400

So whoever wants to study the art of shipbuilding as a historical science finds himself short of illustrative material to start with. Because we have pyramids, ruined temples, and treasures found in the tombs of pharaohs to look at, it is easy to study Egyptian art and architecture. Lecturing on Gothic cathedrals is no problem because an abundant number of representative examples have been preserved. The excavation of Pompeii aroused widespread interest in Roman art; both Winkelmann's research and a knowledge of the art of antiquity would be unthinkable without the availability of adequate study material.

But when it comes to ships, that is original, historical vessels, hardly anything has been handed down to us. Is it fair to say then that a recorded history of the art of shipbuilding does not exist because of the lack of the necessary material for research? Investigation of this question, and the encouraging discovery that there is sufficient evidence (though largely of a secondary nature) to make research into this ancient and little known but extremely interesting branch of art appear worthwhile, gave rise to the publication of this book.

What does the available material consist of? The secondary evidence consists of graphic representations from which the historical evolution of the ship can be deduced: prehistoric rock paintings, paintings of Nile boats on the walls of the royal tombs of ancient Egypt, paintings on Greek vases, early medieval miniatures showing ships, lines and building plans of ships of the Renaissance and Baroque periods, marine paintings and drawings of the 17th and 18th centuries, the naïve 'ship's portraits' popular at a later period, and even early photographs of sailing ships of the last century. There are, furthermore, some contemporary models of vessels which have themselves long since perished.

There is also some primary evidence still available, although it is very scattered and not always easy to find. It consists of a few North European ocean-going ships from the first centuries before and after Christ, as well as from the Viking era, which were discovered during excavations; ships that sank a long time ago and have only been salvaged in recent years, like the 14th-century Bremen cog which sank in the Weser, and the *Vasa*, which went down in Stockholm harbour in 1628; some relatively recent historic ships, which have been preserved, like Nelson's *Victory* at Portsmouth, the whaler *Charles W. Morgan*, built in 1841 and now lying at Mystic, and the sailing ship *Cutty Sark* at Greenwich; and finally remains of old ships and fragments of their ornamentation which, when collected together, give an impression, if not a complete record, of the historical development of ships and their ornamental and artistic splendour. Wood carvings, especially, played an important role in shipbuilding and were often of amazing artistic quality.

13

Primary and secondary evidence of this kind form the substance of this book. It does not deal with the so-called classical marine paintings like those of the 17th-century Dutch school of marine painters, with which anyone interested in ships is familiar and which have always had a place in the history of art, or rather the history of painting. These painters, as well as their French and English contemporaries, concentrated mainly on seascapes with ships as accessories. Only in a few rare instances did they portray ships as such, and these, too, have long been recorded in the history of art (though not necessarily as illustrations of the art of shipbuilding). The same is true of a large part of the secondary evidence.

We have devoted a lot of space to the specialized field of ship portraiture, an internationally popular kind of amateur painting which flourished from the middle of the 18th century onwards and is in many ways related to the very much older practice of painting ships on votive tablets. Particular attention has been paid in this book to the latter, as well as to art in ancient and non-Western shipbuilding. We have included ship portraiture not only because it illustrates so clearly the architectonic history of ships in the last two hundred years, but above all because as far as we know no survey has even been published of this branch of art, and our object in this book would certainly be served by one. Not least, we have included them because of the naïve artistic charm of these pictures, especially of the glass paintings. Many of them were painted by seamen themselves and as such are the products of a purely maritime folk art. For the same reasons it has been both logical and interesting to include examples from the many different forms of seamen's crafts.

None of the objects presented in this book – providing in their entirety the material for a history of maritime art – are to be found in art or craft museums. Some are in the maritime museums of a few seafaring nations. Without exception these museums have only been built during the last few decades and concentrate primarily on the technical aspects of ships. A few are in the possession of long-established shipping firms and shipyards, or in maritime sections of local history museums in large ports as well as in local history museums of moderate-sized ports with important traditions.

We have attempted to obtain details and illustrations of all the objects that are of interest in connection with this work; and we have inspected many of them personally and had them photographed especially for this book. In this task we have been backed by the experience and active co-operation of experts of many countries, whose assistance was enlisted in many cases in the course of personal discussions. They readily put their knowledge at our disposal. The editor's special thanks go to them, for although the idea of this publication was his, he could never have hoped to realize it by himself. Thanks are equally due to the publishers in various countries who, by arranging

14

J. Bureus, 1626

publication of this work in their own language, made it possible to have a large international edition, without which the cost of producing a book with such lavish illustrations and splendid presentation would have been excessive.

The result of our efforts is intended to provide no more or less than a basic introduction to the subject and inspire more intensive research into the history of art in shipbuilding throughout the world. In order for this inspiration to be fruitful we have had to provide convincing visual aids; and for this reason great stress has had to be laid on the number of illustrations and the quality of reproduction. It has been more important to give prominence to a few characteristic chapters of an art history of shipbuilding than to try and give a complete and balanced critical survey. This will only be possible in the future and will result from further detailed research by many individuals.

We hope that this book will give them a stimulating basis on which to work, but that it will also give pleasure to all lovers of ships, experts and laymen alike. Although looking at ships from an artistic and scientific point of view calls for technical objectivity, this does not mean one need be insensitive to the strange attraction of the sea, to that peculiar romantic mixture of homesickness and sea fever with which everyone who has ever sailed the Seven Seas has at some time or other been afflicted.

Island of Amrum, July 1966   Hans Jürgen Hansen

The Architecture of the Ship
History and Design of Water-borne Craft

Shipbuilding, which means the construction of vessels which are to serve as water-borne vehicles, poses technical, scientific, political, economic and sociological problems; but at the same time aesthetic and military considerations can play a considerable role.

The shipbuilder must adhere to certain principles of physics; otherwise his work is, literally, doomed from the start. Shipbuilding calls for specialized craftsmanship in the handling of the materials, and the vessel must be so built that it can fulfil its particular purpose with maximum economy, and in addition offer the best possible living conditions for the crew and, where applicable, the passengers. These are the problems which characterize the nature of our vessel.

Man has always felt the need to make articles of everyday use not only practical but also, as far as possible, aesthetically pleasing and beautiful. It would be enough to make them merely functional, but by giving them visual appeal they are lifted above their immediate practical purpose and more or less made into works of art.

When considering the ship historically and aesthetically, one is inevitably forced into comparisons with domestic architecture. The house, too, is first of all a functional structure whose main purpose is to afford shelter to man in every possible way. It was probably in the design of religious edifices that aesthetic aspects first played a noticeable role over and above the considerations of practical necessity. Later this trend developed both in other public buildings and in the houses of the ruling classes and the rich, who could afford the luxury of a building either modelled on a temple or made more attractive in some other way. This is how palaces, castles and other ostentatious buildings came to be erected amid ordinary dwellings.

Art as a science strives to compare the different periods and to point out their peculiarities, their aesthetic laws – in short their style. It is not only the building itself which is of interest but also the 'artist', its creator. In other words the building represents the architectural achievement of a certain person, a certain era, a whole country, or perhaps only a small region. A building was frequently erected for its own sake or to the glory of God (like temples and cathedrals). On the other hand, many domestic buildings, like, for instance, farmhouses, fall into the category of folk art as far as their aesthetic appeal is concerned because they are clearly purpose-built, and it is merely as a result of their proportions, or a modest amount of ornamentation, or simply their colourful rendering that they appear pleasing.

As far as pleasant design and the human need for decoration are concerned, ship-building, too, can be art. In classifying it as such we must differentiate between the basic shape and the ornamentation added to it. One can search in vain throughout the whole of literature for a comprehensive presentation of the history of art in ship-building. The reason for this is that the necessary research is beset by two difficulties: to start with, there is only very little material that can be drawn from authentic sources. Among them we can number excavations of whole ships or parts large and numerous enough to enable the original ship to be reconstructed with a minimum of guesswork. Technical drawings have been available since the Renaissance and technically correct models since the Baroque period, and a very small number of actual ships from the past have been preserved in museums or at other exhibition sites. The large numbers of pictures of ships on which we can draw must be used with the utmost caution for judging what ships of the past looked like, especially when it comes to considering the ship as a 'work of art'. After all, the artist is hardly ever obliged to make his paintings faithful reproductions of the originals, and he is quite at liberty to alter the shapes of ships or add embellishments as he likes. The same goes for models of ships and for receptacles in the form of ships which are only intended as ornaments or symbols (votive ships). Secondly it is by no means easy for a layman without a specialized knowledge of naval architecture – and even an art historian must be regarded as such – to appreciate the aesthetic appeal of a ship.

The expert differentiates between the underwater body of the ship, which is the 'live' part, and the part of the hull above the water, which could be said to be 'dead'. Whether or not a vessel looks good depends only on the latter. The shape of the underwater body is determined solely by the requirements imposed by the laws of physics, and the builder is bound by laws of nature which he must not violate. However, the boundary between the underwater part of the hull and that which projects above the water is not marked by a fixed line, say the waterline, but it changes according to the degree to which the ship is loaded. The volume of the hull above the water is determined by considerations of safety. Besides, this line is only straight when the hull lies motionless in calm waters. In a seaway and when the ship is under way it is constantly broken by wave motion, which is partly due to impact waves created by the hull itself as it moves through the water. Furthermore, one must take into consideration the fact that during the construction of the vessel the shipbuilder never sees it as it will look later in the water. Aesthetic problems are much more difficult for him to solve than they are for the architect ashore, because he has to satisfy the need for beauty in the part of the hull above the water and the need for functional design in the underwater body. The development of the lines which delimit the predominantly curved hull must meet both requirements. If the shipwright shapes the hull on the stocks, everything depends on the level from which he looks at it, because the boundary curves are seen in different perspectives according to the distance of the eye from the ship and its height above the keel. When designing a ship by means of a 'lines drawing' (also known as a 'sheer-draught'), the outer dimensions of the hull only are drawn up by projection. Perspective drawings are not usual in shipbuilding except for modern welded steel construction. Such plans of ships were only drawn in 1768 by the Anglo-Swedish master shipwright F. H. af Chapman in his illustrated work *Architectura Navalis Mercatoria*.

It is probably on account of these difficulties that the arts have so far been discouraged from undertaking research into the history of art in shipbuilding, so that even J. M. Ritz confines himself to the remark that the ship, in general, is a purpose-built structure but can sometimes be a product of folk art. The shipbuilder, though, likes to talk of the *art* of shipbuilding; and not without justification, for research into the natural sciences, which have managed – since the introduction of iron as a building material and engines as means of propulsion – to bring their influence to bear on this ancient craft, did not begin until approximately two hundred and fifty years ago. Before this, an eye for beautiful lines and experience gained from empirical observation of the ship in the water played the most important part in designing a hull – and this is still so today in the case of small boat design. It did not matter whether the hull was built *ex tempore* on the stocks, as it was as far back as the Bronze Age, or whether a wooden model was carved, the lines of which were then transferred to paper, the ship being built from this drawing. Before flexible laths and curved timbers came into use, the arc of a circle was frequently used to determine the sections of ships. By this method the builder becomes, so to speak, involved in a conflict between aesthetic appeal and functional design. The problem is solved in favour of aesthetic appeal when it comes to the forward and after ends of the ship and the upper edge, the sheer line.

Whereas Egyptian ships (3000 to 1500 B. C.)∗ had long, slender hulls (similar in shape to but on a larger scale than the vessels made by the man who hewed out the kneading troughs) without stem- and stern-posts or with them added merely as

∗ See Notes

Rock carving from Hammer, Norway

Right: a, Dionysus at sea in a sailing boat with stem and stern ornamentation, painting inside a cup by Exekias, 2nd half of 6th century B. C., Ma; b, Isis as patron goddess of sailing ships on a Mediterranean vessel. Reserve side of Imperial Roman coin, Bl.

18

a

b

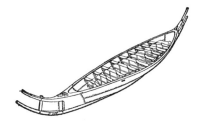

The Hjortspring Boat, about 400 B. C.

Dürer school, about

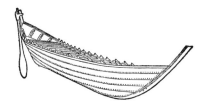

The Nydam Boat, about 400 A. D.

Left: Sperm whale crushing a boat, water-colour by a seaman, about 1840, Nb.

embellishments (around 1500 B. C.), ships indigenous to the Atlantic had stem- and stern-posts which together with the keel formed a spine, an integral part of the hull. This method of construction may have been derived from the Bronze Age log canoe. It is interesting to note that illustrations of Greek ships with rams at the stem bear a distinct resemblance to these boats. The Greek ship had a round stern, though, and the similarity in the shape of the stem, too, is only superficial, for in the Bronze Age boats, which were propelled by oars, the stem-post served to facilitate beaching on the rocky coasts of Scandinavia. While the Greek ships, some of them with several banks of oars, had an overall length of about 78 ft., the Bronze Age boats were only about 40 ft. long. Their stem-posts were topped by fearful dragon heads or the heads of other animals. The Greeks, on the other hand, had animal heads with large glaring eyes painted on their battering-rams, the aim being the same – namely, to frighten and terrify the enemy. In this way the ship was given a personality. Both types had in common their long, slim hull which was essential for high speeds. The rounded stern of the Greek trireme was shaped like a shell and swept forward to protect the officers and captain from the wind and sea and from enemy attacks. Although all of these larger ships had a mast and sails, they were really rowing boats with auxiliary sails, because their sail area was too small to make them into proper sailing vessels. Besides, their freeboard – that is, the part of the hull above the water – was too low because of the oars.

All we know about Bronze Age and Greek ships derives from illustrations of them, but in all probability they are correct. Pictures of Bronze Age ships in Swedish rock paintings have been proved authentic by the discovery of the Hjortspring boat, a vessel from the Early Iron Age (La Tène), about 400 B. C., on the island of Alsen.

The Nydam Noor find, originating from approximately 400 A. D., represents a typical rowing boat of the kind the Angles and Saxons may have used for their voyages across to England under their leaders Hengist and Horsa. This boat has parabolic sections and was very fine fore and aft, terminating in raked stem- and stern-posts with which, going ahead or astern, it could slice through the waves and ride over them. This vessel, too, had a very low freeboard. It was built of five broad planks on either side which were of equal width, and the way in which they were bent round to meet the stem- and stern-posts resulted in a beautifully upswept sheer line. Since these boats were clinker built (that is, the planks were not fastened edge to edge but over-lapped at the edges like roof tiles, so that their run was clearly marked) the curve of the sheer was accentuated by the sweep of the planking. It was this sweep into the stem and stern and the pronounced sheer of the gunwale which inspired the Germanic shipbuilders to curve the stem- and stern-posts farther and farther back to increase upper beam of the cove overhung aft was also equal to the height of the bulwark. That means that the deck of the stern-castle was bigger by that much than the part of the main deck lying immediately beneath it. Already in the 15th century this stern-castle deck reached as far forward as the mast and today it is called the half deck. Timbotta's drawing corresponds with a votive ship's model which is now in Rotterdam and is said to have come from Mataró; both depict a small hut with a gabled roof, the gable facing fore and aft. A bulwark on either side as well as aft provides some shelter against wind and weather, and a rail forward guards against anyone falling off.

a   b

   In the years of the Renaissance period under consideration here, a significant technical revolution took place. Timbotta's drawing and the model from Mataró represent sailing ships with only one mast and one sail. Around the middle of the 15th century, to which these two pieces of evidence are ascribed, the earliest copper engravings depicting ships made their appearance, executed by a master signing himself W A. They show hulls of the kind described, with slight modifications here and there, but differing from the former by being rigged with three masts. Presumably the single-masters differed in length from the three-masters and for this reason made the setting of several sails necessary.

   Mast, rigging and sails, strictly speaking, are meant merely to serve the propulsion of the ship, and questions of beauty apparently play no part. Since an inexpertly rigged and canvassed ship may be disabled or shipwrecked, considerations of aesthetics are strictly of secondary importance. Nevertheless, a sailing ship with its sails 'full and by' and swelled out by the breeze is a majestic and beautiful sight. But how often has anyone been able to watch a ship under full sail from the shore? The sailing ships of

Right: Ship models; a, Church ship from Mataró, Spain, about 1450, Rm; b, Staatenjacht (state yacht), 17th century, Rm; c, Warship, Lübeck, about 1650, Lb; d, 'De Grote Jung', 1779, Bt.
Page 26: After part of a model of a Flemish galleon, 1593, Mn.

24

a

b

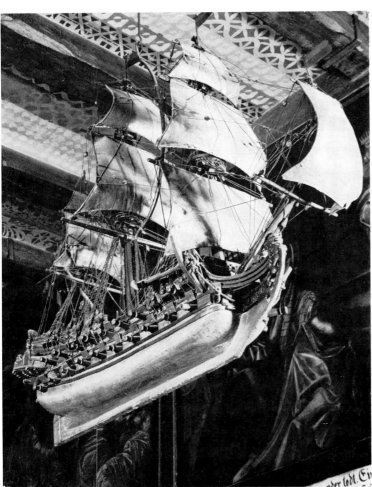
c

d

a

b

c

d

the past, surging along in all their splendour or battling against the elements in a storm, are known to us only from paintings, either the classical marine paintings or the rather less accomplished ship portraits. It is not too difficult, though, to get near one of the few remaining sailing ships when they are in harbour and admire the intricacy of their standing and running rigging and wonder what the many different parts are used for. The arrangement of the rigging, which was entirely empirical and determined by the captain more often than the shipbuilder, was little (if at all) influenced by questions of beauty. It is obvious, though, that the position and rake of the masts and the height of the yards influence the appearance of the ship as a whole quite considerably. In fact, people had got so used to the sight of rigging that they would not part with it on the first of the big steamships and pretended that it was essential for reasons of safety. It is certainly true to say that a sailing ship without sails and rigging looks like a plucked bird, no matter how beautiful the hull may be. Besides, the rig characterizes the type of ship.

In the Schlüsselfeld Gold Cup at the Germanisches Nationalmuseum in Nürnberg we have an attractive model of a Renaissance sailing ship, even if its proportions are not entirely correct technically. In the 15th century fire-arms began to have an influence on shipbuilding. It was then, especially towards the end of the century when the French master shipwright Descharges began to build ships with gun ports, that the first real warships were built. A separate deck beneath the main deck was provided to take a row of guns, and was called the gun deck. It is not improbable that there was some connection between this innovation and another change: that of replacing the previously rounded stern by a flat surface called the 'transom'. The stern being no longer round it was deprived of any special reinforcing timbers, so the transom had to be not only flat but strong and watertight. This was achieved by several layers of planking, which also made it possible to cut gun ports into the transom and use them to shake off pursuers. It goes without saying that this change in the shape of the afterbody of ships decisively influenced their looks. The hull which was otherwise rounded and curved was suddenly cut off by a sharp edge which clearly showed off the after section of the hull.

In two copper engravings by the Flemish master W A the ships portrayed are named as types. One is a *barze*, the other a *kraeck*. The latter in particular deserves our interest, since the Flemish word *kraeck* corresponds to the Spanish *carrack*, a much quoted type in naval literature. In the 16th century this nomenclature was used for ships of an entirely different type, which Pieter Brueghel the Elder painted in great detail. These ships carried an enormous after-castle over the transom, so large that they must make the modern shipbuilder wonder how much stability the hulls had. Not

Olaus Magnus, 1539

Page 27: Catalan xebec, 18th-century votive ship, Bc.
Left: a, The Victory of Samothrace on her pedestal shaped like a ship with outriggers for oars on either side, about 180 B. C., Pl; b, Clay model of Greek ship, Pl; c, Bronze votive ship, about 122 B.C., Be; d, Stone sculpture of ship on the fountain near the church of Santa Maria in Domenica o alla navicella in Rome, about 1 A. D.

29

only did they have after-castles, they also had mighty forecastles with threatening guns protruding from their ports. One must suspect Brueghel of a certain amount of exaggeration, for the castles appear more like modern multi-storey blocks of flats, and the risk of capsizing would not have permitted superstructures quite so high. However, we do know that when the invincible Spanish Armada was defeated in 1588, nineteen years after Brueghel's death, sixty-three out of a hundred and twenty-seven giant carracks and galleons sank off the west coasts of Scotland and Ireland.

24a
see frontispiece

Brueghel's workshop produced pictures of two other types: the caravel and the galleon, both of them types which quite obviously originated in the Mediterranean. It can be assumed that the caravel was developed from a fishing vessel of the same name. The galleon probably belongs to the family of galleys, although it is purely a sailing craft. The dimensions of a large Swedish caravel from the year 1534 are recorded in the Swedish National Archives: she was 174ft. 6in. long, 39ft. on the beam, drew 21ft. 6in. and had a height aft of 52ft. 7in. above the waterline. The half deck was 78ft. 8in. long, the hut above it 33ft. 2in. and the forecastle 39ft. 4in. The caravels were generally less beamy and lower than the carracks. We can assume that both W A, who obviously had not mastered perspective in ships, and Pieter Brueghel have made certain use of artistic licence in their drawings, and consequently their works cannot be credited with unqualified authenticity.

Apart from their slim lines and low superstructures there is one further indication that the galleons were related to the galleys: the long, beak-like projection at the stem-post which in galleys was called the *sperone*. It has often been maintained that this was a ram, but it was quite obviously not suited for use as such. 15th-century engravings already show a simpler form of this consisting of a knee that was simply fastened to the stem. It took on a new function when it had to serve as a support for the bowsprit, which around that time was rigged with an additional square sail forward of the stem: the spritsail. The *sperone* was then renamed *galion*. The massive bulk of the hull provided the main visual impact, coloured paint was little known and wood carvings are not much in evidence.

Galliot

Besides the *barze*, the *kraeck*, the caravel and the galleon, Brueghel has portrayed two other very important types of vessel: the galley and the *fluyt*. In the 14th century the Italian city republics of Genoa, Venice and Pisa developed a type of warship modelled on the galleys of classical antiquity, with a long, narrow hull, pointed at both ends. The oars, which were up to 50ft. long and were handled by between three and five men each, rested on an outrigger on each side of the ship that ran parallel to the bulwark. This was called the *drapera*. With an overall length of 130ft. and a beam of 16ft., the galley drew approximately 6ft. 6in. The afterbody of the ship was narrow and tapered

Galley

and had a curved stern-post. Over it sat a platform where the officers and helmsmen stood. The bulwark which ran round this platform was often richly decorated. A light awning served as protection against the weather. There was a second platform in the forward part of the ship on which the guns were placed. The two platforms were connected by a raised bridge, the *corsia*, from which the overseers of the oarsmen (who were usually slaves and convicts) could survey the scene. Galliots, galleys and galeasses, all of them vessels propelled by oars, differed from each other only in that the galliot had one mast, the galley two and the galeass three. Each of these masts was rigged with triangular lateen sails. These very low, slim and elegant vessels which were built with many variations, with the sailing aspect emphasized in the Northern European type, survived in many places until the 18th century because of their ability to be used for all kinds of manoeuvres independently of the wind. For this very reason they were also used as flag ships and state vessels. Since the year 1526 the commander of the French galley fleet had a galley by the name of *La Réale* as his flag ship: it carried the flags of both the king and the admiral. The *La Réale* built in 1680 (a model of which

143a

is kept in the Musée de la Marine in Paris) was particularly richly decorated at the bow and stern by the well-known sculptor Pierre Puget, who had been trained by an Italian shipbuilder. The state galleys of the Republic of Venice, called *bucintoros*, were magnificent, gilded vessels with nothing to distract the eye in the way of nautical gear except the projecting oars. These ships, covered all over with exquisite wood

58b; 134b

carvings, were used for a symbolic act: the doges of Venice sailed out into the Adriatic in them and threw a ring into the sea as a sign of the marriage of the city to the sea. These craft are probably the best example of ships built purely as works of art, with sea-worthiness playing a very minor role.

The other type portrayed by Brueghel is the *fluyt*, a vessel which according to old chronicles was first built in 1595 at Hoorn in Holland. Brueghel's engraving from the year 1564 makes this appear doubtful, even if his ship does not quite correspond to later drawings and models of *fluyts*. The characteristic feature of the *fluyts* was their very full and rounded shape at the bow and stern. They also had an extremely narrow deck so that they could attain a favourable measurement for the Øresund toll. The measured tonnage was based on beam at deck level, length and depth of the hull. By building ships with full sections and a pronounced tumble-home which resulted in a narrow deck, the actual loading capacity could be made larger than the measured tonnage indicated. Ships with a flat bottom, rounded at the bilges and with round, almost spherical ends, were developed in Holland as early as the 15th century, and even in our own day Dutch and Friesian coastal vessels and inland water craft have been built like

31

this in wood as well as iron. They look comfortable and portly, which is why many of these former cargo ships and fishing vessels are now used as yachts and pleasure boats, even as houseboats in Holland. The 16th-century *fluyts* underwent yet another change: the cove, which we can see on Brueghel's engraving, and which had a helm port in it, through which the tiller entered the ship, disappeared. Instead, the helm port was enlarged and framed by a generous surround of heavily gilded wood carvings. Above the helm port was the rear bulkhead of the poop, which now became the stern. This, too, was framed in carvings and further decorated with an illustration, a taffrail or other sculptured embellishments. All this made for a very impressive stern. Since stability was impaired by the round sections and the tumble-home on the topsides, these ships could carry topsails only above the mainsail. But the bowsprit had another sail added to it, which was carried on a small mast at the bowsprit end and was called the spritsail topsail. The poop was at least one deck higher than the half deck so that the officers could have a good view of the whole ship as far as the forecastle. The uppermost wales were drawn right up to the helm port and the bulwark ran parallel to the wales. At the level of the half deck it was only marked externally by a rubbing strip. In the same way the bulwark of the half deck and the poop ran parallel to the wales, thus giving the impression of a rather more pronounced sheer aft. In this way the step profile of the superstructure aft was less noticeable and the ship presented a more compact shape. Besides, a large part of the main deck bulwark was hidden behind the many rigging stays with their blocks and chain plates. The *fluyts* were very economical as cargo vessels, but on occasion they were also used for military missions and, above all, for the whaling trade which developed rapidly after 1614. When a new rating system was introduced for the Øresund toll in 1669, the *fluyts* began to be built with decks of more normal width.

Two other types of ship similar to the *fluyt* were built in Holland in the 17th century: the *hooker* and the *buys*, which were primarily fishing vessels for catching cod with rod and line or trawling for herring. Since these two types did not have very high superstructures, the man at the helm was protected by a special shelter called the *statie*. It soon disappeared in the *hooker*, though. In the second half of the 18th century yet another variation of the *fluyt* was built, with a less pronounced sheer and a much wider stern area which in some cases even projected beyond the rounded part of the stern below it. This type, which we can see on many pictures of whaling in the Arctic, was called a *bootschip*. Since it was broader aft, it frequently had additional windows above the transom, which was another point in which it differed from the *fluyt*.

Yet another type similar to the *fluyt* which was built in Holland from the second half of the 18th century was a kind of pinnace. It had finer underwater lines and the flat part of the stern reached down to the waterline. Often there was a second deck beneath the main deck. This 'pinnace' was used as a merchantman as well as a warship, and it played

Amsterdam, 1544

45a

Right: Stern of a model of the Dutch flagship 'Zeelandia', 1662, Rm.
Page 34: Details of 18th century ship models; a, b, Beak-heads, a, about 1750, Lg; b, of the 'Naseby', 1655, Lg; c, d, Gilded carvings on superstructures, As; e, f, Stern view of the models 'Store Christianus Quintus', 1697, Co, and 'Wapen von Hamburg', 1720, Hh.
Page 35: Stern of the model of the 'Naseby (Royal Charles)', 1655, Lg.
Pages 36/37: Detail from the stern of a warship, early 18th century, Lg.

32

a

b

c

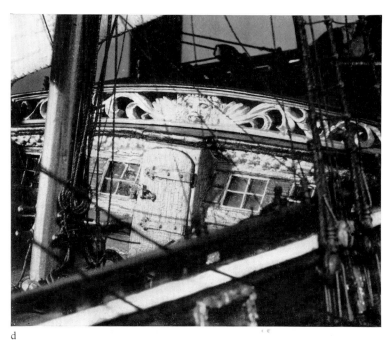

d

e

f

a

b

a

b

c

d

Amsterdam, 1566

34e, f; 38a

89; 90; 91; 92; 98a, b; 110a; 111d

41

an important part in the second half of the century when, after the Thirty Years War, Dutch trade expanded and Dutch shipbuilders concentrated on building beamy ships with shoal draft to ply the shallow Zuiderzee.

The English could make use of far greater draughts and under Italian influence started to build ships with finer lines in about 1630 in which, among other things, a new wooden framework of horizontal knees connected the ribs to the sternpost from the keel up to the transom in their stern parts. In their effort to achieve naval superiority both England and France built triple deckers, that is vessels with three gun decks one above the other in addition to the half deck, the poop and the forecastle. The two lower gun decks had gun ports which could be closed with port lids; most of the upper, through gun deck had open ports. From the lowest deck two or four guns could also be fired aft from ports below the transom. The part of the stern above the transom offered abundant scope for ornamental wood carvings. Special wood carvers' workshops were opened which were kept busy by the shipbuilding trade alone, and their artistic achievements were scarcely inferior to those of their contemporaries who carved altars and chiselled statues out of marble. The sailors, of course, were not enamoured of these masses of ornaments, which were often bulky and projected from the ship in an awkward fashion. The baroque figures which decorated the quarter galleries (used as the officers' toilets) and the stern galleries, as well as the lanterns over the poop, frequently caused the rigging to get caught and greatly interfered with sail handling. This passion for wood carvings reached its climax in the 17th century. After that the ornamentation became more modest again. One obviously could not do entirely without them, for nothing looks more bare than the unadorned stern of an old ship of the line. This was illustrated in 1961 when the *Vasa*, while being salvaged from Stockholm harbour, was fitted with a temporary stern to seal the hull. The *Vasa* had been built in 1627 for the King of Sweden by a Dutch shipwright and had sunk during her first outing in Stockholm harbour in 1628. She was raised 333 years later.

Large, flat sterns were usually broken up by the windows of the officers' quarters and the poop, and the space below the transom was pierced by gun ports. The artist designing the stern decoration was consequently forced to build his work round these windows.

The practice of emphasizing the sheer line by letting the wales run parallel to it was continued in the 17th and 18th centuries. As a result some of the gun ports, which were cut into the sides at regular intervals, had to be cut through the wales, thus interrupting the continuity of the line. This created problems not only as far as the appearance of the ship was concerned but also with regard to the strength of the hull. While the latter could be solved the former remained, for the eye could not be deceived.

Naval warfare in the 17th century called for some kind of comparison between different vessels, and so all great naval powers started to divide their ships into rates – usually six – according to the number of guns they carried. The hull shape was based on sections which were determined by the arc of a circle, as was the stem-post. Although hydrodynamic laws were still largely unknown, and despite many new problems which arose from military requirements, these kinds of sections had proved themselves satisfactory. The result was a very round, full forebody which was in no way conducive to speed. The foremost mast, the foremast, was placed on the forward third of the forecastle and decisively influenced the appearance of the ship when seen from the bow. The fore-bulkhead of the forecastle, which was often gaily painted, and a railing round the top of it, dominated the impression one had of the hull after the eye had got over the confusion of the forward rigging, bowsprit, spritsail, topsail spritsail and the figure adorning the beak-head with its supporting timbers on either side. Compared with 19th-century ships the hawse pipes were not very noticeable. In Swedish ships a heavy wooden platform leading in a curve from the stem-post to the forecastle was particularly noticeable; it served to protect the planking from chafe by the anchor. Whilst in most European ships the beak-head projected far beyond the stem, many French vessels had a rather more steeply angled beak-head which was much more imposing and powerful, especially when it was adorned with a full-size gilt lion. This ornamentation, along with the platform inside the beak-head, largely concealed its real purpose, which was to serve as an anchorage point for the ropes with which the bowsprit was made fast.

The bulwark of the upper deck between the forecastle and the half deck was raised above its original height, estimated to have been between 3ft. 3in. and 4ft. 3in., to afford the soldiers who stood behind it protection from the sea and hide them from the enemy. So it reached the same height as the forecastle and half deck and provided a visual connection between the two.

In the 18th century the sheer became straighter, probably because the hull had to be strengthened internally to counter sagging caused by pitching in seaways and by the heavy load of the guns. This is the reason why warships of this period, particularly the big ships of the line, which were only decorated at the ends with very modest carvings appeared like colossal boxes. In some of the big ships of the line the stern was relieved by galleries. In 1610 Phineas Pett built the *Prince Royal* with three projecting galleries on the stern. Around the middle of the 18th century the galleries were usually set back into the stern to afford better protection to those standing on them. The ornamentation applied to them often incorporated features from domestic and palace architecture, like balustrades, window frames and vignettes typical of this period. The stern, as well as the quarter galleries which survived until the middle of the 19th century, provide the only possibility for dating ships of that period by characteristics of style.

Drawings by Charles Davis, 19th century, Sa

Sloop

Topsail schooner

Brigantine

Full-rigged ship

42

Three-masted schooner

Barquentine

Hermaphrodite brig

Brig

Barque

It is not surprising that the large merchantmen of the British, Dutch, French, Danish and Swedish East India Companies were always modelled on the warships of each particular nation, especially since these cargo vessels and passenger ships were heavily armed to enable them to combat attacks by pirates.

Apart from the large, multi-decked ships of the line a naval power also needed light, fast warships called frigates, which had up to forty guns and were used for special missions. Because of their more moderate size there was less room for wood carvings. The part of the hull above the water was little different in frigates from that of the ships of the line, their superiority was derived from finer underwater lines. An even lighter type, the corvette, which was used for reconnaissance, convoys and privateering, was armed with about 18 guns only and could be propelled by oars if necessary. The fore and aft superstructures were low and light, and the stern ornamentation and the quarter galleries were modest compared with the ships of the line.

The ever increasing and very varied tasks merchant vessels were called upon to perform resulted in the course of the 18th century in a whole series of other new types derived from the Dutch *fluyt* and pinnace. The *pink* was developed from the *fluyt* and the *bootschip* and was less rounded at the ends. In contrast to the merchant frigates, which will be dealt with later, it had no cove or counter, and the stern was flat only above the transom, not below it. The *cat* and the *barque* had no beak-head.

All merchantmen in the 18th century still had a slight tumble-home, probably to make it more difficult for pirates to board them. The builders seemed to have forgotten, though, that this made loading and discharging difficult too. The five types of merchantman classified by F. H. af Chapman could be rigged in various different ways, which shows that basically the hull shape and the rig were independent of each other.

In the Mediterranean – probably in Spain – very fine-lined and slender sailing ships with up to three triangular lateen sails had been developed to fight the pirates of the Barbary states. These were the *xebecs*. With their long beak-heads, which carried only the bowsprit, and their very fine stern lines they must have been spectacularly fast sailing craft. The *brig*, too, was initially a fast, two-masted pirate vessel whose home was the Mediterranean. It differed from the *snow*⋆ and the *brigantine* only by its rig. These types were very low in the water and sometimes had a decorated beak-head. Their stern areas were small but attractively decorated with carvings and paintings.

It would be too big a task to describe all the small merchantmen in detail: the *cutters*, *ewers*, *tjalks*, *kofs*, *galleasses*, *galliots*, *hookers*, *boejers*, *jachts*, *smacks* and *luggers* with their U-shaped, V-shaped or rounded sections, with spherical, wedge-shaped or punt bows,

43 ⋆ A *snow* is a small brig-like sailing vessel with a supplementary trysail mast.

with straight, curved, raked or S-shaped stem-posts and flat or overhanging round or counter sterns. In some types the two ends were nearly identical. They were coastal vessels with a very modest draught to make them suitable for shallow water, and they often had to navigate far up the river estuaries to discharge their cargoes. Very often they were the work of ship's carpenters who, following their old family traditions, built them 'by eye' without first drawing up plans. Most of them were easily recognizable as such. They were typical examples of shipbuilding by small craftsmen, simple vessels with a flush deck and skilfully conceived lines, whose ornamentation was limited to a few carvings, usually done by the ship's carpenter himself, or, especially in the 19th and 20th centuries, to colourful paint. In the last two hundred years they have been frequently copied in iron and equipped with engines.

About 1700

Special mention must be made of a type developed chiefly in Holland in the 17th century: the *staatenjacht*, i. e. state yacht, which was used for representative purposes or as a pleasure boat by rich Dutch merchants on their inland waters, either as a sailing boat, rowing boat or *treckjacht* towed by horses. Elaborate carvings decorated its transom, sides, rudder, skylights, deck-house and other parts. Even the jackstaff was included in these ornamentations, which can be seen up to the present day in some of the typical Dutch yachts which once plied the many Dutch waterways as cargo or fishing vessels.

25b

Pleasure yachts became a common sight in other seafaring European countries, too. Even on the rivers and lakes round Berlin, in the very heart of Europe, magnificent state yachts were kept by the princes and kings of Prussia. The existence of these craft is rather less incongruous in the large trading towns, especially the free towns, where they had to fulfil official functions. The National Maritime Museum in Stockholm possesses the stern and cabin of the schooner *Amphion* designed in 1777 by F.H. af Chapman and built in 1778 for King Gustav III (1771–1792) to be used by him on Lake Mälaren and in the archipelago. The luxuriously appointed cabin and the lavishly decorated stern and stern-post are in the classic style called 'Gustavian' in Sweden. They can be regarded with some certainty as the work of the famous shipwright, who at the time had the rank of Lieu-tenant-Colonel. One of the most unusual features about this ship is the accentuation of the bilges by a long, dark blue plank which merges into the raked stern in an elegant curve. Chapman had already incorporated this feature in the frigates of the archipelago in 1767.

117

Right: a, Model of a fluyt, about 1700, Lb; b, Water colour design for the bow ornaments of a yacht, early 18th century, Rm. Page 46: Sterns of ship models; a, English Admiralty model, 1652, An; b, British warship 'St. Michael', 1669, Lg; c, Ship of the line 'Boyne', 1692, Lg; d, Votive ship from Brittany, 17th century, Pm.

The turn of the 18th century witnessed no particular changes in the architecture of warships, since there had not been any decisive modifications in naval warfare either. In the 18th century the rigs had undergone certain changes, which greatly improved the manoeuvrability of the large warships, but as far as the hulls were concerned they were simply given a changed appearance by painting them a dark colour (black, navy blue,

44

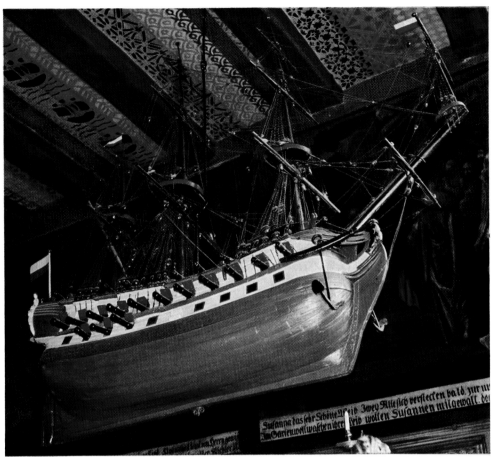

a

b

a

b

c

d

a

b

c

d

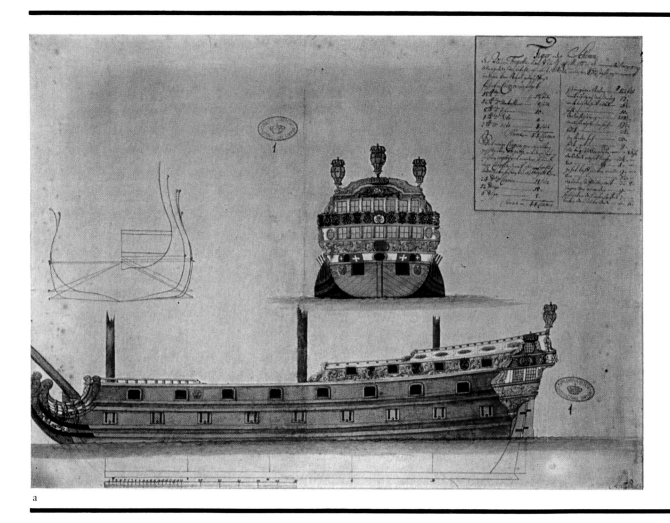

a

b

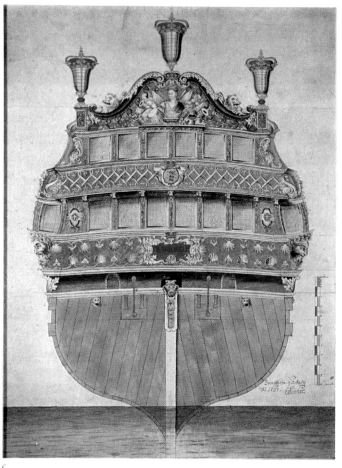

c

dark red, dark brown) alternating with light-coloured bands (white or yellow) in line with the gun ports. When the ports were open the character of the warship was clearly shown by the bright red paint on the inside of the covers. These features and the remaining decorations, almost neo-Gothic in their simplicity, remained characteristic of the sailing warship until the requirements of steam power, armament and armour plating imposed practical alterations.

Merchant ships, on the other hand, came under the influence of yet another change, this time from the other side of the Atlantic. Up till the Declaration of Independence (1776) the building of large ships in North America had been influenced by the English mother country. Small vessels, which were involved not only in honest trading but also in smuggling and piracy, had developed into fast sailers. Initially it was the smaller ships like the schooner which were given finer underwater lines, but after the discovery of the Californian gold fields this style of construction was adopted for the larger sailing ships as well. This is how the famous clippers came into being, magnificently fast ships with impressive rigs, which set up one speed record after the other and for a long time even outclassed the steam ships.

Their particular hallmark was the curved, projecting clipper bow, which filled the space that had previously been taken up by the beak-head, and through which the bowsprit, too, was gradually incorporated into the hull. The timbers that supported the stem knee and the decorations on them were kept rather flat in profile alongside the name plate. The figure-head swept out long and slim from under the stem knee and had to be shaped to suit this position. The slim afterbody of the hull terminated in an overhanging stern, which had developed from the cove. The flat, narrow transom was usually slightly curved until around 1850 when designers began to make it round or elliptical. In the sixties these very fine lines were abandoned because it was found that whilst restricting the loading capacity of ships they did nothing to improve their average speed, which was

60

after all the prime consideration. From now on cargo-carrying sailing ships were built longer and, as a result, narrower. This made it possible to increase the sail area without adding to the height of the rig and, in so doing, jeopardizing stability. The resulting type lent itself perfectly to conversion from wood to iron; in fact it could be increased in length even further. On these huge sailing ships the superstructure (forecastle, bridge, poop) only played a secondary role and influenced the ship's appearance far less than the colour of the paint. In the first half of the last century, when pirates still constituted a certain danger, merchant vessels were often camouflaged to look like warships with sham or painted gun ports. By the middle of the century this façade had become purely ornamental in character. The improvement in ship paints and their increasing cheapness led to hulls being painted in more colours, and certain combinations frequently became

Page 47: Sterns of ship models; a, Warship, early 18th century, Ms; b, Warship, about 1685, Lg; c, East Indiaman 'Padmos', 1722, Rm; d, East Indiaman 'De Jonge Jacob', 1724, At.
Left: Water-coloured design drawings of ships and their ornamentation; a, Elbe frigate 'Stormarn', Neumühlen nr. Hamburg, 1703, Co; b, c, Beam and stern view of the stern of the 'Prins Wilhelm', Bremerholm nr. Copenhagen, 1697, Co.

established as a shipowner's house colours.

Model Ship Building
Votive Ships, Builders' Models and Ornaments

Because of the almost complete lack of original vessels, our knowledge of shipbuilding in bygone days would be extremely sketchy were it not for a considerable number of historical models. In their time they were made for widely differing purposes, yet the fundamental motive behind them has probably always been the same. This can best be illustrated by a true episode from our times: a small boy stood on the beach not far from a large port and threw all manner of objects like tins, buckets and boxes into the water, clapping his hands as they floated on the waves and crying delightedly 'Ship, ship, hurrah!' as he had often heard at his father's yard when a ship was launched. He later became a shipbuilder himself and took over the family business. There must have been many boys like him who played by the water with tins and boxes or home-made boats, until one day what had been a game became a serious matter and they learned to build real ships or went to sea.

It is certainly thousands of years since the first child or grown-up built a ship in miniature, a model ship. In recent centuries such ships were also made for very practical purposes, such as predicting the characteristics of real, life-size ships prior to their building. But floating models, built either as toys or aids in shipbuilding, were not the only kinds of miniature ships made. We know of model ships which were put into graves as burial gifts: some from the beginning of the third millennium were found in King's Tomb 289 excavated by Woolley in Ur; many Egyptian tombs yielded scaled-down replicas of the Nile ships on which the dead made their burial voyages; and a find in Nors in Jutland revealed many small boats from about 1200 B. C., all of them made from thin sheets of gold and decorated with spiral ornamentation. We find ship models hanging in churches as votive offerings, in the town halls of ports and in the houses of the shipping guilds. We find them in museums, in the banqueting halls of princely castles and in the offices of shipbuilders and shipping companies. Seamen built model ships during their watches below, shipbuilders used them as an important aid to planning and building, and gold- and silversmiths created valuable miniature ships purely and simply as show pieces. All these models (for our purposes we are excluding the more modern ones of the last hundred years) are more or less technically accurate and show varying degrees of perfection in their workmanship and aesthetic qualities. In the first place they are interesting to the history of shipbuilding for their documentary value, but at the same time they are noteworthy as products of arts and crafts peculiar to the maritime sphere.

The burial gifts mentioned earlier show that ship models played a role as votive offerings from a very early time. In a similar way, models of Chinese junks, South Sea outrigger boats, ornamented ships from ancient Siam and Indian canoes from America had a religious significance. Many of these models may have been put into the graves with the thought of the long journeys which the dead had to make in the hereafter.

10 Egyptian models of burial ships, up to 3ft. long, were usually carved from a single block of wood, but despite their simplicity they were provided with decorative accessories and small figures. The most beautiful example, which is now in the Cairo museum, comes from Tutankhamen's tomb. Together with the reliefs and wall paintings in the temples and burial chambers they provide an excellent source of information for the study of Egyptian shipbuilding.

There are practically no model ships from ancient times in the Mediterranean – with the exception of a few examples such as the primitive terracotta model of a trireme from Hermonthis in Egypt, today in the National Museum in Copenhagen, the model of a Greek ship in the shape of a bronze urn in the museum in Beirut, and several stone

28a, b, c, d sculptures of symbolic significance: the Nike (Winged Victory) of Samothrace in the Louvre, and the fountain near Santa Maria in Domenica o alla navicella in Rome.

The oldest known votive ship from a church is in the Prins Hendrik Museum in Rotterdam and is said to have originated in the middle of the 15th century. It is rather crudely built but gives the impression having been completed by an expert, perhaps by a seaman who donated it as a thank offering to a saint for a successful voyage. This probability is supported by the fact that it is supposed to have come from the chapel of San Simon of Mantaró on the coast of Catalonia. With all its technical details the model is important evidence on shipbuilding in the Mediterranean at that time. Numerous ship models have found their way in a similar manner to the churches in the ports of all countries. Many a seaman used the involuntary periods of rest imposed by calms to make a model for the church in his home port, his own vessel perhaps serving as a pattern. In almost every church in the coastal towns of Scandinavia such ship models can be found. They also occur in the towns of the Baltic and North Sea

51 coasts of Germany.

53a, b, c, e

Another kind of votive ship is to be seen among the offerings in the churches and chapels in places of pilgrimage, in particular on the shores of the Mediterranean. They are small model ships made of wood, wax, sheet iron or silver, consecrated mostly to St. Nicholas or St. Antony in gratitude for a safe homecoming, for a successful fishing expedition or for having been saved from a disaster at sea. There are old, high-sided 18th-century ships alongside modern motor boats made of sheet steel. Among the largest *ex voto* ships of this kind are two big sailing boats, 5ft. long, in the church of Madonna dell'Arco in Naples. Numerous votive ships are to be found in the pilgrimage church of Santa Maria above Rapallo. Some of them are made of wood, some of sheet silver, and some are kept under glass in cases with gold frames. Many model ships given as votive offerings hang over the altar of the crypt of San Nicolo at Bari, the place where the relics of St. Nicholas, the patron saint of seafarers, are kept.

Both religious motifs and old heathen customs play a part in processions in which model ships are carried. 'Historical processions', such as are occasionally held these days, often carry with them models of quite considerable size. This custom is by no means confined to coastal towns. Far inland by the great rivers, where the river shipmen have joined together in guilds, models of the local barges are carried in procession, mostly at the annual winter celebrations: in Lauenburg it might be an Elbe barge, in Schleswig a tench fishing skiff, on the Danube an 'Ulmer Schachtel'. In the days when shipbuilding was still in the hands of craftsmen of the guild such models were also carried in ceremonial processions, and many a museum houses a collection of ship models of unknown origin which may once have served this purpose.

As far as their decorative purpose is concerned votive ships can be compared to those ship models which one can find hanging from the ceilings of town halls, inns and houses of the seamen's guilds. These, too, were often made by seamen in their spare time.

One thing about these models which is surprising is that despite their intimate familiarity with items they handled daily many seamen were quite capable of getting the proportions wrong. Quite often the masts are too high and the yards much too thick. Nor is it uncommon for the hull to have the wrong shape, but a seaman can hardly be blamed for this since he never sees what his ship looks like except above the water and only gets a look at the underwater part when the ship is slipped for repairs. However, not all of the faults we can detect in these hanging models are unintentional. Some of the distortions in the dimensions are deliberate and aimed at correcting the very acute upward angle at which the ship is viewed. This accounts for the fact that in many cases the cannons protrude much too far from the ports. Some models are not only very crudely carved and rigged but painted untidily and in unpleasantly

25c, d; 45a

Right: a, Church ship Solen, 17th century, Ss; b, Church ship of about 1640, Lg; c, Church ship from Madonna dell'Arco in Naples, 18th century, Vn; d, East Indiaman 'Jonge Jacob', 1724, At; e, Frigate 'Freidrig d. 6.', 1825, Ho; f, Frigate 'Princess Mary', in bone, 1796, Hg.
Page 54: Stern details of models; a, Stern of a Mediterranean galley, about 1700, At; b, Helmsman's seat on a Dutch yacht with stern board, rudder head and gilded top of jackstaff, 1714, As; c, Stern of the 'Hollandia', 1664, As; d, Stern of a Dutch warship, 1665, replica of a model once in the possession of the Hohenzollern-Museum in Berlin, Lg.
Page 55: Dockyard model of the British warship 'St. Michael', 1669, Lg.
Page 56: a, Danish royal frigate 'Elephanten', builder's model by Francis Sheldon, 1687, Co; b, Tuscan builder's model, mid 18th century, Vn; c, French warship 'Valmy', builder's model, 1867, Pm; d, Friesian 'boejer', model, about 1800, Sn; e, Earthenware bowl in the shape of a warship with boats, Schleswig, about 1750, Fb.

a

b

c

d

e

f

a

b

c

d

a

b

c

d

e

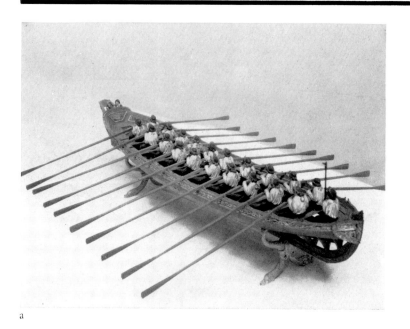

a

b

c

d

e

f

a

b

c

bright colours, although this can scarcely be noticed, since they are normally viewed from a distance. The maker of the model is not always responsible for such features. In some instances the room with the model was redecorated at a later date, and in the process the ship was cleaned and repainted to match the room. At the same time the rigging was restored, frequently by an unskilled hand. This explains many mistakes on ship models which were not originally there.

There are other models which only partly resemble a particular type of ship and for the rest are full of errors. These include features which may look pretty but on the original ship would have been entirely absurd. In the 'Schifferhaus' in Lübeck, for instance, there is a model which is obviously meant to represent a *fluyt*. But the rigging is wrong, because the masts, in addition to the topmasts, have topgallant masts with topgallant and upper topgallant yards and are very high indeed. *Fluyts* only had topsails over the mainsails. They were not stable enough to take more. On the other hand the model may be meant to represent a *bootschip*, in which case a small topgallant sail would have been possible over the topsail. But even on the *bootschip* only one square sail could be permissible on the mizzen mast above the mizzen gaff sail.

Although it is the part of the ship above the water which reveals important architectonic details, we usually see the underwater body first if the model hangs high up on the ceiling. Surprisingly there are many models in which the underwater body is superbly shaped, conveying a perfect impression of the beautiful run of the lines. It may not be commonly known that marine artists occasionally use ship models when painting their pictures, just as other painters use small clothed puppets to study drapery. Whoever has tried to draw the complicated lines of a ship in correct perspective will understand how useful such aids can be. We can assume that even the Dutch Baroque marine painters, van de Velde, Simon de Vlieger, Ludolph Backhuizen or Jan van de Capelle often used models, but they did not have to build their own since the master shipwrights at that time habitually made small models of their future ships so that the customers, shipowners or captains could see what the builder had in mind. Many marine painters in the 19th and 20th centuries built themselves models of the ship they were about to paint complete with all the details of deck gear and rigging.

The Altonaer Museum in Hamburg possesses such models, though one several yards long was destroyed in the Second World War. They are not absolutely true to life since the artists did not work from technical drawings but from a series of freehand sketches with some dimensions added. The paintwork, too, is fairly rough and the knots and splices can hardly be called expert, although some painters may have been keen sailors and had a command of these nautical skills. For the purpose of making a study of the history of shipbuilding these painters' models are often very valuable since the artists

45a

Stern of a crusaders' ship

Page 57: 'Ville de Dieppe', ivory model, Dieppe, 1811, Pm.
Page 58: Models; a, English state barge, about 1672, An; b, Venetian ceremonial galley 'Bucintoro', 1727, Vn; c, Maltese galeass, 18th century, Co; d, Brig 'Elisabeth', about 1830, Ha; e, Three-master 'Loire', about 1871, Pm; f, Aviso 'Hussard', 1884, Pm.
Page 59: a, b, Bow and stern of Nelson's flag ship 'Victory', 1765, Portsmouth; c, Figure-head of the tea clipper 'Cutty Sark', 1869, Greenwich.
Left: Four-masted, full-rigged ship 'Wendur', model, 1884, Lg.

61

recorded in them many small details which would otherwise have been forgotten, like the position of the winches, the shape of the tiller and the leeboards, the arrangement of the companionways, hatches, bollards, spars and anything else which the ship's carpenter and the captain worked out together.

As has been mentioned, many small scale models of ships were built in the 17th, 18th and to some extent the 19th century as well, for the purpose of enabling the shipwright and shipowner to work out exactly what was wanted. There were several reasons for building these miniature ships, which were called builders' models or Admiralty models in England, where they were built especially for submission to the British Admiralty.

46a, c

From the 16th century the shapes of warships were drawn with arcs of a circle. These were supplemented by other drawing methods in the 17th century, but the construction proper, the determination of the dimensions and the shape of individual pieces like frames, beams and knees and the way they were made up into keel, stem, deck beams and such like, could not be expressed yet by drawings. Even if the master shipwright had known how to do it, his workmen would not have known how to interpret them, since they had insufficient technical knowledge. Nor did the captains, the naval officers and the Admiralty officials understand a technical drawing of a ship. And yet important points of construction had to be discussed with them, for example the strain which individual parts of the ship would have to bear in a battle or in a seaway. A painting by Seymor Lucas in the Victoria and Albert Museum, showing a conference of marine experts round a builder's model of a 17th-century warship, illustrates this state of affairs. There was nothing else to do but to make a scale skeleton model of the ship from the initial drawings, on which every detail of construction could be viewed and discussed. Such a frame model was also useful in explaining to the ship's carpenters how a particular job had to be done. Some of these models have survived and can be seen in Annapolis, Greenwich, Paris, Amsterdam, Copenhagen and Stockholm, among other places. In them the ribs have been planked up at gun port level and the wales added, no doubt to show up the discrepancy between the sheerline and wales on the one hand and the true run of the decks on the other. In some cases the topsides have been completely planked up, while below the waterline the timbers have been left uncovered. One 17th-century English model not only has its topsides planked up with all the carvings in place, but all the rigging completed as well. Other builder's models are complete in every detail, exterior as well as interior, although the inside cannot be seen except with the aid of a mirror and a light or felt by hand through the hatches. It is conceivable that the models were built at the same time as the real ship but were always one stage ahead so that the carpenters could be given their instructions. On an

56a, b, c

18th-century Russian warship in the possession of the Grand Duke of Oldenburg the stern was sawn off after completion to show the interior arrangement and later screwed on again and the ship then rigged. The Grand Duke's collection also contains a model that has been stopped up with pitch inside, probably to enable experiments to be made by which such physical characteristics as buoyancy, stability, trim and resistance could be determined, bearing in mind that there was no known way of calculating these data arithmetically at that time.

There are also models of warships in which only half the hull is completed both inside and out: half-models which are open down the centreline so that the whole of the accommodation can be seen. The Technical High School at Hanover possesses a model of the 100-gun English warship *Royal George* in which the accommodation can be inspected by lifting off the upper works. It is not possible to see right down into the bowels of the ship because the underwater body has not been built up on frames but carved out of a solid block of wood.

These detailed and meticulously constructed models are objects of great value. They were built to various scales, and it was on the scale that the recognizable rendering of small, important details depended. The navies of the great sea powers had special workshops set up in which trained model makers worked solely on the construction of these models. It seems that they were first introduced in England around 1660, since one of the oldest models of a warship is that of the three-decker *Prince* built in 1670. When the English master shipwright Francis Sheldon went to work for the Swedes in 1659 he took with him by way of 'credentials' a frame model of an English warship which is today in the Maritime Museum in Stockholm. The Royal Shipyard in Copenhagen opened a special design room in 1696 and model builders worked there for the first time. After the Peace of Roskilde with Denmark (1659) the Swedish King Charles XI founded the naval base of Karlskrona at Blekinge on the island of Trossö, where there was a shipyard for building warships. The models which were built in the course of constructing warships were collected in a building and in 1752 were declared an official model collection by King Adolph Frederik, in other words a museum of shipbuilding. It formed the basis of what is today the Swedish Marine Museum at Karlskrona, where we find models made by the descendants of Francis Sheldon who worked there since 1686, as well as many built under F. H. af Chapman. There is also an old model on show which was used around 1717 for towing tests, together with the second pendulum which served as a speedometer for comparing the shapes of different hulls. From 1782 to 1785 Chapman used models to prepare rationalized building plans for ten ships of the line and ten frigates, which come very close to modern design methods. For each type there was a set of four models scaled 1 : 16. 1. frame model, 2. completed hull,

3. half-model, 4. fully rigged model. They can be seen in their original form, unmutilated by restoration. As a result of these rationalized plans the building time from laying the keel to launching the ship was reduced from one hundred and eleven days to forty-five days. The important role the rigging played in these models is shown up by the fact that in Thomas Miller's *The Complet Modellist* (1655) the setting up of the rigging forms the major part. In fact one of the most useful functions of the models was to provide a means for experimenting with the arrangement of the standing and running rigging, which obviously had to differ on a warship from the arrangement on a merchant ship, since the former had to fulfil the requirements of battle and for strategic reasons be capable of carrying out different manoeuvres from a merchant vessel.

It can be seen from all that has been said here that builders' models were very important in the construction of 17th- and 18th-century warships. There are few models of merchantmen, with the exception of the ships of the East India Company, which, on account of their special colonial service, were built on military lines. With merchantmen, different from warships, models were used to find the best hull shape for optimum cargo carrying capacity, speed and stability, stability here varying greatly – according to the way the cargo was stowed and the ballast distributed. From some suitable wood the ship's carpenter carved a half-model, i. e. the starboard or port side only of a ship. The work called for a skilled hand and an eye for a good hull shape. He then cut this solid half-model into sections at the intervals of the frames and traced the shape of each one onto paper. In this way he finished up with a set of small-scale drawings of the ship's sections, which could easily be enlarged to the actual size. This method came into use in about the middle of the 17th century and is still in use nowadays for the construction of small coasters and fishing vessels.

In America a similar method was employed for constructing fast merchant sailing vessels and yachts. These craft had to have fine waterlines, and in order to determine them accurately the American shipbuilders did not make their models from a solid block of wood but from a pile of small boards laid on top of each other and held together with wedges, pegs or dowels. After the model had been carved they could easily be taken apart and used as curves to draft the waterlines. There are two such models left (of 1795 and 1796 respectively) which originated in the New England towns of Salem and Newburyport in Massachusetts. But this method of model building probably dates back further. It is clear that originally both methods were a mere matter of expediency. In iron shipbuilding, on the other hand, half-models were at first made only for decorative purposes, but later became useful for determining the shape and size of the plates. In many of the older shipyards half-models can still be found hanging on the walls as ornaments. Even today the marriage of technical science and architecture

Right: Stern of the Oseberg ship during excavations, early 9th century, Ou.
Page 66: Model of British warship 'Royal George', 1756, Lg.

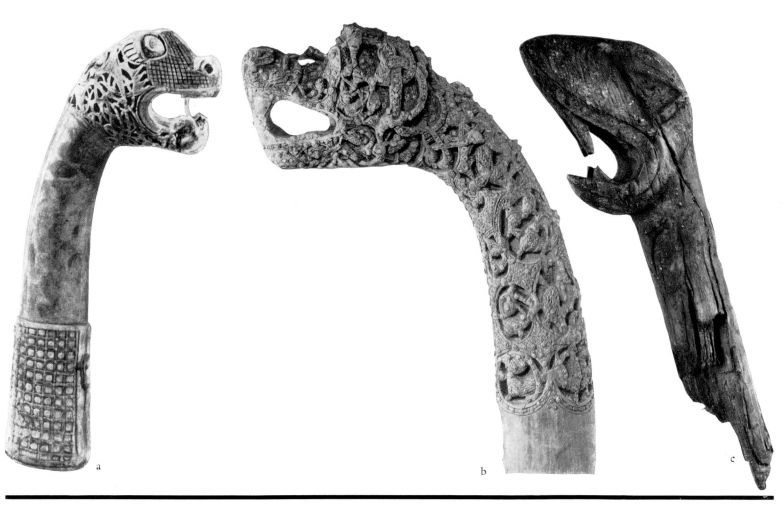

a

b

c

d

e

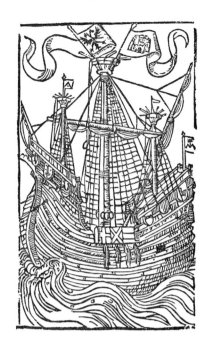

presents the shipbuilder with a problem which has not yet been solved satisfactorily. A number of half-models have found their way into museums, and this is where the myth may have originated that they were originally carved as complete ships and sawn in half, one half to go to the owner and the other to remain in the yard. But whoever has carved a solid, two-sided model of a ship knows that it is much harder to get a perfectly symmetrical hull this way than by making a half-model in which the midships plane serves as a surface for resting on the work bench, which in turn serves as a support for the jigs.

It is obvious from the important part which ship models played in the construction of warships in the 17th and 18th centuries that sea powers went to considerable trouble, even in times of peace, to get hold of ship models of possible enemies. It is also well known that in 1667, during the Second Dutch War, the famous English master shipwright Peter Pett carried his ship models to safety when the Dutch Admiral de Ruyter approached the English coast, and when he was questioned about this later replied that the models would have been more useful to the enemy than actual captured ships. When at the end of the 17th century Russia started to build warships, Czar Peter the Great stayed for a long time in Holland and England in order to learn about shipbuilding. He brought home several valuable ship models, which formed the basis of the present-day a collection of models in the Leningrad Maritime Museum.

Owners of small boat building yards, too, made models of their craft in their spare time. These models frequently reveal that their builders were certainly at home with saws, adzes and planes, that they were thoroughly familiar with every part of the ship and knew how to determine its dimensions, but that small chisels, gouges, rasps, drills and files for finer woodwork were out of place in their large hands. Instead of wooden pegs and thin nails they used simple wood screws which may have been practical but spoilt the look of the model. Models of this kind are certainly accurate but not always pretty. On the other hand, they have considerable documentary value.

Almost all the large maritime museums, but also the smaller regional museums in coastal towns, house vast numbers of such models of coastal and fishing vessels, mostly of recent origin. The Altonaer Museum, for example, possesses a collection, inspired by the Association of German Deep Sea Fishermen, of models made by boat and ship builders of fishing craft they have actually built. They are entirely authentic as far as shape and scale are concerned.

Since the last century models of a different type have been made of steel ships, which are intended primarily to serve advertising and prestige purposes. In the beginning the yards built such models in their own workshops, and there are still shipyards today which have model building workshops. But when these miniature ships started to be built to a much smaller scale and became more difficult to build, independent concerns began to specialize in their manufacture. They drew their staff mostly from the field of precision tool makers who are accustomed to making very small detailed objects from scale drawings. Several such firms went in for making model machines for teaching, advertising and experimental purposes as the main part of their business. They built ship models as a side line only. The hull in such cases is made by a woodworker, everything else by precision tool makers who work mostly at lathes, drilling machines, special milling and planing machines. The owner of a well-known Hamburg model-making firm, for example, was trained as a precision tool maker in a Bremerhaven compass factory. It is obvious that modern ship models of this type possess a high documentary value.

Museums which concern themselves with shipbuilding, shipping, deep sea fishing and other aspects of the sea very rarely have the room to exhibit full-size ships. In most cases they have to make do with models, which has definite advantages from several points of view. They are able to show the development of a complete series of vessels, or collections of types characteristic of a particular country or region, as well as to demonstrate methods of construction and specialized uses of individual vessels: for fishing, passenger transport, pilot, customs or war service and so on. All this can be demonstrated very effectively with models, always providing that they must be authentic builders' models to be of historical, technical and scientific value. It goes without saying that builders' models are highly sought after by museums. In their absence models have to be made according to information from reliable historical sources. For older ships such information is hard to come by because drawings were rarely made in past centuries and the few which are available of older vessels – from about 1600 onwards – are confined to lines drawings. From the 18th century on drawings of the sail plan were occasionally made to find the sail area and centre of effort for calculating the relative stability of ships. They also served to determine the scantlings of the spars which were then made by the spar maker. All the deck equipment, deck houses, hatches, winches and windlasses, bollards, hatch covers, railings, companionways, bunks and so on, were made and installed to the master shipwright's and captain's instructions and were the products of their experience. This state of affairs changed with the transition to iron ships, for the construction of which technical drawings were indispensable.

An example can be cited here which might be valid for other maritime museums. From lines drawings contained in the archives of the Altonaer Museum a number of models have been made, their rigging being copied from paintings of the original ships kept in the same museum. The group which built the models consisted of a shipbuilder, a block maker and a sail maker, all three of whom had had considerable experience in working with wooden craft. The most important man among them was the block maker who as a turner in a shipyard had to carry out much of the delicate work and possessed the greatest manual skill.

All the old original vessels which are still left today should be measured and drawn and models should be made to provide a permanent record. This brings us to the question of reconstructing historical ships. If the reconstruction is based on the dimensions, drawings or pictures of similar ships only, the model is merely a 'type' model. This applies for example to the model of a herring catcher (a so-called *Heringsbuise*), the *Perl*, from the year 1776, now in the Altonaer Museum. On the basis of the dimensions given in the measurement certificate of this vessel, further data needed for the lines drawing were determined according to F. H. af Chapman's rules from the year 1775 and the lines drawing was then prepared with the help of Chapman's parabola. Deck equipment and rigging were taken partly from Chapman's *Architectura Navalis Mercatoria* published in 1768, partly from the model of the last of the Emden *Heringsbuise* kept in the museum at Emden. What resulted was the type model of a herring catcher; a genuine model of the *Perl* could not be made because no picture existed of this particular vessel. An extremely valuable reconstruction of a ship is published in *Souvenir de Marine* by Vice-Admiral Edmond Pâris, then curator of the Musée de la Marine. It is the 72-gun ship of the line *La Couronne*, which was built in 1633 at La Roche Bernard by the shipbuilder Charles Morieu. It was described along with the methods of construction of the period by Father George Fournier in 1667 in his book *Hydrographie*. An engraving of the ship, that is a portrait, not a technical drawing, is also reproduced in this work. In addition, from the time that warships were divided into five classes, the French navy had tables and rules for the determination of the principal measurements and the rigging of these ships. Concrete data of this kind are also available in the museums in Greenwich, Copenhagen, Stockholm and Amsterdam, and with these as basis it is possible to build faithful historical models of ships. By comparison the task which Carl Reinhardt had to solve in the 1930's was far more difficult. He reconstructed both the *Adler von Lübeck* (1566) and the *Jesus von Lübeck* (1540). Although there was a certain amount of contemporary data to be had, the shipwrights in Lübeck at that time did not build to fixed rules. Nor is the pictorial material from that period very useful. For instance, there are no illustrations of such famous ships as *Peter von Danzig* and Columbus's *Santa Maria*. Only their main dimensions are known, which is why the numerous efforts that have been made to reconstruct these ships must remain of doubtful historical value. All the models of the emigrant ships *Halve Moen* (1609) and *Mayflower* (1620) are based on nothing but hypothesis and can have no claim whatsoever to authenticity.

If we have dealt here mainly with authentic and technically accurate models which are displayed in museums to illustrate the development of shipbuilding, shipping and fishing, then this is not meant as a criticism against exhibiting votive ships, pieces made by seamen and models of ornamental character in a maritime museum. Quite the contrary. But they should not be exhibited together with technically accurate scale models unless the difference between the two types is clearly set out.

Miniature copies of ships quite frequently served purely ornamental purposes, whether in the shape of drinking cups (quite unsuitable for practical use), ink-pots, centre-pieces, lockets, chess pieces or similar articles. There are many splendid examples of this kind of thing, often masterpieces of the silversmith's art. The Schlüsselfeld gold cup in the Germanische Museum at Nürnberg, made around 1500, might be described as the most valuable work of this kind; other noteworthy pieces are an early 17th-century silver cup in the shape of a *fluyt* from Middelburg in the Amsterdam Rijksmuseum, and the gold and silver drinking vessel in the shape of a ship with sails, rigging and small figures of the crew, made by the Augsburg goldsmith J. Ch. Pfeifelmann at the end of the 17th century. Among the ink-pots there is an original example which was made in the 17th century for a jubilee of the Brotherhood of Pilots at Hamburg-Övelgönne. Equally charming are the bowls and terrines in the shape of ships which occasionally crop up as pieces of tableware. They usually consist of the hull of the ship only, with the deck forming the lid, which can be lifted off by means of a handle.

Another interesting peculiarity is the ivory models of ships which members of the seafaring fraternity presented to the rulers of their countries on festive occasions. The oldest example of this kind, representing the warship *Norske Löve* built between 1652 and 1654, is to be found in Rosenborg Castle near Copenhagen. Another example is the model of the *Ville de Dieppe* in the Musée de la Marine in Paris. It was given to Napoleon at the birth of the King of Rome. Similar models, often of astonishing artistic skill, were made from bones by seamen who were prisoners of war during the Napoleonic Wars. Some of these are to be found in museums at Greenwich, Hamburg, Amsterdam and Annapolis among others; a particularly fine example is contained in the private collection of Dr. Grimm at Hamburg.

57

53f

The most unusual among the decorative models are undoubtedly the sixteen small ships worked in silver which were presented to the last German kaiser in 1913 at his jubilee. They portray the development of the large sailing ships and their construction called for a great deal of preparatory research – only possible because the design office of the German Navy Department was just then engaged in research into the problems of reconstructing old ships. Considering what was known of the history of shipbuilding at the time the project was handled extremely well under the direction of Carl Busley.

Right: Figure-head of the corvette 'Ajax', Rotterdam, 1832, As.

Of course, there have always been accurately scaled and technically faithful model

ships which have served representative or decorative functions, and many of the ones decorating the town halls of coastal towns, lobbies of shipping companies and living rooms of private collectors fall into this category. It is not always possible to tell the difference between models made as votive offerings and those made for purely decorative purposes. When looking at the more important private collections of ship models today one comes to the conclusion that the motive behind them is not merely a love of the sea and technical interest, which the collector may share with many a public museum, but equally an individual aesthetic pleasure and a desire for ornamentation on the part of the collector.

Many amateur collections have been built up on the basis of builders' models which never got beyond the development stage which, since they only cluttered up the archives of naval establishments or the workshops of yards, were eventually given away. Of course there can have been few people to have the rare good fortune of the American collector Henry Huddleston Rogers who was lucky enough (and had the means) to acquire fifteen 17th- and early 18th-century builder's models from English royal shipyards from the descendants of Charles Sergison, who was a kind of finance minister in the British navy around 1700. They had stood undisturbed for 225 years in their own special store room on Sergison's estate in Surrey, having once been used for demonstration at British Admiralty conferences when the following year's building programme was under discussion. During the thirty years he was in office, Charles Sergison regularly took home those models which had not been chosen for building. It seems that he was the first authentic collector of strictly accurate scale models. Curiously enough, no real

46a

ships have ever existed for these. Rogers bequeathed them together with his whole magnificent collection to the United States Naval Academy in Annapolis.

Left: Model of the Dutch East Indiaman
'Oostrust', Amsterdam, 1721, At.

Art in Early Shipbuilding

Egypt, Mesopotamia, Mediterranean, Northern Europe

We know from paintings and reliefs that even the earliest ships were decorated. Rock paintings in the Nubian Desert, believed to have originated in Egypt's pre-dynastic period, and early Stone Age rock paintings in Scandinavia, sketchy as they are, show that the upswept ends of ships carried decorations which may be regarded as the forerunners of the later figure-heads. In what is presumably the oldest picture of a sailing ship, on an Egyptian vase dating back to 4000 B.C., the after end of the ship, which is drawn up to a considerable height, is topped by a figure strongly resembling a bird, whereas the sternposts of the Nubian boats remind one of bulls' heads. It is conceivable that these were simply the skulls of sacrificial animals (we shall have more to say about their ritual significance later on) but it is much more likely that they were man-made, hand-carved ornaments. Apart from simple dugouts, of which many have been found in various parts of the world, it is quite certain that the earliest known ships already possessed certain ornamental features.

Austrheim (Norway), about 2000 B. C.

The vessels depicted in the prehistoric Egyptian rock paintings might be boats made of bundles of reeds of the kind still used on the White Nile today. This method of construction was very common in the Old Kingdom. The shipyards were near swamps in which papyrus grew thickly, and all the illustrations show peasants picking, bundling and carrying these plants to the yard. Judging from these old pictures the operation required great physical effort, which the artist often managed to portray very vividly. It seems that after the yard workers had cut off the heads they used the bundles just as they were, supporting them on a kind of rough trestle which made them easier to handle. The boat was given its ultimate shape during this building process. Wall paintings in tombs illustrate the same scene over and over again: men engaged in the important process of binding together the almost completed boat. After this was done the whole boat had to be sealed to prevent water from leaking in. This was achieved by pouring resin or a tar-like mixture between and over the top of the bundles.

The Egyptians also used wooden boats. The Greek historian Herodotus reports that they were built by putting pieces of acacia wood about 6 ft. long on top of each other like bricks and fastening them together with pegs. In older illustrations this method is only depicted once, around 1900 B.C., in a grave from the Middle Kingdom at Beni Hasan. It is quite certain, however, that the boats were made of acacia wood, since carvings from the Old Kingdom often show yard workers standing by acacia trees which are just being felled by woodcutters. The pieces of wood were not all of the same size but were cut roughly to size before building started. It is obvious from pictures in the tomb of Ti that the boats consisted of seven parts: the bow, the stern, three baulks of timber to form the hull and a plank to top them on either side. Towards the end of the Fifth Dynasty the latter became the bulwarks. The pieces were fastened together by means of pegs and holes. The tools used were the axe to shape the tree trunks into squares, the saw to saw them up into planks, the adze for the preliminary and final stages of building, the mallet to force the pegs into the holes, and the hammer. Shipbuilders also needed thick rope, a crutch and poles with which to bend the hull. There are few scenes depicting this process. The finished hull was put on stocks. It is possible that each part of it was impregnated before being put into place, and probably the whole of the outer surface of the hull was covered with a kind of resin. Since acacia wood itself gives off some resin, this would have contributed to the effectiveness of this method of leak-proofing.

Wooden boats were frequently of the same size and shape as papyrus boats and like the latter came in two types: one with symmetrical ends and the other with asymmetrical ends, that is with the stern higher than the prow, the after end being convex and the forward end concave. Sometimes one end or even both were curved to point inwards. The fore-post and the part supporting the rudder were frequently shaped like the head of a papyrus plant, similar to papyrus boats in which the tied-up ends naturally resulted in this shape. In the Old Kingdom the heads of animals sometimes decorated the bow, among them that of a hedgehog. In some of the wooden ships the bindings of the papyrus boats were simulated by painting vertical bands down the sides of the hull.

Pharaoh Sahure's ship, about 2500 B. C.

Cargo ships, like the one of King Scesse in the Fifth Dynasty, had a kind of rail made of ropes knotted in a zigzag pattern above the top plank of the hull. The zigzag pattern was later retained as an ornament, presumably painted, on the topmost plank of ships, especially Egyptian sea-going vessels, and survived for a long time. It appears on the ships belonging to the fleet of Pharaoh Sahure about 2500 B.C. which are known to us from a relief in the temple of Anubis. They seem to have had a platform in the stern, projecting beyond the hull and surrounded by a rail. The upright stem- and stern-posts bear symbolic signs, the stern-post a hieroglyphic figure which recurs elsewhere in the relief, the stem-post an eye, the 'oculus', which we encounter again on Greek, Mediterranean and Eastern ships, painted on the side of their bows.

This relief found in the tomb of Pharaoh Sahure and now in the Berlin Museum is the earliest known illustration of sea-going vessels, and it shows that ships of that period were obviously painted, probably in bright colours, for which the Egyptians had a special liking. This is revealed again later in the ornamental treatment of the bows of Egyptian royal vessels. There is no reason why they should have been less colourful than the brightly coloured boats found in the Mediterranean today, whose 'oculus' need by no means be the sole ornamental legacy from the Egyptians.

The papyrus boats were usually propelled by either poles or paddles. Wooden craft modelled on them, although sometimes driven in the same way, were mostly fitted with oars. Wood was occasionally used for small, light boats, but its chief use lay in the construction of large ships intended for long journeys by river. They went down under oars and came up under sail. The Egyptians worked the oars with both hands, which means they could never handle two oars at the same time. Two oarsmen shared one thwart, at least on the larger vessels. On passenger vessels the same number of oarsmen sat to port and starboard all the way from the stem-post to the rudder. In cargo vessels the oarsmen sat in the forward part of the vessel only since the after part was taken up with the cargo. Three stages of rowing are depicted in Egyptian illustrations: dipping the oars, pulling them through the water, and recovering them, and accordingly the oarsmen were first shown standing up and bending forward, then sitting up straight, and lastly sitting and leaning backwards. The first of these positions, the one taken up during the dipping of the oars, is the one most frequently depicted. The oars usually rested on the bulwark, which formed a railing. They were almost certainly fastened to this in some way, but it is difficult to ascertain exactly how.

When these large boats were under oars the mast was lowered, the sail rolled up and both sail and mast rested on the cabin roof or in a crutch. While the boats were under sail the oars were stowed away out of sight inside the boat where there was sufficient room, or they were shipped against the hull with the blades resting just above the surface of the water. In this way they did not inconvenience the men whose job it was to work the sail.

The mast in the Old Kingdom was nearly always a bipod, that is, it had two legs meeting at the top; towards the end of the Old Kingdom this bipod mast was replaced by a single mast, which subsequently became the only one commonly in use. The two legs of the bipod mast rested in two steps in the bilges. If the boat had a deck they were held by a kind of iron yoke. In their upper part they were connected by cross pieces so that the mast looked rather like a ladder. Occasionally the two legs of the mast were simply tied together with rope and held together with pegs at the top. A strip of metal projected above the top of the mast to help with the fixing of the stay. In the Fourth Dynasty the mast was only supported by one stay which went from the masthead to the stern-post aft of the helmsmen. Later on a forestay was added to make the mast steadier. The mast was steadied laterally by ropes, which appear in large numbers in illustrations of Old Kingdom ships. The Egyptians drew them in a rather ambiguous way, making them seem to run from one side of the mast to the quarter. In fact, they were made fast to the face of the mast, one set to port and the other to starboard, and led off at right angles to the centreline of the ship. By a peculiarity of the drawing, the mast, too, looks as though it was set up with its two legs in line fore and aft with the centreline, whereas actually it stood astride the centreline.

The sail in reliefs from the Old Kingdom is higher than it is wide and extends from the masthead right down to the topmost plank of the hull, tapering slightly towards the foot. The canvas is bent to two yards; the top one is always visible while the lower one is frequently hidden by the bulwarks or by pieces of gear. The panels in the sail are not vertical as they were later and still are today, but horizontal. In many cases the ships belonged to kings or princes and their sails were decorated. It is very likely that the sails were fitted with boltropes, but this is not apparent from the reliefs. The lateen sail, which is triangular and has no yard along the foot, was not in common use. There is only one example we can quote, and that is questionable: it is a relief in a tomb at Deir el-Gebrawi, dating back to the end of the Old Kingdom. The simplest form of upper yard is a horizontal wooden beam corresponding in length to half or one-third the height of the mast. It could be hoisted at either end and was often thicker in the middle. In the Old Kingdom the sail was bent to the upper yard along its entire width by means of lashings which were depicted as vertical loops in a dark colour that showed up well against the light wood. This method did not give the sail much freedom and was later changed. The lower yard was usually straight and thicker than the upper yard and sometimes it was thicker in the middle.

The upper yard was fitted with an eye in the middle and in some cases with two similar eyes on either side, all of which played a part in the handling of the rigging. We do not know for certain whether brails were used in the Old Kingdom. In their stead the rope with which the yard was hoisted, the lift, was often depicted between the two legs of the bipod mast. This must have been present on all ships, even though some reliefs do not show it. In some of them, especially the one of the *Mastaba* in the Louvre, the crew can be seen hauling on the lift hoisting the sail. Since the Egyptians did not have blocks and tackles until very much later, the lift was led through a hole in the top of the mast which was probably smeared with some kind of grease to prevent the rope from breaking too often. When the sail had been hoisted to the requisite height, the lift was made fast at the foot of the mast.

The lower yard was sometimes worked by hand, sometimes with the help of sheets. It is conceivable that the oarsmen, who were otherwise unoccupied, were entrusted with this task. The upper yard was braced by means of sheets which are always shown very clearly in illustrations. The member of the crew whose job it was to brace the yards is seen standing in the stern of the ship or occasionally sitting on the cabin roof. The various sailing manoeuvres required great precision and complete co-ordination and seem to have been the responsibility of the captain and his mate. In principle the king, when he was on board, was the person in command. He delegated authority to an expert, probably the commander, who stood in the bow holding a pole to sound the depth and a piece of cloth, a kind of signal flag, with which to give his orders. It is well known that sandbanks make river navigation dangerous, and the ship was obviously manoeuvred according to the depth of water. The commander made his signals to an officer who nearly always stood on the roof of the main cabin and whose job it was to interpret the orders and pass them on. They clearly used a code of signals with which both had to be thoroughly familiar. There is one last thing worth mentioning in con-nection with sail handling: whenever the angle of the sail to the wind had to be altered it was no longer sufficient to brace the yard, but the pull had to come on the sail directly. This was done with the help of bowlines which can be seen very clearly in some reliefs. This, too, seems to confirm that the Egyptians bound their sails with boltropes, although, as we said earlier, they never appeared in illustrations. This would have made it possible to fasten the bowlines directly onto the sail, although with some difficulty. In the Old Kingdom the Egyptians had no steering rudder. Instead they used oars, which looked like the rowing oars but were much bigger and were made fast to the gunwale by means of strops. These oars, which many ships had in large numbers, were handled by men standing upright in the stern, presumably half of them to port and the other half to starboard. Some cargo vessels, however, are depicted with one centrally placed steering oar, which seems to have passed down the side of the hull. The reason for its introduction is obvious: the stern platform was entirely taken up with cargo, and there was no room left for the helmsmen to stand. Thus the central stern rudder, which came into common use from the Fourth Dynasty, may have developed through its practical necessity. Another innovation made its appearance in the Fifth Dynasty: the pole of the steering oar had a cross piece on it near the top to make it easier to use. In another cargo vessel o the same period the steering oar is resting on a short post on the stern platform and operated by a cross piece.

Large ships always had a kind of cabin which served either as a retreat for the king and his court if they wanted to rest or as stowage space for the cargo.

We have dealt with the ships of the Old Kingdom in some detail because they possess very nearly all the features which we find in later Egyptian ships and also because we have a large number of fairly precise pictorial records from this period. We shall now try to give an account of what few noticeable alterations were made in the periods to follow, most of which represented a definite step forward compared to the old methods.

In the Twelfth Dynasty (i.e. the middle of the 19th century B.C.) the funeral boats were given a very special shape derived from the sacred barques: the stern-post was sickle-shaped in profile, while the stem-post was drawn up vertically and widened out slightly towards the end. These boats were equipped with two steering oars, one to port and one to starboard, each lashed to a post. They had neither mast nor sail, since they were always towed. Apart from funeral boats there were other types of vessels in the Middle Kingdom that were customarily towed. They had the same shape as the craft by which they were towed but possessed no rigging whatsoever. They had one single central steering oar supported by a short post and operated by a cross piece. There was a cabin for the king, and one illustration at least shows his litter on which he could have himself carried to his final destination immediately the boat had tied up.

As a rule the boats of the Middle Kingdom (1991–1778 B.C.) had a stern-post which was slightly higher than the stem-post and curved forward at the upper end, while the stem-post ended in a sharp point. Undoubtedly the shape of the stern-post had something to do with the introduction of the single stern rudder, since it provided a simple way of lashing the latter to the stern and at the same time giving it the necessary play. When the boat was being rowed the sail was rolled round the mast and thus could be lowered and stowed on top of the cabin as in the Old Kingdom ships.

The sail was always rectangular, sometimes wider than it was high, and the panels of the cloth were no longer horizontal but vertical. The yards were straight and had braces attached to them.

While the funeral boats were hardly changed in the New Kingdom (1570–1085 B.C.), other vessels underwent a number of innovations. The stern-post was no longer curved forward, a shape which we assume was dictated by the central position of the stern rudder. In the New Kingdom the problem presented itself in a different way: in most boats the steering rudder, though still aligned on the centreline, passed down the side of the hull forward of the stern-post, a custom we have already met in the Old Kingdom. With this arrangement it was no longer necessary to tie the steering oar to the stern-post. Another solution was to have a deep groove in the top of the stern-post for resting the steering oar. Cargo vessels primarily used this method, and frequently the groove can be seen even when the steering oar passes down the side of the hull, which suggests that

Queen Hatshepsut's ship, about 1480 B.C.

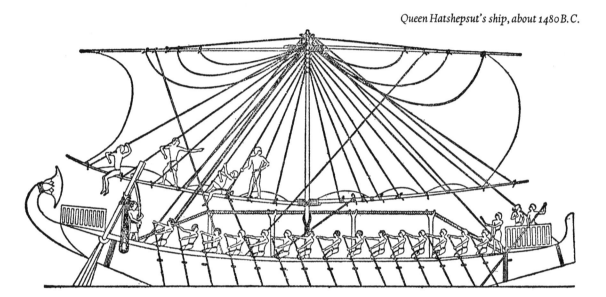

the crew could utilize either method. The second change is that the mast was no longer lowered when the boat was being rowed but remained upright, supported by its two stays. Besides, the mast must have been permanently anchored in the deck, since it appears that shrouds were no longer used. The sail was much wider than it was high. Along its upper edge it was no longer bent to the yard with tiers which were very close together but simply with three lines, one at each end and one in the middle. In this way the sail could catch the wind more efficiently. Nor were the yards of the same shape: the upper yard was convex, the lower concave. The brails are clearly visible, especially those of the lower yard. These 'false lifts' were much more useful in the New Kingdom since the lower yard was no longer level with the bridge, as it had been previously, but considerably above it, about half-way up the mast. It was more common for ships in the New Kingdom to have a platform both fore and aft round which ran a rail decorated with flowers or symbolic motifs.

Reliefs in the temple of Deir el-Bahari describe the expedition of Queen Hatshepsut (who reigned from 1492 to 1472 B.C.) to the land of Punt, which was probably Somaliland. This suggests that the ships depicted were sea-going vessels built for the Red Sea. They had platforms contained by a railing, and ornamented stem- and stern-posts, the latter

Right: Model of a warship carved from bone, 1815, Lg.·

82

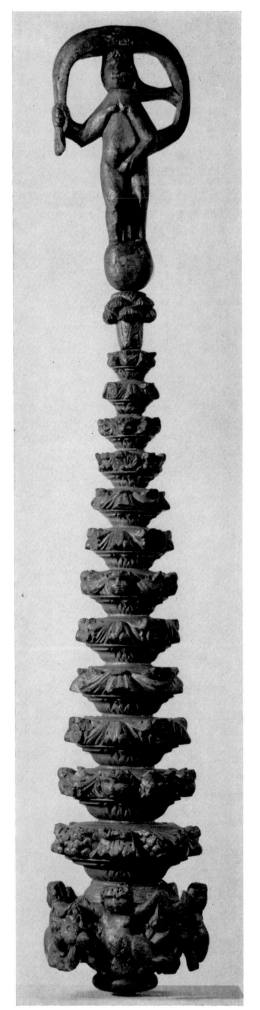

a

b

c

Khorsobad, 706 B. C.

Left: Carved and gilded mastheads of 18th century ships, a, Rm; b, As; c, Fb.

85

curving forward and terminating in a flower. The model boat from the tomb of Tutankhamen, which has been mentioned before, has decorations painted on its sides and large figure-heads in the shape of ibex heads at the bow and stern. Similar heads, facing in the same direction, can be found on the sacred bark of the god Amen-Ra depicted in a very well preserved relief from around 1300 B.C. in the temple of Sethos I in Abydos.

The first portrayal of a sea battle is to be found in a wall relief in the tomb of Pharaoh Rameses III at Medinet Habu. Rameses' warships in it clearly betray the influence of shipbuilding among the Mediterranean countries with which Egypt waged war, one particularly noticeable feature being the ram at the bow, which we meet again in Greek and Roman warships. In Rameses II's warships it is decorated with a lion's head.

On the subject of ornamental art in old Egyptian ships Köster's remarks may be quoted: 'In a country where since time immemorial arts and crafts had reached a very high level of perfection it was natural that ships and their equipment should have been decorated and embellished. Already there existed in the Old Kingdom a number of ornamental art forms which gradually developed into displays of magnificent splendour. Nevertheless, they always betray their origin. From the very beginning the Egyptians never chose the motifs with which they decorated their ships haphazardly. They grew organically from constructional forms, one example being the lashings on papyrus boats, which were later adopted as ornaments on wooden ships. Similarly, the ropes tied round the forward and after ends of ships to serve as anchorage points for the thick rope that was stretched along the entire length of the ship to give fore-and-aft support were subsequently retained as ornaments. The artist may not always have been aware of the original function of the ornaments, of course. The stern-post especially was always lavishly and spectacularly decorated – indeed it has always been a favourite part for ornamental treatment all over the world. Very often it was shaped like a flower, open or closed, bent forward to face the bow or aft to face the sea, and sometimes pointing upwards to serve as a base for a sundial. The bow was customarily painted with symbolic signs such as the hieroglyph signifying life or prosperity. The 'oculus', which has recently been interpreted as the 'eye of Horus', was given a marked predominance.

'The flower is occasionally replaced by an animal head, either purely ornamental or as symbol of a deity. Processional barges and royal yachts had richly decorated sails, often with squares in different colours. The way in which red, blue and white squares alternated with each other made the sail look as though it had been made from interwoven panels. At first sails were obviously made of mats of interlaced reeds until finer cloths came into use. They in turn were given an ornamental treatment which had its origin in the weaving technique used for these mats.

'If the pharaoh himself, or possibly the deity represented by his or her statue, was on board, a magnificent pavilion was erected amidships or in the after part of the ship, made of wooden pillars which were carved, painted and possibly even gilded, and had precious cloths and carpets spread over them as protection from the sun. Here again we come across the chessboard pattern, reminiscent of interwoven reed matting, sometimes with pictorial patterns woven into it. Carpets with lavish patterns were often draped over the sides of the vessel. A throne made of precious materials stood in the pavilion, and in front of it was erected the standard of the king or god.

'The gear of the ship was decorated as well; some items may even have been made of precious materials. We are told of oars that were made of ebony and inlaid with rolled silver. The oar and rudder blades were freely decorated with lotus and papyrus motifs as well as with geometrical patterns. The stem-post frequently terminated in a hawk's head, and the stern-post was also shaped into the head of a divine animal.

'We can imagine these state vessels decorated down to the last detail, painted in many bright colours and glittering with gold and silver and other precious materials. A procession of these ships under the sparkle of the southern sun must have been a magnificent spectacle indeed.'

In Mesopotamia, too, a river navigation similar to that on the Nile had been developed in very early times. This is confirmed by finds, among them the silver model of a boat from Ur, which scarcely looks any different from our present-day rowing boats. Beyond the Euphrates and Tigris deltas sea-going ships plied the Persian Gulf, and it is conceivable that they established a sea connection with the seafaring people of the Indus

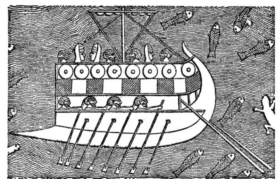

Reliefs from the palace of Sennacherib, about 690 B. C.

Ships on Cretan seals

culture. But we possess no pictorial records of early ships in Mesopotamia as we do for Egypt; the only representative example belongs to Assyrian times. One of the earliest records is a large relief in the palace of Sargon in Khorsobad from the year 706 B.C. depicting what are obviously Phoenician sea-going ships. The stem-posts are shaped like horses' heads, the stern-posts like fishtails. Both come up very high. From ancient cuneiform inscriptions we know that they were called the horns of the ship, and in fact genuine bulls' horns were sometimes fitted on top of them. It is thought that

Boat from the Cyclades

Boat from Cyprus

Greek ship

Greek ship

this shape of stem- and stern-post, as well as the Phoenician method of building ships with a keel and frames which is still used today but which was unknown to the Egyptians, originated in Mesopotamia and was later taken over by the Phoenicians. Stem-posts in the shape of horses' heads already appear in pictures of Phoenician tribute ships in front of the palace gates of Balawat, dating back to the reign of Shalmaneser in the 9th century B.C., while Sargon's son Sennacherib had his palace ornamented with reliefs of what were obviously Phoenician war and cargo ships. In both types we can see round shields decorating the topsides, which remind us of the shields hung on the gunwales of Viking ships and also of the painted coats of arms on royal vessels of the late 15th and early 16th centuries, for example Henry VIII's *Henri Grâce à Dieu*. Sennacherib's warships had the long ram typical of fighting vessels in the Mediterranean.

In those days the Assyrians, and later the Persians, employed Phoenician seamen and possibly even 'chartered' ships complete with crews from the Phoenicians. This illustrates yet again the decisive influence Mediterranean shipbuilding had from the 2nd millennium B.C. on the subsequent history of shipbuilding. Crete was the first to dominate the Mediterranean and probably acquired its prosperity, to which the palace of Minos at Knossos still bears witness, by extensive sea trading. The Cretans' traditions were passed on to both the Phoenicians and the Mycenaeans in early Greece.

The inhabitants of the widely scattered islands and peninsulas of the Greek archipelago were destined by their very geographical situation to turn towards the sea. In fact, the most illustrious epochs in the history of the Greeks are the ones when their ships could navigate the whole Mediterranean freely from end to end.

'According to tradition Minos was the first to own a ship: he made himself ruler of what is now known as the Hellenic Sea; he conquered the islands of the Aegean and became the first to colonize most of them.' Thus wrote Thucydides, but while the pictures of small, rather delicate ships on vases from the 3rd millennium tell of the riches of the island of Melos, which at the time yielded a very precious stone, obsidian, it is not until much later, after the golden age of Crete, that the existence of a ruling fleet in the central Mediterranean can be confirmed. It sailed east as far as Egypt and Syria and westwards beyond Sicily. The so-called Mycenaean culture seems to have spread even further between the 14th and 12th centuries B.C. It was then that the export of merchandise grew considerably – clear proof that then a real fleet existed and that proper sea routes were mapped out, linking well-known ports of call. We also know that at a date over which historians are still in dispute but which was certainly no later than 1183 B.C. (the year Eratosthenes names for the capture of Troy) the Greeks sent out a real 'armada' in search of Helen.

We know very little about the ships that were in use at that time. Not that art in the 2nd millennium has left no records of them, but the pictures, mostly on rings or engraved in stones, are of such diminutive size and so sketchy that details cannot be recognized. They only show the boats in profile, with a full and capacious hull, a main mast and a rather large sail which required permanent rigging. The detailed descriptions by 'Homer' are of little use since he lived several centuries after the events he writes about, and it is precisely during those centuries that the Central European peoples overran the Greek peninsula and the surrounding islands, and destroyed the Mycenaean culture. They did not concern themselves with the sea, being too preoccupied with settling down in the conquered land, and they allowed the maritime power which their predecessors had built up to decline. They left the sea to pirates and to those who, for some time to come, were to dominate the Mediterranean as a new sea power: the Phoenicians.

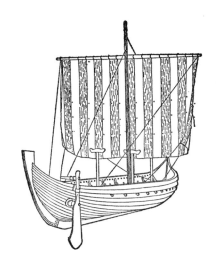

Gokstad ship, about 800

At the same time that Homer wrote his epics the Greeks were building up another fleet, and the descriptions from the *Iliad* and the *Odyssey* refer no doubt to these new ships. The enthusiasm with which the poet lists the ships of the Greeks in the second song of the *Iliad* and his preference for adventures in foreign lands which is borne out in the *Odyssey*, are evidence of the renaissance of shipbuilding and navigation in the 8th century B.C. Hundreds of Greeks from many towns, above all Corinth, Megara, Chalcis and Miletus, crossed the seas to Southern Italy and Sicily, to Macedonia and Thrace, as far as the other side of the Bosphorus, to found new towns and resettle the overflow of population. The vessels in which these courageous pioneers went to sea were galleys, the longest of them about 88 ft. long. They were propelled by oars, but each possessed a mast which could be lowered and which was used whenever there was any wind. The mast was rigged with a peculiar sail made of strips of canvas stitched together side by side. These ships were very light and fast, with a shallow hull and a bow that came sweeping up like a horn. They had no decks to speak of but two narrow platforms fore and aft for the watch, the captain and the mate. When one was used as a warship a long, narrow bridge was added which ran from one end of the ship to the other. On this the warriors stood. There was a space on either side for the oarsmen, and the bow was fitted with a ram for attacking smaller enemy ships. Undoubtedly there were also cargo vessels with much fuller lines, but there are neither pictorial nor written records of them. In any case, they could not have been very numerous at a time when piracy was so widespread that every ship had to be equipped for battle.

We cannot trace in detail the development which from the end of the 6th century B.C. led to the design of those types of ships that remained in use till more or less the end of antiquity. Progress showed itself in the improved strength and speed of the vessels. They continued to have oars as well as sails, but the number of oarsmen increased and the sails became larger in size. Once the threat of piracy had ceased to exist, the difference

Right: Lion's head, detail of picture b on page 90.
Page 90: a, Stern decoration from the 'Vasa', royal ship of King Gustavus Adolphus of Sweden. Two griffins support the crown above an idealized picture of the king, below it the initials GARS (Gustavus Adolphus Rex Sueciae); oak, originally gilded, 1628, Sw; b, Royal coat of arms on the stern of the 'Vasa', oak, escutcheon originally painted in polychrome, lions and crown gilded, 1628, Sw.

a

b

a

b

c

Prow

see Notes

Page 91: Decorations from the 'Vasa'; a, c, Caryatids from the port gallery, spruce, originally gilded, 1628, Sw; b, Figure of Hercules with club from the port railing of the upper deck, oak, originally gilded, lower part of mask originally painted ochre and red, 1628, Sw. Left: Lower gun deck of the 'Vasa', 1628, Sw.

93

between warships and cargo ships became much more clearly marked. The warships, which served as escort vessels in an emergency, were designed for battles in which numerous fleets took part. There were rather more sea battles in Greek history than there have been in more modern times.

These ships were built with several banks of oars, with the galley slaves sitting at different levels and staggered so that they did not hinder each other. This principle underwent certain variations in the course of time: the old five-banked warship, which was much too heavy, was replaced at the end of the 5th century by the three-banked vessel, the *trireme*, which had a beam of at least 20 ft. and an overall length of 125 ft. It had fine lines but was so ingeniously designed that it could hold a crew of two hundred (three banks of oarsmen, a military command group and presumably a few men to handle the sails). These light and easily manoeuvrable vessels could reach a speed of seven knots. The marble pedestal on which the winged 'Victory of Samothrace' stands in the Louvre represents a small part of the bow of such a trireme.

Towards the end of the 4th century ships developed a tendency to become enormous without otherwise changing their basic conception. Some of the ships built were almost unusable and much too difficult to manoeuvre: the four- and five-banked vessels of Alexander's time were followed by eight-, nine-, ten- and eleven-banked ships built under the Diadochi. The invention of heavy machinery like catapults made it possible to go even further. There was a thirteen-banked ship that needed eighteen hundred men to move it along; Demetrius Poliorcetes constructed one with sixteen banks at the end of the 3rd century B.C.; and at the same time Ptolemy Philopator proudly launched one with forty banks which was about 400 ft. long and 50 ft. in beam. Its figure-head rose 70 ft. above the water. Four thousand oarsmen, of whom the ones in the lowest bank had to handle oars 55 ft. long, were needed to push this monster along, which was so heavy that it was only used for ceremonial occasions.

As far as ornamental features on Greek ships are concerned we know from all the available pictorial records that they were richly painted. We can see large eyes on either side of the bow and the characteristic prow with its horn pointing upwards as well as a ram projecting horizontally from the bow. The ram is often shaped like the head of an animal whose eyes then stood for the oculus, which was otherwise painted on either side of the bow. The horn is sometimes decorated with wood carvings, and the forward-curving stern-post frequently terminates in an animal's head, too, or in a kind of fishtail, the *aphlaston*. On many of the drawings and sculptures of ships that have been found we can make out ornaments in relief, doubtlessly carvings, as well as rows of shields hung up on the rail, in the same way as they were on the ships of Sennacherib. Carvings and paintings along the gunwale and the sides of the hull seem to have been quite common.

The votive ship in the Beirut museum has relief ornaments at the bow and stern. Among the many paintings of ships on Greek pottery one of the most impressive is that on the bowl of Exekias now in the Munich Antikensammlung. 28c

Roman shipbuilding was based on Greek tradition. Basically the type of the large, multi-oared Mediterranean rowing ships did not change right up to the galleys of more recent times. As always the extent of their ornamentation will have depended on the purpose for which they were intended, which means that flag ships and pleasure craft of rulers will undoubtedly have been the most splendidly decorated.

We know from a relief found at Ostia what Roman trading ships looked like. The curved stern-post terminated in a swan's head, and beyond it projected a platform, while the stem was decorated with the figure of a goddess, maybe Isis, who was regarded in early Imperial Rome as the protectress of mariners. She was also protrayed as such on Roman coins, holding a billowing sail. She must not be confused with Nike, who was occasionally portrayed as goddess of victory on warships, one example being the 'Victory

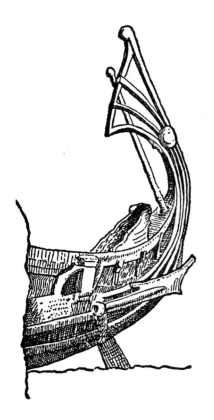

Aphlaston

Roman merchant ship

of Samothrace'. The merchant ship in the Ostia relief had figures carved in relief at the bow and stern, and the ship fountain in Rome, too, has a figure on the bow, possibly a lion's head. We may assume that even in those times figureheads stood for the name of the ship. Name plates on the bow were not unknown in antiquity either. Many of the names of ships are preserved in records, and we can gather from these that the Greeks and Romans, as is now common practice everywhere, already preferred to give their ships feminine names.

Köster points out that Greek and Roman shipbuilders and designers were known and mentioned by name, which proves that shipbuilding in antiquity was regarded as more than mere craftsmanship and manual skill was not all that a shipwright was credited with.

In Northern Europe a number of prehistoric carvings of ships on rocks and cave walls have been preserved, some of those in North Scandinavia dating right back to the Neolithic period, as far back as 2000 B.C., while the large group of the Southern Scandinavian ones belong to the later Bronze and Iron Ages.

There are no signs of pre-Christian influence of Mediterranean shipbuilding in Northern Europe, even if the broad dissemination of the Megalithic culture, which originated in the Eastern Mediterranean and from 2000 B.C. spread along the coasts to Spain, France, Ireland, England, Northern Germany and Southern Scandinavia, is proof of extensive and continuous sea traffic.

Many other rock paintings, for example the ones found in Bohuslän in Sweden or in Austrheim on the Nordfjord in Norway, show boats with sledge-type runners extending horizontally from the keel. The Hjortspring Boat found in a bog on the island of Als is a live example of this type. Thought to have been built in the 3rd century B.C., it is a wooden boat with planks that were not nailed but tied to the frames with animal sinews. It has been argued from this that ships of this type were modelled on boats similar to Eskimo kayaks, which are made from animal hides stitched together and stretched over wooden frames. This theory would explain the nature of the many vertical supports which can be seen connecting the gunwale and keel in the rock carvings: they represent the ribs of the wooden skeleton.

There are no ornamentations to be found on the Hjortspring Boat, but as in later excavations the possibility cannot be ruled out that it might have been painted in one or more colours. The fact that no traces of paint are left disproves nothing, since even the *Vasa*, who sank with her paint still fresh and was well preserved in the waters of the Baltic for a mere three centuries, had hardly any paint left on her when she was raised. Most of the rock carvings of Scandinavian boats have their curved, decorated ends in common, often topped by animal heads resembling those of early Egyptian and Mediterranean ships. Nor do any of the finds of Northern ships of the following centuries, when planks were no longer sewn together but nailed together in clinker fashion, feature any carved ornaments to speak of. The most important amongst the ships of this period are: the Nydam boat excavated from a peat bog in Schleswig which was built during the time of the Anglo-Saxon conquest of Britain; the Sutton Hoo ship built about 670 A.D.; the Norwegian boats from Kvalsund (about 700 A.D.), Fjörtoft, Holmedal, and Bårsal; the Swedish ones from Runa, Äskekärr, Vendel, Valsgärde and Rasbokill. Most of these are Viking vessels dating from the time when Norse warriors invaded the coasts and ports of Europe. With the exception of the large and lavishly decorated Oseberg Ship, believed to have been a kind of pleasure ship belonging to a Viking princess and dating from about 800 A.D., very little of the decorations that adorned the famous ships of the fearsome Scandinavian conquerors remains. The slightly later Gokstad Ship has no decorations on it either, but the numerous pictorial stones from the 5th to 8th centuries on the Island of Gotland portray Viking ships very similar to the Oseberg Ship, all of which have ornamented stem- and stern-posts, usually a spiral like the Oseberg Ship aft and an animal head forward. In this they strangely resemble the Phoenician ships with their horses' heads and fishtails. Two dragons' heads from Viking ships have been retrieved from the mud of the Scheldt, and written records confirm that Norman warships were fitted with dragons' heads at the bow and stern. They are shown on the famous Bayeux Tapestry which portrays William the Conqueror's fleet during its crossing to Hastings in 1066. There are quite a number of long-ships of the Gotland, Oseberg and Gokstad type on this tapestry, and their colourful treatment seems to confirm that all these early Germanic vessels were painted in different colours, apparently in certain significant combinations and following the lines of the clinker planking. Church murals on Jutland painted 300 years later still depict very much the same treatment of ships' sides. In the Bayeux Tapestry the animal heads on the stem-posts are remarkably colourful. In shape they still resemble the strange heads of the Oseberg treasure, probably the most outstanding artistic evidence of the Viking period, whose exact purpose, though, is still unknown. They are painted and some are liberally covered with silver nails. According to contemporary accounts, some of the awe-inspiring dragons' heads on Viking ships were gilded.

Himmelstadlund (Sweden), Bronze Age

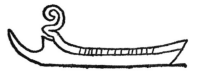

Bohuslän (Sweden), Bronze Age

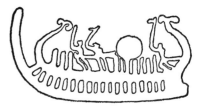

Bohuslän (Sweden), Bronze Age

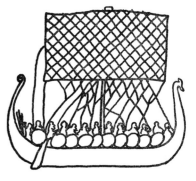

Gotland (Sweden), about 700

68c, d; 96

68a, b

Right: Figure from the stern of the Hamburg ship 'Die Admiralität von Hamburg', oak, 1691, Hh.
Page 98: a, b, Capitals in the shape of heads from the 'Vasa', oak, originally gilded, 1628, Sw; c, Jackstaff socket early 19th century, As; d, Lion's head, figurehead from a Swedish East Indiaman, early 18th century, Ss.
Page 99: Figure from the stern of the Hamburg ship 'Kaiser Leopoldus Primus', 1669, Hh.
Page 100: a, Royal coat of arms of King William III from the stern of a British warship, about 1700, Lg; b, Carved equestrian figure of Charles XI of Sweden from the stern of the 'Carolus XI', 1678, Ss.

Flag ship of William the Conqueror, Bayeux Tapestry 11th century

a

b

c

d

a

b

a

b

c

d

e

f

a

b

c

d

e

f

g

h

i

a

b

c

d

Wood-carving on Ships

The Ornamentation of Bows, Sterns, Masts, Rudders, Decks and Cabins

see Notes

Since ships have always been at the mercy of the ravages of nature – in other words, the hand of God – more than any other product of human invention, they have always and everywhere had an extraordinary mythical and religious importance. This is to be seen in the rites of sea-going primitive races, in the mythology of the ancient world, in the ship burials of the Vikings and certainly not least of all in the fact that nowhere is there as much handed-down superstition – even in our enlightened age – as among 'Christian' seafaring peoples.

This explains why, as the technical and architectural feats in shipbuilding became more and more spectacular over the centuries, shipbuilders, just like temple and church architects, had to give more and more attention to the ornamentation of their works. Indeed, the ornamentation was frequently extremely lavish, be it to humour the gods, or to satisfy the extravagant tastes of the rulers representing the divine or worldly authority.

Throughout history, ships have been richly ornamented. Because until a hundred years ago they were made almost exclusively of wood, the ornaments consisted nearly always of wood carvings, often gaily painted, if only to protect them against the sea and weather. We can say that wood-carving in shipbuilding corresponds to sculpture in architecture.

Wood carvings on ships can be mainly divided into bow and stern decorations and mast and rudder decorations, although there is scarcely a part of the ship which has not come in for decoration at some time, particularly in the Baroque period when ships were virtually overladen with ornaments. In the Western world the art of ornamental wood-carving in ships undoubtedly reached its peak in the 17th and 18th centuries, and this applies to quality as well. Unfortunately there is so little original material available that we must refer to whatever few and fortuitous discoveries there have been, irre-

Page 101: Rudder head, 18th century, Bf.
Page 102: Rudder ornaments; a, From a Genoese galley, 17th century, Vn; b, From a Neapolitan state barge, 18th century, Vn; c, 18th century; d, 20th century, At; e, 18th century, Sn; f, 18th century, Rm.
Page 103: 18th century rudder-heads; a, f, Rm; b, i, Sn; c, e, As; d, Ou; g, Bf; h, Je.
Left: 18th century rudder-heads, a, Sn; b, Bf; c, d, Rm.

spective of their artistic quality and state of preservation, in compiling this chapter on the art history of shipbuilding. This must always be borne in mind when evaluating the rôle that wood carvings played in shipbuilding. Of all the wood carvings on Renaissance and Baroque ships (let alone earlier ones) not even a ten-thousandth part has survived. After all, ships had a short life. Those that did not go up in flames and sink in battle were broken up and their wood carvings used on other ships. In this way they were either dispersed or finally destroyed. What is left of them today are a few insignificant remnants, far too few in number to form a reliable basis on which to construct a scientific survey of this important branch of the history of art. Nor do the large numbers of pictures of old warships yield sufficient information to allow for a thorough study of the subject and for it to be analysed from every angle. And although it is touched upon in the many books that have been written on the development of ship types, it is always considered of strictly secondary importance and treated in general terms only.

Stern decorations on Roman warship

It is therefore impossible to answer the question as to when man first started to decorate ships or, for example, to trace the development which led from primitive tribal symbols to painted and carved stem ornaments and finally to figure-heads (a development which is of particular importance in this connection since no type of ship decoration has been as universally popular as the stem ornament, whether symbolic, heraldic or figurative), without frequently resorting to hypothetical interpretations of the available material.

Apart from a few finds like the Norwegian Viking ships, the Swedish royal flagship *Vasa* and a few surviving fragments of original carvings, the material on which we must base our research consists of model ships made as votive offerings or burial gifts, models made for various other purposes, pictures of ships on pottery, coins, seals, tapestries, glasses, mosaics, tombstones and sculptures and in paintings and drawings. Their accurate presentation by the artist cannot always be relied upon.

The earliest ships were undoubtedly tree-trunks, from which the dugout canoe developed. It is conceivable that ships were first given signs or symbols to mark them as common or personal property, and from this was born a desire for decoration. The basic concern of primeval man was procuring food, more specifically meat. When he went out hunting he used animal skins and heads as a camouflage under which to stalk his prey. In many cases he probably did this standing or sitting in the bow of his canoe so that this need for camouflage may have been the first stage in a development that resulted in the figure-head.

see Notes

However, the main reasons underlying the ornamentation of ships must have been mythical and religious. This becomes quite clear in the chapters on shipbuilding in antiquity and shipbuilding outside Europe, as well as the one on votive customs in the Mediterranean. As man battled against the sea in its unpredictable moods he imagined that he was facing a deity whose temper might be one of either fury or benevolence. In all probability he thought that the god might punish him if he made him angry, and so he offered up sacrifices of humans or animals to placate him. Consequently it became the custom to display the offerings on a pole to show the god that the sacrifice had been made. This explains why ships, even in modern times, have carried the symbols of such offerings on board, for instance the symbol of a lamb's fleece.

179a, b

There are still fishing ports today where one can see boats displaying the horns of goats or other animals or a sheep's fleece with which their owners hope to placate the furies of the sea.

Informative details about Roman, Phoenician, Greek and Egyptian ships can be derived from pictures on coins, vases and mosaics, to name but a few things, which

168c, d

portray contemporary vessels and items of gear. Many of them show the oculus, the eye painted or carved on the bow. This is the earliest form of ship ornamentation we know, and it can still be seen today on many Portuguese, Chinese, Italian and Indian ships.

Roman merchant ship

The earliest Egyptian oculi were elongated, those on early Chinese ships round, while present-day ones take many different forms. It is likely that both the story of the god Ra, who drives across the sky in his sun chariot, and the myth of the eye of Horus, were responsible for the oldest forms of ship ornamentation we know – the sun wheel and the oculus.

On the ships of earlier seafarers we find pictures and carvings of swans, horses, bulls, geese, ibises and bears, as well as fan-shaped lotus flowers and gilded statues of gods which indicated the ship's home port. Athenian ships carried the statue of the goddess Pallas Athene, those of Carthage the god Ammon. All ships belonging to one state carried the statue of the same god or goddess, but their figure-heads were often designed to mark individual ships. The same was true of painted ornaments and carvings. Not everybody could understand a name spelt out in letters, but a figure or a picture was an obvious means of identification. Painted decorations and bronze reliefs were common on Roman ships about 200 A.D., while the use of figure-heads can be traced back to the year 50 A.D. Egyptian ships, on the other hand, had painted or carved figure-heads as far back as the 2nd millennium B.C.

The Bible tells of a journey which the Apostle Paul made from Malta to Syracuse on board an Alexandrian ship and mentions a sign which is thought to represent a figure-head. The passage is *Acts* 28. 11. In the Authorized Version it reads as follows: 'And after three months we departed in a ship of Alexandria, which had wintered in the isle, whose sign was Castor and Pollux.' The Moffat Bible expresses it even more precisely: '...with the Dioscuri as her figureheads...' The heavenly twins were probably represented by a carving, or even a simple painting, on the bow. It may even have been a bronze relief. We know from the fittings on the Nemi ship (now in the Naples museum) that cast-bronze ornaments were used at that time.

Even in more recent times there have been ships in Venetian waters bearing stars and other symbols that resembled very closely the oculus of antiquity, and on Lake Garda in Northern Italy one can still see boats with ornamented stem-posts, figure-heads and painted ornaments. Another reminder of ancient customs is a fishing boat in Venice whose bow is decorated with very attractive, old-fashioned paintings made up in part of female figures. In Sicily we come across innumerable brightly painted boats, many of them with oculi. On ships in Asian waters we find traditional ornaments which have been handed down over many centuries and are part of a religious ceremony accompanying the building and launching of the vessel. The *Jafna Dhoni* has a stem-post terminating in a spiral and an oculus on either side of the bow. The Masula boats of Madras have the ends of their stem-posts carved into peculiar little knobs and crudely shaped figures carved into them. In Europe we find Portuguese ships decorated with a fleece on the stem-post and various kinds of ornaments, particularly coloured stars and oculi, which may be the direct descendants of Phoenician traditions.

The ancient Chinese junks were decorated with wooden dragons, either carved or cut in relief and painted. Today the imaginative decorations on these vessels consist mainly of geometric patterns and the old-established oculus. Sometimes the Phoenix, the immortal bird, is featured as well. The Ning-Po junks have very splendid paintings decorating their sterns. The stem-post of the Viking ship found near Oseberg on the Oslofjord and believed to date back to the beginning of the 9th century is crowned with the spiral of a snake ending in a head with glaring eyes. The stern is shaped like the tail and rolled up like the forward end. An intricately carved motif extends along the stem-post from the waterline upwards and a short way along the bow and stern. The similarity of this ornamentation and that on canoes used in the Pacific e. g. by the Maoris, is quite striking. The Bayeux Tapestry provides us with information on the way the Vikings decorated their ships. In it we can see ships painted in horizontal stripes of red and yellow, red and black, or blue and yellow. The stem- and stern-posts are crowned with carved dragons or, as has been argued recently, leopards. Two such heads from Viking ships have been found in the mud of the Scheldt; one of them is now in the British Museum, the other in the Nationaal Scheepvaart Museum in Antwerp. They are very much cruder than the heads found with the Oseberg ship, which are similar in type but very finely carved and adorned with silver nails. What purpose the Oseberg heads originally served is still a matter for conjecture, but it is very likely that it had nothing to do with the ship itself.

Gable heads on tent supports of Gokstad ship

65

see Notes

Right: a, Venetian heraldic lion from a ship, about 1700, Vn; b, Carving from the port quarter of a galley, second half 17th century, Vn.
Page 110: a, b, c, Lions' heads from gun port lids; a, From the 'Vasa', 1628, Sw; b, 18th century, Rm; c, Lion's head off a sailing ship, about 1800, Rm; d, e, Figures of lions decorating rudders; d, 1776, Rm; e, 19th century, At; f, 18th century, As.

a

b

a

d

b

e

c

f

a

b

c

d

e

f

a

b

c

Bergen (Norway), 1376

Detail of sculpture from the 'Vasa'

Page 111: Coats of arms from stern decorations; a, Arms of the Morosini, late 17th century, Vn; b, Coat of arms from the 'Belgica', 1897, At; c, Swedish royal arms, 17th century, Go; d, Family arms of the house of Vasa, from the 'Vasa', 1628, Sw; e, 18th century, Os; f, Coat of arms from the 'Royal Charles', 1656, Ar. Left: Coats of arms used as stern decorations, Vn; a, 1866; b, Galley, mid 18th century; c, Neapolitan ship, 18th century

When round bows came into fashion they put an end to the high, carved stem-posts of the long ships, and from then onwards the bow was decorated with an insignificant coat of arms or a small tapering animal. The method of building lent itself less to lavish ornamentation. But when the prow and beak-head were introduced new possibilities for ornamental treatment were opened up. Signs and symbols on the bow and stern seem to have disappeared, but at the same time a new genre of embellishment developed when the high forecastles and aftercastles came into fashion with their Gothic pillars, arches, tracery and heraldic shields. The latter were a relic of the times when soldiers hung their battle shields over the railings of the castles, as the Vikings had hung theirs on the sides of their ships. It is possible that this form of decoration originated during the Crusades, when so many nations took part that the recognition of friend and foe was of some importance. It was in the 16th century that art in shipbuilding really began to flourish. Its main function was to provide the big warships with painted or carved figures and ornaments. It played a particularly notable role in the 16th and 17th centuries and the beginning of the 18th century, which in the history of art corresponds to the Renaissance and Baroque periods. For various psychological reasons big warships were decorated in such a manner as to emphasize the military and political power of a country. The leading humanists and artists in each country were called upon to draw up the iconographic plan for a ship's ornamentation and to make sure that the work was done according to the ruler's instructions. This was an important branch of artistic activity in seafaring countries, and wood-carving in shipbuilding at that time must not be overlooked as an aspect of art as a whole. Already in 1543 one Jeffrey Bytharne considered the subject of ship ornamentation important enough to write about at length. He lays down precisely the various forms that ship decorations ought to take: the exterior decorations from the waterline to the top of the castles were to be painted in the colours and with the device of the admiral; the fore and after decks were to be decorated as splendidly as possible, the shields bearing the arms of the admiral.

Elizabethan ships were painted in the colours of the Tudors, green and white, red, scarlet, yellow and blue. As figure-heads the dragon and lion were popular, and the stern had the royal arms painted or carved on it. This was more or less universal throughout Europe. The preference of the Tudors for bright, contrasting colours lasted through the whole of their period. During the reign of James I carved and gilded ornaments became fashionable, which represented a notable departure from Elizabethan ships. Stern galleries had been introduced before this, and soon they became a dominant decorative element. The long, low prow and the point of the beak-head carried the same kind of ornamentation till after the middle of the 17th century and gave ships a very warlike appearance.

89; 90a, b; 91a, b, c; 92; 98a,b; 110a; 111d

In the *Vasa*, the ship of King Gustavus Adolphus of Sweden, one of the most powerful rulers of this time, we have an example of a splendidly decorated and gilded state vessel and warship. Equipped with 64 cannons she sank in Stockholm harbour on 10 August 1628. Rediscovering and salvaging her provided a new and better basis for scientific research into shipbuilding and ship ornamentation of that epoch. In the 333 years during which the *Vasa* lay at the bottom of the sea her nails and bolts were eaten away by rust, her forecastles and after-castles collapsed and the carvings and ornaments fell down into the mud and sand, where most of them were protected from damage. Since the water of the Baltic contains insufficient salt for teredo worms to live, the ornaments, and indeed the entire hull, escaped the ravages of this voracious marine borer which does not shrink from devouring the most massive of oak hulls. So far seven hundred carvings and ornaments belonging to this ship have been retrieved from the mud. As the ship is restored it is planned to replace them exactly as they were originally, thus making the *Vasa* look just as she did before she sank. Although it may yet take a good many years before the work is completed it is not too difficult at this stage to imagine where most of the carvings belong and to get a pretty good idea of what the ornamentation on a 17th-century ship looked like. The stern section of the *Vasa*, the part that was most severely damaged, has been reconstructed to such an extent that the shape of the after-castle can be determined. It was evidently built in 16th-century style, comparatively high and narrow (about 13ft. wide at the top) and with two steps in it. In the history of shipbuilding the *Vasa* thus represents an interesting example of the transition from the 16th to the 17th century. In the 16th century ship ornamentation was mainly painted. We know this from some very good models and pictures. The Museo Naval in Madrid is in possession of a model which, according to the records, was presented to Philip III by a Flemish ambassador and probably dates from 1593. All along the sides from fore to aft it is decorated with purely ornamental patterns in the style of the Renaissance, either gilded or painted in bright colours. In a well-known painting showing Henry VIII embarking at Dover, we can see that the upper parts of the forecastles and after-castles are decorated with heraldic shields. On the stern is the coat of arms of England, which was probably painted on, not carved. It is repeated on the after bulkhead of the forecastle. In the Statens Sjöhistoriska Museum at Stockholm there is a votive ship which was originally in the possession of the Storkyrka in Stockholm. The sides of the hull from end to end are painted with male heads framed in colonnades and arches with a frieze of legendary animals underneath them. Apart from creeping plants, which are taken from the repertoire of Renaissance ornamentation, the painted decoration consists of a symbolic picture of the five senses on the after-castle. Whereas at one time it had been assumed that this model came from somewhere outside Sweden, the discovery of the *Vasa* and her carvings has confirmed that it is in fact

26

Right: Stern designs, Lg; a, Warship 'Edgar', Woolwich, 1779; b, Warship 'Princess Carolina', formerly 'Rotterdam', about 1770
Page 116: Stern designs, Lg; a, Warship 'Glory', Plymouth, 1788; b, French warship 'L'Achille', about 1790
Page 117: Stern and cabin interior of the schooner 'Amphion', built by F. H. af Chapman, 1779, Ss.

114

a

b

a

b

a

b

c

d

e

f

g

Cherub from the 'Vasa'

119

of Swedish origin. It is without doubt a very good example of the painted warships of the Renaissance period. There is also a very handsome and gaily painted contemporary model of a Dutch three-masted ship of 1560 in the Nederlandsch Historisch Scheepvaart Museum in Amsterdam.

During the 17th century and the Baroque period carved ornaments predominated. In the *Vasa* the after-castle was still built in 16th-century style, but from an artistic point of view she is a 17th-century ship. She was built by a Dutch shipwright who had emigrated to Sweden and by Dutch ship's carpenters especially recruited for the job. Most ships built by the Dutch during the first decades of the 17th century were rather sparsely ornamented. The splendour of the *Vasa* must be attributed to the political position Sweden then held. The time was the middle of the Thirty Years War, and the country was busy consolidating its supremacy in Europe, which it was to retain for the remainder of the century, and it was intent on impressing friend and foe alike with imposing warships.

A close analysis of the carvings and the parts of the vessel, assisted by reference to models and pictures of ships of that time, has enabled research workers to state fairly conclusively, even at this early stage, where everything on the *Vasa* had its place. One ship that has been of particular assistance in this respect is the French ship *Saint Louis* built in 1626 in Holland, which appears amongst others in a popular engraving by H. Hondius.

The *Vasa's* sculptures are typical examples of the ornamental art of the Renaissance with its classical style. They are entirely in keeping with the decorative façades of German-Dutch domestic architecture which was fashionable in Sweden, and Stockholm especially, between 1620 and 1630.

The *Vasa's* figure-head was a large, gilded lion flanked by two supporting timbers carved as heads of Hercules. Along the beak-head or on the bow were placed rows of Roman emperors crowned with laurel wreaths. The inside of the gun port covers had masks of roaring lions on them so that if the ports were opened they would glare at the enemy as symbols of the destructive force of the menacing guns. Most of the sculptures were concentrated on the after part of the ship, the stern and the galleries. The long quarter galleries were supported by figures of warriors in antique style, which no doubt refer to Vitruvius' reports of Persian warriors whom the Spartans took home with them to serve as human temple-pillars. The heads of these warriors probably acted as corbels, and some of them may have been grotesquely contorted. This motive is common enough in Renaissance art, especially graphic art. The roofs of the galleries were occupied by caryatids, their lower parts shaped into fishtails, and wearing all kinds of headgear like oriental crowns, winged helmets or cardinals' hats. At the ends of the galleries there were small, turret-like oriels with slender pillars and domed roofs which were topped by orbs decorated with sprays of flowers and fruit. The stern bore the Swedish coat of arms 6ft. high. It was framed in knobs and scrolls and held by two powerful lions. Flanking it were two hovering cherubs pulling aside a cloth draped in typical baroque style. Above the coat of arms sat the most important of the stern sculptures: a carved bust of Gustavus Adolphus, idealized in appearance, with two griffins holding the royal crown over it. Below this sculpture was the inscription 'GARS', which stands for 'Gustavus Adolphus Rex Sueciae'. Lower down on the stern was another heraldic carving, a shield with a gilded sheaf of corn and a crown over it. This shield, which was held by two cherubs, symbolizes the name of the ship, *vase* meaning sheaf. The sheaf was the emblem of the reigning house of Vasa and appears in their family coat of arms, which at the same time was the centre-piece of the national coat of arms.

Design for a figure-head by Griffiths, 1850

What else can be said about the iconographic conception of the ornamentation? Gustavus Adolphus was considered by his contemporaries a Gideon who would come to the aid of the oppressed Protestants in Germany. This is symbolized by a number of small figures of warriors which might have had their place on the stern. They wear Roman armour and carry torches and trumpets in their hands, true to the passage in the Book of Judges describing Gideon's victory over the Midianites.

Hercules, the best known figure in ancient mythology and in the 17th century a symbol of courage in warriors and learning in humanists, is represented by several sculptures. Five life-size figures of warriors in 17th-century armour might possibly be mythical kings from Sweden's remote antiquity. It has been established by colour analysis that most of the sculptures were once gilded.

Detail of a stern-gallery, design drawing, about 1750

The unique treasure of material provided by the *Vasa* and her ornaments can be taken as a natural departure point for further research into the development of ship ornamentation during the 17th century. It reached its peak about the middle of the century, and a large number of models and pictures have been preserved from those decades. The drawings and paintings of the two Dutch artists van de Velde, father and son, give a very good idea of Dutch and English warships. The detail in them and the meticulous way in which they were painted makes them valuable aids in research into art in shipbuilding.

One of the best known 17th-century warships was the English *Sovereign of the Seas*, launched in 1637. Although not a single part of the original ship has been preserved we have a fairly good idea of what her decoration looked like from pictures and written records. She was designed by Phineas Pett and is thought to be the most lavishly decorated and gilded ship that ever left the stocks of a British shipyard. Her ornaments were extravagant, and the gilding alone cost over £6,000, an immense sum at that time.

120

Design for a figure-head by Griffiths,
1850

35, 111f

The ornamentation was designed by Anthony van Dyck, pupil of Rubens and court painter to Charles I. The quarter galleries bore the national coat of arms, and the upper part of the stern was occupied by the goddess of victory surrounded by Jupiter, Jason and Hercules. The figure-head was in the shape of King Edgar on horseback trampling seven kings underfoot, and there were also a cupid riding a lion and six allegoric figures representing the Virtues. The ship was certainly an impressive manifestation of Britain's claim to rule the waves.

Some of the original sculptures of this period have been preserved and, in the light of the *Vasa* find, deserve renewed attention. There is, for example, the large British coat of arms which came off the flag ship *Royal Charles*, now in the Rijksmuseum in Amsterdam. Originally named the *Naseby*, she was built by Cromwell in 1655 and was the only vessel to be given lavish ornamental treatment in this sober era of Puritan simplicity when ships were almost bare of ornaments and gilding except for the Commonwealth coat of arms. She carried a figure-head of the Lord Protector himself with a wreath that had 'God with us' written on it. She was later taken over by Charles II and re-named *Royal Charles*. In the Battle of the Medway the ship was captured by the Dutch naval hero, Michael de Ruyter, whose own flag ship, *De Zeven Provincien*, built in 1666, had the Dutch royal coat of arms on her stern, surrounded by the seven shields of the United Provinces.

While the court painter van Dyck was enlisted by Charles I of England to work on what was probably his biggest ship, the great French Baroque sculptor Pierre Puget was busy running a workshop in the naval port of Toulon. The figures on the *Réale* in the Musée de la Marine in Paris are said to be by him. We are told that his rule was absolute and none of the naval experts got a word in when it came to deciding on the ornamentation of ships. Overloaded with figures of mythological warriors and heroes, they became much too bulky and awkward to manoeuvre, and it is quite possible that the captain, once out of harbour, took the opportunity of stripping his ship of some of the ornamentation to make her easier to handle.

143a

During the reign of Charles II (1660–1685) no fundamental changes were made to the appearance of ships as compared to Cromwell's times, except that more use was made of royal emblems and coats of arms. A minor innovation were the carved garlands that surrounded the gun ports. Amongst other small alterations the beak-head was shortened. Despite an official injunction from the Admiralty prohibiting the use of carved ornaments, these continued to prosper.

Towards the end of the 17th century the solid sterns were given a more open appearance by splendid stern galleries and balconies with decorative carvings. The beak-head disappeared and the figure-head was fitted to the stem-post in the way we are used to seeing it now. The most remarkable figure-heads were mainly equestrian statues of reigning monarchs, many of them of considerable artistic quality. Small models, often made in wax, of figure-heads and stern decorations were frequently submitted to the sovereign or the Admiralty for selection before the final order was placed. A number of these models dating from the end of the 17th to the 19th century have been preserved; some of them can be seen in the Prins Hendrik Museum in Rotterdam and in the Danish War Museum in Copenhagen. It may be noted in passing that the famous Danish classical sulptor Thorwaldsen was a pupil of a figure-head carver named Willerup.

146a–d

In 1732 William Kent designed a state barge for the Prince of Wales. The figures on it, which consist of dolphins, lions with fish tails and two graceful nymphs support- ing the Prince's coat of arms, were carved by James Richard and mounted and gilded by Paul Pettitt.

135a; 136

A popular choice for figure-heads on ordinary warships in the 17th century was a fierce lion with gaping jaws. It remained so for over a century. Lions and lions' heads were commonly used as ornaments on other parts of the ship, too. In the general fight for supreme power and national prestige each country copied the others' ship- building methods and ornamentation, especially any improvements which could be gleaned from captured ships. This explains why almost identical figure-heads can be found on ships of different nations. In 1703 and again in 1796 the Admiralty ruled that extravagant bow ornaments would have to go and decorations be con- fined to simple figure-heads and cast heraldic shields. But in England as elsewhere the tradition died hard, and the seamen themselves clung to it with superstitious stubbornness. Eventually the realization that heavily ornamented warships were a handicap in sea battles must have hastened the steady reduction in the amount of artistic embellishment which had characterized the appearance of warships since 1700. Figures gradually gave way to merely ornamental patterns. More stress was laid on beadings, friezes, emblems and *cartouches*. Figures were confined to smaller sculptures of dolphins, masks and cherubs, while the only larger ones were those of the figure- head and coat of arms. This development was parallel to and linked with a reduction in the size of the after-castle, which naturally reduced the size of the surface on which ornaments could be applied. The process of elimination continued through the 18th century until all that was left in the way of ornamentation was the figure-head, coat of arms and name symbols.

90d; 155b
98d; 110a–f; 111e

115a, b; 116a, b

It may be of interest to list a few outstanding 17th- and 18th-century features: there were the ornate mastheads, mostly gilded; the stern-boards commonly decorated with scenes from the Bible, which were found on Dutch coastal and inland vessels

84a, b, c
127a–f; 128
118a, b, c, d, f

102e

102a, b, c

103a–i; 104a–d

behind the helmsman's seat; the boards flanking the accommodation ladder on ceremonial occasions, which were carved with ornamental patterns and Biblical scenes; and the many forms of rudder decoration. The upper part of the rudder blade often bore carved decorations, and the end of the tiller was frequently carved into a lion's, dragon's or dolphin's head. The most original decorations were found crowning the rudder stock; amongst them were lions, dragons, dogs and the strange heads of allegorical figures which were very popular then, soldiers, and maidens with bare bosoms, some frail, others very generously proportioned.

Among the exterior and interior decorations on ships there were some which were not of wood. Even on antique ships some ornaments were made of metal, as is proved

68e

163; 164

268a, b

268c, d, e; 265a–f; 98d; 155b

by the bronze ornaments from the Nemi ships. In Sweden there exists the gilded weather-vane from a Viking ship, and Antwerp possesses a number of cast-iron masthead decorations from the Baroque period. Examples in Paris, Amsterdam and Venice show that great care was also lavished on ships' lanterns. An especially attractive feature were the hanging compasses suspended from the ceilings of captains' cabins and often used as chandeliers. Occasionally name plates and coats of arms were cast in bronze or iron instead of being carved from wood.

The red and gold lions on the bows of larger ships survived until the end of the 18th century when they were replaced by brightly painted full-length figures portraying the name of the ship. The development then progressed through three-quarter length figures to the simple white bust of the 19th century. Despite Admiralty directives to reduce the amount of ornamentation, tradition and superstition had such deep roots in seafaring men that it was difficult to enforce these laws. Although the final aim was to do away with figure-heads altogether, the Royal Naval College at Portsmouth actually conducted art classes for the express purpose of introducing apprentices to the art of wood-carving. The Admiralty injunctions had one good result, though, in that they reduced the unshapely groups of figure-heads to more sensible

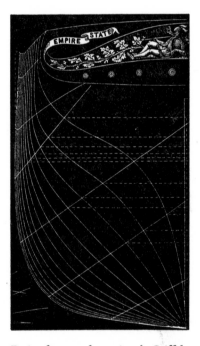

Design for stern decorations by Griffiths, 1850

167d, g

proportions. Busts became fairly common now. Some of them, like that of Nelson winking, which came off the *Horatio* (1807), reveal a humorous touch which is no doubt to be attributed to the influence of Rowlandson and other contemporary cartoonists.

As armour-plated ships became the order of the day, the navies of all nations adopted the use of heraldic devices such as shields with ornamental accessories. As faster types, notably in iron, were developed, ornaments disappeared almost completely. The last ship of the British Navy to have a figure-head was the *Espiègle* which was wrecked in Bombay in 1923. There are some exceptions in other parts of the world. The vessels of the Japanese Navy still carry their chrysanthemum device on their bows, and shields

are still common on German warships and merchant vessels.

The first to put an end to bow ornamentation were the French, who had attached so much importance to their figure-heads and produced some really first-class examples. Even they realized that ornaments could become an embarrassment when they interfered with the intended function of the bow and beak-head. When things got to the point where the value of a ship was judged by the fame of its wood carver rather than its seaworthiness and usefulness in battle, the great days of wood-carving on ships had come to an end. The French, too, had an art school where wood carvers-to-be could learn the art of draughtsmanship. Some of their drawings have been preserved, among them the one of the *Carmagnole*'s unusual figure-head, which was a guillotine, and that of the *Le Revenant*, whose figure-head is casting out a coiled line. These two are in the Musée de la Marine in Paris and several more can be found in other French museums.

166c, g, l; 167c, d

American figure-heads were mostly similar to those on English ships, but in the 19th century in particular they developed a style of their own, especially on merchant vessels. Contrary to the European practice of letting the figure-head 'grow' out of the stem-post, so to speak, the Americans put it on a shelf or volute, standing upright with one foot pointing outwards. The same volute and framework of acanthus leaves were used for busts. There were also some very impressive eagles among American figure-heads, and a number of beautifully made American Indians. They aroused considerable interest when their ships called at European ports.

167c

The Americans apparently know much more about their figure-heads and ship ornaments in general than other nations do about theirs. Brewington's investigations are very informative in this connection. The works of American wood carvers, especially of those who worked in the New England ports, are certainly worthy of attention. Many of them have found a place in American museums. Canada, Australia and New Zealand, too, have preserved examples of the art of maritime wood-carving, but they are usually modelled on British or American originals or were even made in those countries. There is one example, though, of an indigenous New Zealand work: the sculpture of the Moa bird in the Naval College at Auckland.

It is strange that with so many thousands of figure-heads and other ornaments so little is known about their artists and their working methods. Occasionally one comes across a clue referring to the finished work, but there is still a lot of documentary research to be done to bring to light all the small clues that many sources undoubtedly contain. The *Vasa* is one of the few exceptions in this respect. We know that most of her sculptures, and probably the best of them, were made by the wood carver Maarten Redtmer who, in 1625, according to the records of the Stockholm yard that built the *Vasa*, received an annual salary of 354 Riksdalar, which was a sizable sum

124

in those days. Johan Törnström, who from 1782 to 1818 was the official figure-head carver in the Swedish naval dockyard at Karlskrona, is one sculptor about whom we know a great deal, thanks to the works of Cederlöf. At one time a furniture carver in Stockholm, he belonged to the circle surrounding the great Swedish sculptor Sergel, and we know whence he drew the inspiration for his massive classical figures, which now stand in the Marinmuseet at Karlskrona and are among the best-preserved figure-heads of that period.

142b; 147b, c; 148a, b

In Germany, too, a number of figure-heads have survived. The largest collection is to be found in the Altonaer Museum in Hamburg. Most of them date from the 18th and 19th centuries. One very early one from about 1600, representing a twin figure with a wheel, can be admired in the museum at Heide. Others are in Bremen, Lübeck and other smaller coastal towns. There are numbers of figure-heads in maritime museums and private collections in Britain, Holland, Spain and Italy, too, notably from the 19th century. Altogether they are unlikely to total more than a few hundred in the whole world. Many of them are already of the steamship era when merchant ships still carried decorations on their stem-posts, until the bow shape was changed and the straight stem introduced. This finally led to the disappearance of most of them.

156a

In Victorian England figure-heads on merchantmen were painted in subdued colours. It became customary to paint those of foreign-going ships white. Some sailing ships are still in existence, but they are getting fewer and fewer. Training ships still use figure-heads, the latest, the *Sir Winston Churchill*, has a lion and coat of arms as hers. Comparatively recent sailing ships, like for instance the *Peking* built in 1911, which was once a German nitrate clipper, and the British training ship *Arethusa*, as well as training ships of other countries' navies and merchant marines, were built at a time when figure-heads were no longer considered an important part of the trimmings of training vessels. In this era of competitive merchant shipping, when the old, super-stitious breed of sea-dog has had to yield to the modern mariner of the steam and motor age, even the finest ship has room for no more than a simple ornament bearing her name. It is good to know that there are still many places in the world where we can see and study these old figure-heads and sense something of the ancient, extinct art of carving ships' ornaments.

One of the most interesting collections of figure-heads is that of Captain 'Long John Silver', as he liked to be called. It was originally housed in a building called The Lookout on the Gravesend sea-front. Collecting maritime rarities and talking ships was the Captain's hobby. His house was one splendid museum, and he enjoyed gathering round him as many people as possible who had some connection with the sea and ships. Every time he managed to get hold of a new figure-head to add to his collection he invited everyone to a ceremonial 'launching'. During his lifetime he collected some hundred pieces of varied origin, some of them beautifully made works of art, others the crude products of unskilled hands. The whole collection passed to the *Cutty Sark* Preservation Society when the former tea clipper, now lying at Greenwich, was made into a museum of the British Merchant Navy. It is now part of the interior furnishings of the *Cutty Sark*. The *Cutty Sark* herself, built in 1869, has an impressive figure-head whose carver was still a skilled craftsman in the old tradition. His father had been a carver of figure-heads at Gloucester before him.

59c

Figure-head, 'Bianca Aurora', 1848, Bc.

Right: Carved stern boards, forward-facing sides, 17th century; a, c, e, Sn; b, Wh; d, f, Go.

126

a

b

c

d

e

f

a

b

Art in Shipbuilding Outside Western Culture

Ritual and Symbolic Significance of Ships

To think of beauty as a thing in its own right and consider art as an independent category of culture is a comparatively recent achievement in Western civilization. The recognition of beauty, even outside the environment in which it was created, dates from the end of the 18th century. To assess products of foreign cultures as beautiful and at the same time as expressions of art was only possible after the existence of art as a category had been realized. We have only begun to appreciate so-called primitive art since the beginning of this century, though we have appreciated the artistic creations of the great Asian cultures for somewhat longer. This is not the place to go into details of the origin and development of our Western evaluations of primitive art. Instead, I would like to refer the reader to a very instructive study on the subject by A. A. Gerbrands.

The evaluation of art as a separate category of beauty is characteristic of modern Western culture. It is a phenomenon which is not met among peoples outside the Western cultural sphere. What we describe as art in their cultures is—as indeed it was in Europe in the past—the result of expert craftsmanship, of outstanding manual ability. The creators as well as the recipients recognized no value in the product other than its suitability for the purpose for which it had been made.

Art in shipbuilding among non-European peoples is a very complex theme. Even in Europe, where art has acquired a certain independence, the creative artist remains tied to the society and the culture in which he lives and works. His work is rooted in his personal perception of traditional values with which he has grown up. The exact evaluation of works of art therefore calls for a knowledge of these traditions and of the society and culture in question, even when the environment is not relevant to the recognition of a work of art as such and its principles can be studied successfully outside this context. In our Western culture shipbuilding and navigation are both suitable for independent study; each can be regarded as a subject in its own right, complete in

Left: a, Relief from the stern of the 'Juffr. Anna Magdalena', 18th century, Rm; b, Stern board, 17th century, As.

129

itself. Although a knowledge of our culture as a whole is presupposed, it need not be part of such a study. But shipbuilding and navigation among the primitive races are a different matter altogether. They cannot be studied and understood outside their cultural and social environment. Besides depending on craftsmanship and technical skill they are closely linked to the social sphere and the basic principles of philosophy and religion. The same is true, in even greater measure, of so-called primitive art. Since the latter, as far as it concerns us here, namely in the form of artistic decoration and design of vessels, occurs among very many peoples with essentially different forms of culture, an intensive and systematic treatment of the theme would be outside the scope of this book. We will, therefore, confine ourselves in the following pages to a general characterization and a few elucidatory examples that are typical of this type of art. In doing so it will be expedient to differentiate between primitive cultures and the Asian cultures. As in all other things, we must consider shipbuilding outside Europe and the art connected with it against a background of Western equivalents.

The ship as we know it in the West is a means of transport built according to technical principles and serving as a conveyance for people and cargo. It is primarily of economic importance, but from time to time it has also had military significance. It has even happened that a particular type of vessel has been developed as a powerful weapon, such as was the case with the war galleys of antiquity which could sink enemy ships by ramming them, or the modern submarine, whose chief purpose is to fire torpedoes.

For seamen and all who have anything to do with them, ships have a high emotional value. One of the main reasons for this is probably the fact that the ship is considered a living thing, which explains why, in the English language, it is of feminine gender. In the West, too, ships and navigation are closely linked with all aspects of culture. Without sea travel our society and civilization are scarcely conceivable. However, as has already been remarked, it is possible for us to study shipbuilding and navigation by themselves in isolation.

Primitive cultures are characterized by a much stronger inner unity, an interdependence of all and everything, a connection of all aspects of life to the same central theme. This characteristic of primitive cultures allows us to describe them almost as totalitarian cultures. Their ideology, religion, social structure and economy are always closely linked and intertwined, and the same is naturally true of shipbuilding and art. These peoples' conception of the structure of the world is clearly defined, and the definition is reflected exactly in the religious ritual and the social structure. Even the economy depends on it, and the traditional partitioning of the residential areas is bound by it, as is the division of the villages, the camps and frequently the gardens. The same structure often reappears in the layout of buildings, especially those used as temples.

Roughly the same is true of means of transport, although it is usually less obvious. The shape and layout of ships, too, is influenced by the structure of the cosmological system. In these cultures the ship, in addition to being a means of transport and thereby a technical instrument of the economy, is also in a certain sense a sanctuary, a temple, at least an object of religious importance and ritual value.

The design and ornamentation of these vessels is seldom or never profane, but instead they are the expression of religious concepts and related intimately to the essence of the culture. Ornamentation of a religious nature, like holy pictures of the Roman Catholic church, can certainly be found in European shipbuilding, but the connection is much looser. The religious element does not embrace the ship as such but is related to a particular, individual ship only, which might merely carry a picture of the saint after whom it was named.

168 d

In the foregoing paragraphs we have compared primitive and Western shipbuilding and the art forms connected with both. In the great Asian cultures the relationship between art and shipbuilding stands mid-way between these two extremes. Ships – and sometimes works of art – occupy a more independent position in these cultures than among primitive peoples, without being autonomous entities in as marked a way as they are in Western culture.

see Notes

The belief that a ship is a living being is also fairly general among peoples outside the Western sphere. This is expressed by putting an eye on either side of the bow as decoration, of which James Hornell has given an account. This strange custom can be seen along the whole of the southern coasts of Europe and Asia, from China to the Atlantic Ocean. Hornell's account in a later work clearly points to the identification with a deity from the Hindu pantheon on the coasts of India and Ceylon. The ship is dedicated at its launching to a deity, Amman, Ramaswami or Lakshmi. The bow of the ship serves as an altar, in which is stored everything necessary for worship. Before the onset of each voyage and at other times when it appears expedient the favour of the patron divinity is invoked. A scroll or other ornamentation on the stem-post has a close connection with this divinity. It is not always clear, however, whether they are considered patrons or whether the vessels themselves are incarnations or seats of the deities. In any case, the scroll on the stem-post, which is often very beautiful and carefully carved, is dedicated to the deity, and the crew regard it as holy. Hornell's illustra-

see Notes

tions show several examples of such stem-post ornaments.

see Notes

In contrast to India, where the ship's bow is considered sacred, the Chinese give special attention to the sterns of their ships. The stern is the place where the captain (*laodah*) and his family live. It is also the ship's temple, where the altar is built into the large transom. The outside of the transom is often richly painted in sea-going ships.

In China as well as India rowing races take place from time to time in narrow boats built specially for the purpose, which resemble snakes and dragons in both shape and ornamentation. In the princely courts of India these vessels had very elaborate carvings indeed and were painted in many colours and heavily gilded.

In Asia all these ships occur on the fringe of the centres of culture to which they belong. They are of considerable importance to the crews that man them but of no particular interest to the majority of people. They are in a sense marginal phenomena. In the primitive cultures this is altogether different.

It goes without saying that in primitive cultures, too, the ship is first and foremost a means of transport. As such it usually conforms admirably to the demands made upon it within the framework of the geographical and technical possibilities of the culture concerned. The strong connection of the ship to other cultural elements, religion in particular, explains the deep significance which ships can have in such cultures. The extraordinary care which is taken in the design of the ships and their decoration is rooted in this significance. It follows that religious symbols are employed very frequently.

The important position the ship occupies is very apparent in South East Asia, among other places, and in particular in Indonesia. The Malay archipelago covers a large number of widely dispersed islands. Without sea transport the life of the people in this area would be unthinkable. Not only does the sea serve as a link with other peoples, the larger islands also have many sizable rivers which are navigable by ship and in places cut through thick jungle which would otherwise be inaccessible.

Many ships in Indonesia have cleft stem-posts, a kind of fork, pointing upward or forward. This peculiarity, which is not unique to Indonesia, led many investigators to the conclusion that the ships were identified by their users with more or less mythical animals, the cleft in the stem-post representing the animal's mouth. This assumption turned out to be correct. The split stem may have come about as a constructional peculiarity when the freeboard of a dugout was increased by planks. But it also occurs in forms which have nothing whatever to do with the planking-up of a dugout. The reason why this remarkable custom is so widespread is certainly to be found in the fact that the vessel was identified with an animal. This is quite obvious, for example, from the model of a dugout from East Borneo in the Rijksmuseum voor Volkenkunde in Leiden. Its stem-post consists of a beautiful openwork carving representing the head of the mythical dragon, the Naga, while the stern-post is made into the tail of the animal. Hose and McDougall illustrate the stem-post of a head-hunter's canoe from North Borneo in their book. The point is clearly recognizable as the head of a crocodile holding a human embryo between its gaping jaws. In this case the crocodile is probably

see Notes

173

see Notes

176c

Right: Figure from the starboard quarter of a galley, 17th century, Vn.
Page 134: a, Figure of Neptune from a state vessel of the Grand Duke of Tuscany, 17th century, Vn; b, Figure of the goddess of Justice from a barge, 16th century, Vn.

132

a   b

a

b

the demon of the initiation who swallows the novice (represented by the unborn child) during the head-hunters' initiation ceremonies, so that he can be reborn as a grown man later on in the ritual.

125

At one time small log canoes could be seen on the coast of Bali, their stem- and stern-posts carved into the head and tail respectively of Makara, the fish-elephant of Hindu mythology. Representations of Makara with a small human figure in its mouth are also well-known in India. Archaeological evidence in India suggests that the oldest form of this mythical animal had the shape of a crocodile.

see Notes

From the Dyak tribes in Borneo, which are known by the name of Ngadju, we know a very detailed myth in which two ships play a part: the hornbill boat and the snake boat. In the ritual of these tribes these mythical boats are represented by real boats. They symbolize the two halves of the cosmos: the upper world, principally feminine, associated with the heavenly mountain and the heavenly tree, and the masculine underworld, associated with the mythical dragon (Naga), the snake and the crocodile.

Josselin de Jong has remarked on the very widely developed dualism of the culture of Indonesia. 'The fundamental separation of human society into two: two sexes, two phratries, two lines of descent... is at the same time a cosmic bisection in which Heaven and Earth, Upper- and Underworld and all kinds of other opposites, above all superiority and inferiority, good and evil, are included. This social and cosmic dualism forms the nucleus of a comprehensive system of classification...and a cosmic community in which every individual group has its own special function to fulfil.' In all probability the forked stem in Indonesian boats not only represents the jaws of an animal but is also the symbolic expression of the idea of dualism of society and culture which plays such a dominant role in this group of islands.

It has already been explained that these vessels are not only of value as transport, but also fulfil a function at the initiation ceremonies, those rituals which introduce the youths to the traditional racial and tribal secrets. It is only after they have been initiated into the sacred cultural values of the tribe in this way that they are regarded as grown men. Ships are used in this connection on Borneo, and on Bali, too, there exist dugouts in the shape of Makara which are very likely used for this purpose. In Indonesia the ship is thought of as identical with an animal, and it is the animal which in some cases plays a part in the initiation ceremony.

This latter peculiarity also applies to other aspects of Indonesian culture. For example, the shadow figure with which every performance of the Javanese shadow play, the *Wajang*, opens and finishes and which is also used to signify an interval, has a silhouette in the shape of a leaping flame. There is always enclosed in its centre a small building, surrounded by bushes and trees, in which there are snakes and other animals. This

Page 135: a, Figure from the port quarter of the state barge of Frederick, Prince of Wales, 1732, Lg; b, Figure from the starboard quarter of a Genoese galley, 18th century, Vn.
Left: Figure from the starboard quarter of the Prince of Wales' state barge, see a on previous page

symbol goes under two names: *Kajon*, which can be translated as copse, and *Gunungan*, which is the name for a hilly or mountainous landscape. The Dutch scientist W. H. Rassers has shown that the *Kajon* represents the male shrine in the depth of the forest, where the youths are initiated to manhood and where women are not permitted to enter.

The *Wajang* play is in itself a holy ritual which has the character of an initiation ceremony. The flame and the *Kajon* appear again in the same or similar form on the planks which are fastened to the stem-posts of the community vessels on Tanimbar Island in the South Moluccas. These stem-boards, too, are shaped like flames, slanting as though they were blown by the wind. They are carved into splendid openwork ornaments with the shape of the Naga or a snake or bird on the underside. The whole is more stylized and austere than the Javanese *Kajon*, but the similarity is unmistakable. The ceremonial voyages for which these Tanimbar community boats were originally built were doubtless connected with the initiation rites of the Tanimbar islanders. The Museum voor Land en Volkenkunde in Rotterdam possesses a set of seventeen of these stem-boards, which are among the most beautiful ornamental wood carvings of Indonesia. *176a*

We can see from all this that in Indonesia the ship is a valuable cultural factor which has a certain importance beyond its function as a means of transport. The decoration of the vessels is therefore an obvious necessity, and it is no less obvious that the decorations are connected with concepts of the cosmic system or are even symbolic of them. It is scarcely surprising that great care is devoted to their execution and that among them are to be found examples of the highest artistic skill.

An especially interesting example of a culture in which navigation of the seas occupies a central position appears in the Trobriand Islands east of New Guinea. The most important occupations there are farming and fishing, in which a large part of the islanders are engaged. But alongside these, and closely linked with them, there exists a system of ceremonial barter called *kula*, which joins many of the islands. It involves the exchange of traditional valuables, like bracelets and necklaces, between the leading and powerful men in the communities. In this ceremonial exchange, which is regulated to the tiniest detail by a ritual code, religion, social structure and economy are closely intertwined. *Kula* has an emotional influence on all aspects of community life. Everyone feels part of it or at least takes a lively interest in it.

The ships which are used for the barter voyages are built solely for this purpose and are kept for it alone. Such a ship is the property of the chief who has had it built and who maintains it. But the ownership of one of these ships is not ownership as we know it in the West. The 'owner' cannot do what he likes with it. The whole village community has helped to build it and also has to help to maintain it. It can only be used for the one special purpose: for the great journeys in connection with the *kula* barter system. Malinowski has made far-reaching investigations into the *kula* custom and has published his findings. He reports fully on the building of a sailing canoe intended for the *kula* traffic. The prolonged rituals which are performed during its construction constitute a complete cycle together with those that follow later, prior to and during the voyage. Although such a ship is given its own name, it is more frequently called by the name of its owner. It is identified with its master.

168a

The boat is basically a long dugout canoe with high bulwarks of planks erected along the sides. These are fastened fore and aft to a bulkhead which is higher and wider than the boat itself and rounded at the top. These bulkheads, which also serve to keep out the spray, are richly decorated with wood carvings and painted in many colours. Each is supported by a small, lavishly carved and painted board fitted longitudinally over the stem- and stern-posts respectively. These boards are among the most beautiful specimens of Trobriand wood carving. Together with the strikingly carved and painted Trobriand dancing shields, they represent the culmination of ornamental art in the South Seas and are very much sought after by museums and collectors.

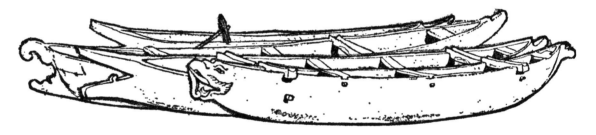

Dugouts from Sanur, Bali, drawing by W. O. J. Nieuwenkamp

There is little to be said about the decoration in detail. In contrast to Indonesia, there is no connection between the communal vessels and the ritual of initiation. Such a ritual is completely unknown in the Trobriand Islands. However, Malinowski says that the youths who take part in a *kula* voyage for the first time are initiated by the older men into the sacred *kula* legends. This takes place as they pass certain geographical peculiarities on the voyage, in so far as these play some part in the mythology of the barter system. Even if the youths do not pass through a formal period of initiation, their instruction on the *kula* boat no doubt serves the same purpose.

We have seen that the *kula* system is a ritual exchange of valuable articles. The community takes an emotional part in every expedition and its outcome. A friendly contest is held between the *kula* partners, in which magic plays an important role. Anyone who receives a piece of jewellery from his partner must reciprocate with a comparable gift.

A necklace must be given in return for a bracelet, or vice versa. The gift made in exchange must have at least the same value. Each attempts with charm and friendliness as well as with magic to move his partner to generosity, without being allowed to ask openly for anything. The reputation and honour of each partner and the community he represents are at stake in these exchanges. If the present given in exchange is too small this might be interpreted as meanness, and meanness is something everyone detests. What is more, a *kula* partner can expect to receive twice as many presents in return if he shows himself to be generous. Meanness defeats itself; the stream of wealth tends to bypass the miser.

Another barter system which is full of ceremony although rather less peaceable exists among the inhabitants of the Asmat territory of south-west New Guinea. These people are notorious head-hunters. Head-hunting to them is a matter of retribution. If a village in this area sets out on a head-hunt it is nearly always an act of revenge for heads taken from among their own people. By cutting off a few heads in the enemy village and taking them home reparations are made. This war-like barter is deeply rooted in the religion of the people. All important religious celebrations go hand in hand with a head-hunt. Since these celebrations play a part in the promotion of the fertility and well-being of the group and as such are held at fairly regular intervals, the need for a head-hunt arises quite frequently. At the same time, because other villages undertake regular raids, there is constant reason for a vengeful attack.

The district in which these people live is a marshy area on the delta of a number of large rivers. Transport by land is quite impossible because the rivers, inlets and their interconnecting channels are all tidal, and the numerous islands and islets can only be reached by water.

Boats, in this case dugouts of every size, are indispensable here. The traffic between the houses and fields, between one village and another, as well as any form of contact with more distant localities is only possible by canoe. The entire social and economic life relies on water-borne transport. Very long dugouts are used for head-hunting and other, more friendly, contacts with neighbouring villages. These boats are considered sacred objects by virtue of their decoration and their consecration prior to launching.

During certain religious festivals the inhabitants of one part of the Asmat Delta carve pictures of their relatives who have been killed during a recent head-hunt on a long wooden post. These commemorative poles (Bisj-poles), which are made from the trunks of trees, are set up with their tapered ends down and one of the roots of each is cut into a large pennant which projects at the top. They remind the relatives of the deceased, whose likeness is carved into the wood, that their lives have not yet been avenged and that a head-hunt is due in the very near future. One part of this pole is

Right: Detail of carving on the side of a Venetian galley, 17th century, Vn.
Page 142: Classical stern carvings; a, Early 19th century, Lg; b, From the warship 'Karl XIII', carved by Johan Törnström, Karlskrona, about 1820, Ss.
Page 143: a, Angel blowing trumpet by Pierre Puget, figure on the port quarter of a French royal barge, late 17th century, Pm; b, Siren, stern figure from the state barge of Marie Antoinette, second half 18th century, Pm; c, d, Crown on the cabin and figure of Neptune on the stern of Napoleon's state barge, 1811, Pm.
Page 144: Stern boards; a, Ship of the line 'Frederik den Sjette', 1831, Co; b, With coat of arms of Liverpool, 18th century, Os; c, 18th century, Os.

a

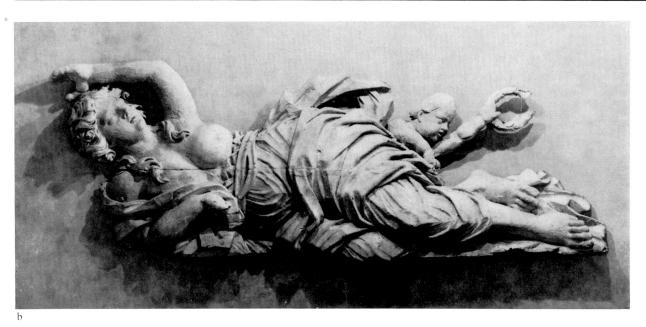

b

a

b

c

d

a

b

c

a

b

c

d

a

b

c

d

a

b

c

d

a

b

always carved in the shape of a canoe. In fact, the pole itself is seen as a canoe, as the boat in which the dead travel to the land of souls after the celebration. The pennant is beautifully carved in openwork with motifs which symbolize the ancestors: the hornbill, the black cockatoo, the nautilus shell, the praying mantis and various spiral-shaped nose ornaments. Bisj-poles are unknown in other parts of the Asmat Territory where, instead, the inhabitants carve ghost canoes without bottoms from the trunks of trees and decorate them liberally with carvings. Inside the canoes there are pictures of the dead, sometimes in the shape of hornbills, and in their midst there is always a tortoise. Big bowls in the shape of canoes, elaborately carved and decorated with pictures, are also well known. As a rule they are used for making the red ochre dye used in the rituals and for painting wood carvings.

174a; 175a, b, c

The big canoes used for head-hunting are decorated with carvings on the stem. They bear likenesses of the beheaded relatives or symbols of them, exactly like the pennants of the Bisj-poles. Sometimes stem-boards carved in openwork project from the bows of the canoes, and these, too, are decorated with carvings similar to those on the Bisj-poles. On the sides of these boats is carved a continuous motif of traditional ornamentation which resembles the footprint of a cassowary and is supposed to increase the speed of the boat.

We have mentioned that among the Trobriand islanders the *kula* barter traffic, in which the reputation and honour of the leaders and of the community as a whole are at stake, arouses strong emotions. Similarly the head-hunt and the war-canoes used for it arouse emotions in the inhabitants of the Asmat region. But in their case it is not only reputation and honour that are at stake but human lives: that of the enemy which is to benefit their own community, and that of the dead relative who has to be avenged. Clearly these emotions must be stronger than those attaching to the *kula*-traffic. If we consider this fact, and the central position which head-hunting occupies in the Asmat culture, we can well understand the devotion and concentration which the wood carvers bring to the task of ornamenting the boats and the long paddles that go with them. What they produce is usually primitive in form but nevertheless very attractive.

Closely connected to the head-hunt in the Asmat region is a long, very formal ritual which prescribes even the smallest detail of the initiation and in which the war-canoe, too, has its place. A head seized by the village as a trophy is prepared, painted and decorated and then allotted to the youth who has reached the age of manhood. One part of this ceremony is for the initiate to remain seated on the floor for several days holding the freshly prepared head between his outstretched legs, pressed against his genitals. The head, shoulders and trunk of the initiate are rubbed with a mixture of the blood of the victim and the ashes of his hair. In this way the young man receives

Page 145: Stern boards, first half 19th century; a, British warship, Lg; b, Bm; c, Whaler 'Mermaid', Nb; d, Whaler 'Eunice Adams', Nb.

Page 146: Models of figure-heads; a, early 19th century, Rm; b, Warship 'Oldenborg', 1740, Co; c, 'Cron-Jagten', 1742, Co; d, 'Fredericus Quintus', 1753, Co.

Page 147: a, Head of the Germanic God of War Tuisko, from a Bremen ship, early 17th century, Bf; b, c, Heads of the figure-heads of the ships of the line 'Dristigheten' and 'Försiktigheten' by Johan Törnström, about 1780–1790, Kk; d, Head of a figure-head from a schooner, 19th century, Gr.

Left: Figure-heads by Johan Törnström, about 1780–1790, Ss; a, Frigate 'Eurydice'; b, 'Dygden'

149

the identity of the dead enemy and, so to speak, takes his place. After he has endured this process he can visit the village of the victim without danger. He is completely safe there and will be received most cordially, looked after and called by the name of the victim. He is then also the ideal messenger and possible mediator when a reconciliation has to be affected between the two villages.

Another part of the initiation rituals consists in the initiate standing in the war-canoe, the human head held before him, as it goes down the river and out to sea in a westerly direction. During the voyage he simulates an increasing state of fatigue until he collapses as though dead. Once they are out at sea his mother's brother, an important person in the ritual, lifts him and the human head up and lowers both into the water. The totally exhausted youth is born again by this action; he becomes a young child, a novice, who has forgotten everything he has learnt up till now. During the journey back to the village his lost memory is restored to him. He returns to his village an adult, ready and able to take his place among the men and to look for a wife. *see Notes*

These examples of the connection between ceremonial vessels, in which decoration is of special importance, and the initiation rituals which are customary among these people, should not mislead one into thinking that the same thing applies to other races. The examples only serve to illustrate the central position which the ship occupies in some cultures and the great care that goes into its construction, especially from an aesthetic point of view, by virtue of which it can claim a prominent place in art.

Quite a number of other tribes might be mentioned in the same context as those *174b, c; 176b* already named, for example the inhabitants of the Sepik River district, the Geelvink-Bay and the Sarmi district of New Guinea.

Then there are the small human figures carved out of wood which are found decorat- *177* ing the bows of certain ships in the Solomon Islands in the same way as the figure-heads of Western ships. Another tribe famous for their wood carving are the Maoris of New *176d, e* Zealand, who apply it to stern and bow decorations of their large, seaworthy canoes.

Turning to an entirely different part of the world, namely the north-west coast of North America, we might mention that here, too, we encounter vessels abundantly decorated with religious symbols and often very tastefully painted. There are also the river boats of Brazil with their fantastic carvings of the heads of animals and people on the stem- and stern-posts.

Even a mere enumeration of all the hundreds of examples of artistic decoration of vessels found outside Europe would be outside the scope of this book. Yet it would seem justifiable to mention two other outstanding features.

The first is the care which some of these seafaring peoples lavish on their boats' gear, such as paddles, rudders, bailers, masts and parts of the rigging. The paddles are not only functional but beautiful in shape and often decorated in the most tasteful way. There are fine examples of this from all over the world. The same is true of the bailers, although there are not so many of them. The best of these come from New Zealand and the Trobriand Islands. The second feature which ought to be mentioned in connection with shipbuilding outside the Western sphere is so obvious that it is easily overlooked. In modern industrial design in the West it can frequently be observed that something which has the best possible shape for fulfilling its practical purpose is at the same time of the highest aesthetic appeal. The same is true of shipbuilding everywhere, but especially so in non-Western cultures. A ship which fulfils perfectly the purpose for which it was built, that is to say as a means of transport derives the maximum benefit from wind and water, will frequently have a shape which satisfies the highest aesthetic standards and on these grounds must be regarded as art. If elsewhere in this *see Notes* book we talk of 'architecture' in connection with ships, we do so on the assumption that a ship, like any building on land, can be a work of art by virtue of its very structure.

Votive Pictures of Ships

A Mediterranean Seafaring Custom and its Origins

The fishing boats have reached open water and surge under full sail across the limitless blue sea. The men on board keep a watchful eye on the helm, on the course and on the nets ready for casting, but the captain watches with misgivings the white cumulus on the horizon which is steadily building up. Suddenly the wind dies completely away, then comes up again from a different direction, while the sea turns grey. Before the men know what is happening a nor'westerly gale is upon them: the masts break under its force and under the weight of the waves which sweep the deck from end to end. It is essential to reach a harbour or bay in which to shelter as quickly as possible, but will they be able to make it in time?

This is the anxious question which from time immemorial seafarers have asked when they realized that there was nothing left to do against the unleashed powers of nature. Overcome by 'terror antiquus', the unreasoned, primeval human fear, they abandoned faith in the rituals and amulets which were to protect their ships. But there was one remaining hope of salvation – 'in Deo ultima spes' – and so the men in their despair turned to God, possibly through a patron saint, and made a vow. There is something sacred and solemn about such a vow: it is a promise to God to fulfil a particular task, which usually consists in offering an object or an image of it, on the condition that God answers a prayer.

The custom is still practised today as it was in the heathen world. We know that myths and superstitions haunted the first seafarers as soon as they ventured out from the rivers and lagoons onto the open sea in their frail craft, for they knew little or nothing of what really awaited them over the horizon. Frightening stories circulated of dark powers and mysterious creatures which were said to live on the land, in the air and the sea. The mountains and forests were believed to be inhabited by titans, dragons and basilisks, and the sea filled with terrifying monsters. Everyone believed

Right: Figure-head, mid 19th century, Ls. Page 154: Figure-heads; a, Clipper 'Wylo', Greenock, 1869, Sn; b, 19th century, Lk.

a

b

a

b

a b c d

e f g h

in the legendary Leviathan, a gigantic snake, which crushed the strongest ships in its coils, and in the colossal kraken which were supposed to emerge suddenly from their caves at the bottom of the sea and devour ships and humans alike. There were also the Gorgons, with hair made of snakes, the 'immani corpore pistrix', as Virgil called Scylla, the abominable monster that could take on various shapes, and the sirens who sat on rocky shores and lured careless seafarers with their enchanting songs. Homer describes how Odysseus had himself lashed to the mast of his ship so that he should not yield to the temptation of those pernicious creatures. The seamen could only ask for protection from the god Nereus and his numerous daughters, the Nereids, the seahorses and the dolphins who sported themselves among the waves.

Even the cartographers of the late Middle Ages still believed that these fabled monsters existed and illustrated them on their maps of the world as probable inhabitants of the unknown seas.

But that was not all: evil powers, which were believed to be emitted by a mysterious eye and which were all the more terrible since they were invisible, threatened the lives of the poor seamen, whose only defence against the 'evil eye' consisted in confronting it with another eye intended to counteract the dangerous powers of the first. Out of the belief that this sinister influence lurked everywhere there developed quite logically the custom of painting the 'apocryphal' eye above the door of the house,

168c, d

on sacrificial vessels, on the shields of soldiers and the bows of ships.

The symbol of the mysterious eye goes back into antiquity and probably had its origin in the pre-dynastic period in Egypt, where it later came into widespread use as the symbol of the god Horus. It crops up repeatedly in hieroglyphic writings and as a decoration on the things which were put into tombs to accompany the dead on their last journey. It is not possible to say with certainty how the oculus became widespread

see Notes

throughout the world, but it is accepted that the Egyptians themselves, in the course of maritime trade relations which developed between them and the cities of the Eastern Mediterranean, initially passed it on to the Cycladic culture and then to Crete. In this way it reached the Hellenic seafaring tribes and appeared in Italy as early as the 7th century B.C. on the murals in the Etruscan tombs at Tarquinia. All the ships portrayed on the coins which were issued by the cities of the classical world have a stylized form of the magic eye on their bows. The same symbol was taken up again by the Roman mint when it issued the *aes grave*. It is characteristic that the bows of the galleys engraved on these coins are fitted with a *rostrum tridens*, the symbol of Poseidon, the god of the sea. A very similar myth, and one which probably had local origins and evolved independently of western influence, is found among certain Chinese fishermen. They believe that a boat is really no more than a fish and therefore needs eyes to be able to move

Page 155: Figure-heads; a, Winged Victory on Nelson's funeral barge, 1806, Lg; b, Lion, 17th century, washed up on the coast of Jutland, He.
Left: Wooden figures from ships; a, Early 17th century, Hd; b, Early 17th century, As; c, 18th century, Os; d, e, h, Figure-heads; d, Late 18th century, Ss; e, Barque 'Lord Palmerston', 1854, Go; f, Figure from a chandler's shop, about 1820, Lg; g, About 1800, Lg; h, 19th century, Rm.

in its element. The concept of the 'evil eye' and its secret powers is still very much alive among the coastal inhabitants of the Mediterranean, who are receptive to superstitions. Even today the oculus is found commonly among the many amulets with which the boats of the Sicilians and Neapolitans are decorated, either by itself or in the strange company of pictures of angels and saints. It is painted on the bows of Venetian fishing and trading vessels; it appears in relief on the Abruzzian *bragozzi* and on the *trabaccoli* along both shores of the Adriatic. It is also present on the Portuguese boats known as *meia lua*. The oculus as such has retained its magic properties unchanged through the centuries, but it has taken on different shapes in different countries. Sometimes it is represented by an eye closely resembling the human eye, but it also appears as a coloured circle, in the shape of a triangle or star, or simply as a white dot.

The colours in which seamen and fishermen paint their craft can have a religious significance – today just as in ancient times. Even if the sides of the ship are painted black for practical reasons, the bow and stern are given bright colours. A red triangle on the bow is a reminder of the distant past when a sacrifice was made at the launching of the boat: the colour symbolizes the blood which flowed over both sides of the bow. Virgil reports that before weighing anchor Aeneas sacrificed a bullock to Poseidon and Apollo, who were by ancient custom the patrons of seafarers. A black sheep was offered up to the storms and a white one to the fair winds; the entrails together with goblets of the best wine were cast on the waves. The seafaring customs of the Italians seem to be completely permeated with these old traditions. Although they survive in symbolic form only, they can still be recognized in such old customs as decorating the bow of certain boats with an image of the animal which it was once customary to sacrifice to humour the gods. This is clearly illustrated in old Neapolitan votive pictures which show ships carrying a sheep's fleece, or a wooden carving of one, on the bowsprit.   *178b; 179a, b*

Through the generations Italian shipbuilders gradually forgot the true ritual meaning of such images and added more and more ornaments to their boats as though they considered it necessary to hide the true shape of the timbers. Not infrequently one or other would confuse the holy with the profane and substitute a carving of the Virgin Mary or a saint for the animal figure-head, giving it the same shape and size as the original heathen symbol. This custom remained unaltered right through the 19th century, and it is safe to say that until the first decade of the present century no *pinco*, no rowing boat, no dinghy or *barca* left Naples, Messina, Genoa or Marseilles without the mythical symbol on its bowsprit. Even today many surviving *trabaccoli* laden with stone and wood ply the Adriatic, and although they no longer carry sails and have lost most of their picturesque ornaments, some still carry the fleece of the sacrificial sheep on their bowsprits. But they are the last of their kind, and to preserve their memory one of these fleeces carved in wood was salvaged from a shipbreaker's and given to the Museo Storico Navale in Venice as a record of an art and a tradition which so strongly, and for so long, influenced the unsophisticated souls of seamen and shipbuilders.

To illustrate the mythological and religious philosophy of these simple seafaring people we should like to refer to the ceremonies which accompanied the launching of a ship and which could take strange forms, differing from one region to the other. In Sicily, for example, a dialogue took place between the shipbuilder and the customer when the latter prepared to hand over the agreed price. The shipbuilder first said three prayers and then asked the buyer if he was satisfied with the work. After this had been confirmed he blessed the ship three times in the name of the Ark of the Covenant and the Holy Trinity, whereupon he scored the sign of the cross on the transom of the vessel with just two blows of the axe.

The fishermen of central and southern Italy harbour a mass of naive beliefs and superstitions, handed down from their forefathers, concerning the struggle of good against evil. Even today it is customary to fix the horn of a ram at the masthead and to drive nails into the ship from the inside or to keep pieces of 'magic' wood under the deck, and the inhabitants of the Abruzzi coast believe that to ward off a threatening storm a member of the crew, the first born in a family, must scratch the sign of Solomon on the mast with a pointed knife with a black handle, at the same time repeating certain mysterious words which his father has disclosed to him (and him alone) on Christmas Eve.

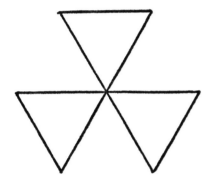

Solomon's sign

In antiquity the custom of making vows to offer votive gifts was very widespread, and numerous inscriptions recall the ritual formula 'votum solvit libens merito', generally abbreviated V.S.L.M. Herodotus calls a gift offered to the deity *anathema*, and old records reveal that the temples of Olympia and Delphi housed wonderful offerings. One of these *anathemata*, which is thought to be one of the oldest, is a small bronze ship found not so long ago in Syria, near the Sidon of antiquity. The beak-shaped bow, the animal-like figure-head, the bulwarks behind which the oarsmen sat, in short everything points to the model being a war galley, in which the donor, as is evidenced by writing engraved

on the starboard side of the ship, had been to sea, presumably round the year 122 B.C.

In Rome even the population as a whole is known to have made vows. The whole of the island in the Tiber was made into an enormous stone galley, dedicated in 282 B.C. to the god Aesculapius as a thanksgiving for freeing the town from a plague which had afflicted it for years. Part of the bow of the ship still exists *in situ*.

On the Monte Celio in Rome there is an old church called Santa Maria in Domenica or 'alla Navicella' (which means 'of the little ship'), which was reconstructed during the Renaissance. It is named after a small ship hewn out of stone and made into a fountain which stands in the square in front of the church. According to documents this interesting piece was originally an offering to the goddess Isis Pelagia, the patron of seamen, 28d and was once kept in a sanctuary built in the first centuries of Imperial Rome by non-Italian soldiers who had their camp nearby. Several authors, pointing out the coat of arms of the Medicis on the base, maintain that this is a copy ordered by Pope Leo X at the end of the 15th century and that the original was destroyed. In any case, the stem shaped like the snout of a boar, the favourite animal of certain deities, is unmistakable evidence of its original religious purpose. This symbol is known from other Roman sculptures.

One of the most valuable votive pictures made by seamen is the well-known marble relief in the Torlonia collection in Rome which was found in 1863 in the ruins of the 94 harbour of Ostia. It shows two Roman cargo vessels which are just about to tie up in the harbour of Claudius at the completion of a voyage with a cargo of wine-filled amphoras. On the poop, near the figure of the water bird, which Apuleius said had to be placed there as a symbol of good luck and permanent unsinkability, the captain or the owner is offering up thanks to the gods by burning incense 'pro salute, itu, reditu incolumitate' (for unimpaired health and a safe voyage out and back), using the formula well-known in old inscriptions, while a sailor has already furled the foresail. The mainsail is still hoisted though already cast free, since the artist obviously needed an area on which to inscribe the two letters V.L. which stand for 'votum libero', i.e. 'dedicated to the free', 'the free' being Dionysus, the god who gave growth and prosperity, and whose image is to be seen in the top corner of the relief. The presence of the apocryphal eye has nothing to do with the second ship but must be seen as part of the magical significance of the votive picture as a whole. The custom of votive offerings has lasted with unbroken continuity up till the present day, just like the temples which were once consecrated to the gods of Olympus and later became Christian places of worship.

Hundreds of churches which in earlier times were filled with votive offerings of the seafaring population lie scattered along the coasts of France, Italy, Spain and Portugal, many on top of steep cliffs, swept by raging storms and often washed by the spray from the sea. Their names are in keeping with the traditions of the places: Madonna Bonaria in Cagliari, Maria Santissima d'Altomare at Andria in Apulia, Madonna dell'Arco in Naples, Nostra Signora del Montenero in Livorno, Nostra Signora della Misericordia in Genoa, San Pietro dei Nembi near Lussino, Notre Dame de Bon Port and Notre Dame de la Garde near Antibes, San Simone de Mataró in Catalonia and many others. Whether big or small, these churches were once full of votive pictures which seamen had painted after surviving a storm at sea. In many cases they probably painted them themselves. Unfortunately their numbers are now steadily dwindling, partly as a result of the neglected state in which many of the churches are today through the effects of wars or natural disaster, but above all as a result of the merciless hunt which the antique dealers have started in pursuit of these objects. They are now considered fashionable because they are 'naive'.

In earlier days these ex-voto pictures were painted on wood, later on, for reasons of economy and on practical grounds, primarily on canvas or paper. The oldest among the ones that are still in existence, like those from the Neapolitan churches which stem from the second half of the 16th century, are painted in tempera, the sea being painted in predominantly dark tones against which the waves breaking on harbour moles and decks of ships stand out in contrast. Later, especially in the 19th century, people went over to oil colours. The dimensions altered little and seldom exceeded a format of 28in. wide by 16in. high, so that they could easily be grouped in a small space, hanging side by side on the wall or nailed to a wooden board. Each picture had the letters V.F.G.A. written on it or on a small plaque underneath it, rarely the whole sentence 'votum fecit gratiam accepit' (he made a vow and received mercy) or other details about the event, since few people at that time were able to read.

The painting of votive tablets, unless they were done by seamen themselves, was usually entrusted to an artist or craftsman in the port who specialized in the work. He needed no special knowledge of ship construction, it was usually enough for the person ordering the picture to describe roughly the type of ship that was to appear in the centre of the picture and its approximate rig, and to give him a few particulars about the weather– i.e., the condition of the sea and the colour of the sky at the time of the event–and finally something about the event itself which had led to the vow. It is interesting to note that these votive pictures, most of them from Madonna dell'Arco in Naples, follow very much the same pattern, so much so, that they might almost be taken as the work of one and the same hand, or at least the same workshop.

The people who painted votive pictures, which might be called a second-rate art but was certainly spontaneous and characteristic of a special section of the population, were called *madonneri* in Venice and *madonnari* in Naples. While most of the pictures from Naples are of anonymous origin, we know the names of some artists who signed those found in Ligurian churches: there is Domenico Gavarrone from Genoa, Niccolò Cammilieri from Marseilles, Franzesco Lizzi from Venice and Basi Ivankovich from Trieste, who also painted some good seascapes. The paintings found in the French churches of La Garoupe are predominantly water colours by members of the Roux family, well-known for their paintings of ships.

All votive pictures follow the same pattern: in one of the upper corners the Madonna is seated or standing with the Christ child on her arm, surrounded by a halo of white clouds. She is a rather stereotyped figure, gazing into the distance and apparently turning a deaf ear to the supplications of the crew of the ship who are about to be swallowed up by the waves. Occasionally the donor of the picture is portrayed in an attitude of prayer in front of the Madonna, but the donor in this case is usually a chance traveller who escaped death by a miracle during a dangerous crossing.

There is a picture of a galley trying to escape the storm with reefed sails and one or another galley struggling to reach a safe port with her crow's nest already lowered and broken in pieces. On yet another picture we see a small ship taken by surprise by a storm near the coast, whose crew has thrown a couple of cannons overboard together with two anchors, clearly with the object of lightening the vessel. The anchors have apparently not yet caught on the bottom. Then there is the episode of the sailor who fell from the yard as the ship rolled and was uninjured, and of the other who fell into the sea and was rescued, and finally of the fire which broke out below decks and by a veritable miracle 180b by the Madonna was prevented from spreading to the whole ship. Another subject which was very popular in the 19th century and reflects the political climate of the Mediterranean at the time is fast pirate craft raiding merchant ships and fishing boats or the coastal villages. Perhaps the memory of these dreaded attacks by barbarians is still alive among the population of Latium, where the exclamation 'Mamma, li Turchi!' is frequently heard. The Turks were once synonymous with barbarians.

One picture shows a boat being rowed by five men and pursued by a pirate galley from which it is trying to escape in desperate haste. The galley has her lateen sail one-third reefed, and her oars are being used to help her along, while her captain is standing at the helm, counting out the stroke and urging his men to greater speed. The danger is great for if the boat is captured the unfortunate crew will undoubtedly end up as slaves in some African market. Another boat with two masts and spritsails which is being chased by two pirate galleys is threatened with the same fate. They are speeding along under reefed sails because of the strong wind. The people on board the Neapolitan *paranza* fear the worst and in their plight are calling upon the Madonna and their patron saint, in this case John the Baptist. According to the inscription on the lower edge of another picture a large *felucca* with a crew of twelve was surprised on 4 July 1608 by a terrible storm, which brought very high waves, half-way between Palermo and Naples and came very close to sinking. The captain, Francesco Dilusi, together with the entire crew, prayed to the Madonna dell'Arco, to Saint Francis of Paolo and the Archangel Michael for help, the latter being portrayed very large in the centre of the trinity. The representation of the apocalypse destroying the devil is an oft-recurring theme in the iconography of Southern Italy and is probably explained by the existence of the popular 180d; 185d sanctuary on the Gargabo in Apulia which bears its name but was already well-known in antiquity as a heathen temple.

Wrought-iron jackstaff socket, Antwerp,
18th century, At.

186a

In 1609 another *felucca* with its sails stowed sought shelter on the coast near an old watch tower. The crew put out to the shore three lines forward and two aft, but the berth was exposed and they were in serious danger of being driven onto the rocks by the prevailing sirocco. An interesting detail in this picture is the skin full of oil which has been lowered over the stern with the obvious intention of calming the seas and creating a relatively calm zone all round the ship. The men are sheltering and are praying to the Madonna dell'Arco.

In one picture seven galleys, almost all of them with their bows pointing towards the shore, lie tied together side by side but with sufficient room between to prevent their damaging each other. This is clearly an emergency anchorage in an unprotected road-stead, where, if the storm increased, they would be in danger of running ashore. On board the first two ships the figures of the captains can be recognized as they pray to the Madonna who is looking down from a patch of light in the sky. There is no doubt that their prayers were heard for at the bottom of the picture someone, probably the donor, has written 'gratiam accepit' in a far from accomplished hand.

There is also the touching offering of a man who was condemned to hard labour on the galleys and is shown still wearing the chains that tethered him to the rowing bench as he thanks the Madonna for his regained freedom. In the background the galley on which he probably served his sentence is sailing away before the wind. Another early 17th-century work shows a fleet of seven galleys of the Viceroyalty of the Two Sicilies which was overtaken by a fearful storm some distance from the coast and compelled to make for the nearest harbour under shortened sail. The admiral's ship has a coat of arms in the shape of a two-headed eagle on the stern, which suggests that it might have been one of the fleet of the Viceroy Don Pedro Tellez Giron y Guzman, Duke of Osuna, which was equipped by him personally and regarded by contemporaries as the most splendid fleet in the whole of the Mediterranean. The painter of the picture has made no technical errors: the order of precedence of the ships is correct, all the ships are sailing in formation under mainsails only, one-third reefed, because of the seas and the wind, which we would probably consider today as being force 7. The oars are shipped and lashed to the gunwales blade up, while the galley slaves sit idle, afraid of what might happen to them since they are chained to the rowing benches.

185a

Another, very much later, votive picture by an unknown artist but certainly painted in the southern style reveals an unusual incident which happened in this confused period of Neapolitan history, when Admiral Nelson's squadron pursued the French ships and the fleet armed by the Jacobite Caracciolo all along the Tyrrhenian coast. A *xebec* with its sails winged out in a fresh wind has opened fire on a group of militiamen who have left their *paranza* on the beach and are replying with their rifles while their comrades seek shelter in the olive groves that slope down to the shore. The *xebec* is obviously a ship which has been captured and re-armed since we know that vessels of this type never belonged to the Royal Navy. The symbol of the *vellum* on the bowsprit confirms its Mediterranean origin.

187a

The fact that the ship has hoisted the pennant and the Red Ensign only means that it was currently under the command of an Admiral of the Red. The inscription on this interesting votive picture merely says: 'Combattimento accaduto al Paron Mauro Simone a Punta Devia con la paranza nomi *li SS Martiri*', which translated means 'The battle of Punta Devia won by Paron Mauro Simone with the paranza *The Most Holy Martyrs*'.

It can be said that artistically the decline of votive picture painting coincided with the end of the era of sail, while at the same time the art of the *madonneri*, who now painted exclusively in oil, lost more and more of its meaning. We will not go deeper, therefore, into the more recent votive pictures which portray the first steamers, their tall black funnels entirely out of place on the open sea, nor will we talk about the adversities which befell the mail steamers and ocean liners, nor about the warships and torpedo boats which occasionally appear on the most recent votive pictures. Paintings have gradually been replaced by photographs and prints, and votive pictures no longer mean a great deal to us, either as paintings or as expressions of ancient maritime customs which were rooted in faith, fear and superstition.

Wrought-iron jackstaff socket, 18th century, At.

Not so many years ago a keen student of naval history, while on a walk through the Old Town of Naples, stepped quite by chance into the church of the Madonna dell'Arco. Inside, in the dim light of candles, he discovered to his surprise that the walls of the naves were literally plastered with maritime votive pictures, while a huge model of an ancient warship hung suspended from the ceiling. It had probably been there since the 17th century, and although it had become blackened by the smoke of candles and incense in its lofty position it was almost completely undamaged, since no-one had ever touched it. There it was, with guns poking out of its ports, the arms of the Sicilian Bourbons on the balustrade of the after-castle and a huge lantern crowning the stern gallery. All the ropes and rigging were in a seaworthy condition and the sails were furled, just as befits a ship in harbour. A particularly interesting feature of this priceless model was the blue and white diamonds on some of the sails, a detail which other historical sources would scarcely have revealed. Apparently this was a privilege accorded only to the flagships of His Majesty King Charles III of Naples to make them immediately identifiable from other ships. The student learned that all these naïve and fragile things, the fruit of patient handiwork done by simple seamen and fishermen, by modest craftsmen and nameless artists, had been condemned to be burnt since they were regarded as worthless plunder. Even the Bourbon ship was to suffer the same fate. But by a lucky chance it was all saved in time and has now found a safe anchorage in the Museo Storico Navale in Venice.

53c

Right: Figure-head of the English warship 'Ajax', 1807, Lg.
Page 166: Figure-heads; a, Corvette 'Saga', by C. A. Sundwall, 1884, Kk; b, Steam frigate 'Vanadis', by Henrik Nerpin, about 1860, Ss; c, American sailing ship 'Indian Maid', late 18th century, Md; d, Frigate 'Minerva', by Johan Törnström, about 1780, Kk; e, About 1860, Ha; f, Mid 19th century, Ss; g, 'White Lady', about 1880, Nb; h, About 1870, He; i, About 1880, At; j, About 1870, Ss; k, About 1860, Ha; l, About 1850, Nb.

a   b   c   d

e   f   g   h

i   j   k   l

a

b

c

d

e

f

g

h

i

j

k

l

a

b

c

d

Ship Portraiture

Paintings Commissioned by Yards, Shipowners and Captains

Page 167: Figure-heads; a, About 1850, Lg; b, 'Magaera', 1864, Lg; c, 'Awashonks' from New Bedford, first half 19th century, Nb; d, 'Benjamin Franklin' from Philadelphia, 1796, Md; e, 'Russell', 1822, Lg; f, 'Daphne', 1861, Lg; g, 'Horatio', 1807, Lg; h, About 1860, Lg; i, About 1850, He; j, About 1850, At; k, 'Harlequin', 1836, Lg; l, About 1870, He.
Left: a, Stern board of a kula boat, Trobriand Islands, Rv; b, Stem decoration from a Venetian trabaccolo, 17th century, Vn; c, d, Painted Sicilian boat with oculus, 20th century

Almost all marine painters, that is painters of seascapes, were to a greater or lesser extent ship portraitists, and none were more prolific in this field than those doyens of the marine painters school, the Willem van de Veldes, through whose drawings we know so much about the appearance of individual 17th-century warships.

When the British school of marine painters emerged in the 18th century, all of them including the best of them, Brooking, Serres and Pocock, accepted commissions from owners or captains to do ship portraits.

During the 19th century there was a tremendous expansion in shipping and a greatl, increased demand for portraits of ships, and also a widening in the class of customer who wanted them. The master of a merchant coaster, for instance, could not afford to commission an established marine painter, even if he would accept such a commission. But as in all human affairs, if a market is created, then people will be found to supply the goods and at the right price. There emerged, therefore, in the second quarter of the 19th century a number of men working in the great ports who turned out cheap and straightforward broadside views of merchant ships for anyone who asked for them. They might or might not have been sailors themselves, but there was no reason why they should have been. They had two things in common: their portrayals of the ships were accurate to the last block, and their work, from an artistic point of view, was generally pretty bad. Necessarily so, since if they progressed to be proper marine painters through their talents, then they really passed out of the category we are discussing. This is a pity, since the successful painters are the only ones we know anything about. The real ship portraitists were probably of a lower class, getting their commissions from the dockside taverns or by going on board ships and offering their services to the captain and crew. They are known to us only by their signatures and from the backgrounds to their paintings, which often indicated the port they worked in.

The lasting charm of many of these ship portraits rests on the beauty of the subject, if they are sailing ships, and the painstaking accuracy of the drawing. There is often a pleasing simplicity in the painting technique, which, however, since it stemmed from a lack of training rather than artistic perception, can be over-admired. Similar, though more delicate, paintings were done for many sailors by the Chinese and the Japanese, when their ships were in Eastern waters.

216a, b

This folk art undoubtedly originated in the Mediterranean, probably in Italy, where those practising the traditional art of painting votive pictures gradually went over to, or simultaneously undertook, the painting of pure ship portraits for captains and ship-owners when they discovered that there was a market for them. The similarity in style and technique between certain votive pictures and contemporary Mediterranean 'captain's portraits' suggests this quite clearly.

As a specific genre in our sense ship portraits came on the scene around 1750. They were usually water colours or gouache on paper, but from the very beginning a number were also painted on the back of glass. Again this was probably first done in Italy. It was not until the 19th century that oils on canvas became the accepted medium for ship portraits and also for votive pictures, which had so far been painted exclusively on wood.

see Notes

A common characteristic of all ship portraits, no matter who painted them or in which port they originated, is their dissemination to all parts of the world. The reason for this lay in their very nature, for all the bigger ports in which ship portraiture was profitable and could develop into a trade were visited by ships of every maritime nation. Consequently portraits from every corner of the earth were in turn taken away to every corner of the earth. This explains why this particular type of painting, though by its nature it really belongs to what is commonly called folk art, was by no means confined by national boundaries. Even the crews, irrespective of their home ports, were sailors of many different nationalities, and this must have contributed to the cosmopolitan style of these pictures. It must also be remembered that many of the artists had themselves been to sea, as captains, mates or naval officers in the war, or if they were professional painters and natives of the ports they worked in they had certainly made a few sea voyages.

Unfortunately very little is known about the beginnings of ship portraiture. Some of the very earliest examples, a number of very fine water colours signed by A. Berlinguero in 1775, can be seen in the Museo Naval in Madrid. It is interesting to compare them with some 18th-century Italian water colours which are now in various museums in northern Europe. They also show very strong similarities to the earliest known glass paintings of ships, which almost certainly originated in Italy. The Norsk Sjöfartsmuseum in Oslo possesses a water colour of a ship with the name, *Sint Johannis*, painted on a scroll in the sky. The style of the painting and the frame, which is without doubt an original rococo

187b; 194a, b, d, e, f; 195a, b, c

see Notes

Ostend East Indiaman, 1729

195d, e, f; 196d; 198a, b, c; 208d

frame, richly carved and gilded, suggest that the picture probably dates back to between 1750 and 1780. A similar portrait of the brig *Mette Catrina* is kept in the city archives of Stade. The museum at Apenrade possesses a water colour of the *Hoffnung* outside the harbour of Ancona, signed in 1792 by Giuseppe Fedi. The water colour of the Swedish ship *Fortuna* dated 'Ancona 1795' (also with the harbour of Ancona in the background), which is now in the Statens Sjöhistoriska Museum in Stockholm, was undoubtedly painted by the same hand, as was the portrait of the snow *Veränderung* from Flensburg, painted in 1799 and kept in the museum at Altona. We know of similar pictures with Livorno in the background from the years after 1800, which suggest the same artist. One exists from 1817 signed by Giuseppe Fedi, now in the museum at Apenrade. This leads to the assumption that the artist moved from Ancona around 1800 to continue his trade in Livorno, where more money was to be made out of ship portraiture.

Special attention was always given to the harbour background, especially if the customer was a captain or crew member to whom the portrait was not only a reminder of his ship but a souvenir of a harbour he had visited. It is not surprising, therefore, that the Bay of Naples with smoking Vesuvius, and Venice with the doge's palace were exceedingly popular backgrounds from the very beginning. Many portraits that originated in these two ports are still in existence today, and it is possible to trace the same harbour scene through the centuries. A particularly representative 'souvenir' is the hand-coloured copy of an engraving made in 1790 by Giacomo Tagliagambe from Livorno which is in the possession of an insurance company in Malmö, showing a Swedish merchantman and bearing an inscription dedicating it to the Swedish Consul General in Livorno at that time.

From around 1800 several ship portraits with a background of Marseilles harbour entrance bear the signature of the Italian Niccolò or Nicolai Cammillieri, an interesting fact which suggests that Italian influences may have played a significant role in this important port in the early days of ship portraiture. The Peabody Museum in Salem has a water colour by Cammillieri, dated 1807, showing the brig *Juliana* built in Newbury. In the same year he painted a portrait of the barque *Victoria* from Flensburg, which is now in the Flensburg museum. Another painter who turned out similar ship portraits in Marseilles in the first third of the 19th century was Honoré Pellegrin.

But it is chiefly due to one family of native Marseillaise marine painters, whose members in their time were world-famous in shipping circles, that Marseilles played such a very important role in the history of ship portraiture in the first two-thirds of the 19th century, which was in fact the heyday of the sailing ships. They were Antoine Roux (1765–1835) and his three sons, Antoine (1790–1872), Frédéric (1805–1870) and François (1811–1882), who ran a shop for nautical literature and chandlery on the quayside of Marseilles harbour between Fort Saint-Jant and the Hôtel de Ville. There, right in front of their very door, they had a close-up view of all the ships moored in the harbour, of all the details of hull construction and rigging. They also owned a small house just above the harbour entrance from where they could overlook the whole bay and watch the frequent naval manoeuvres and the comings and goings of ships.

199a, b; 207a

Antoine Roux and his sons made ship portraits for owners and captains from all over the world, but their chief customers were Americans. Their prolific output threw into the shade the entire production of ship portraitists in other large French ports like Brest, Cherbourg, Dunkirk or Le Havre (where an artist who signed himself 'Montardier' painted some very meticulous and attractive pictures in the twenties and Edouard Adam was well-known in the eighties). The Roux portraits may not be great works of art, but the expert combination of detailed, technically accurate rendering of the vessels and an artistic treatment of the sea, sky and background, which was never matched by any other artist, gives them a very special appeal.

Drawing of a ewer by Otte Steffen, from the account books of the merchants and shipping guild of Stade, 1770/71, St.

The fact that there also exist votive pictures showing ships in a storm or in distress which were painted by the Roux family only goes to show that there is a close connection between the ancient art of votive picture painting and the more recent art of ship portraiture. It can be assumed that votive pictures were painted in French ports from the Middle Ages as they were in Italian, Spanish and Portuguese ports. At least some from the 18th century are still in existence, among them one from La Rochelle painted in oils in 1757, which is now in the Musée de la Marine in Paris.

219b

218g

It goes without saying that England as the most important of all seafaring nations offered a profitable market for the sale and production of ship portraits. In fact we know that they were painted in all the larger British ports. Their average size was about 20 × 30ins., though if the artist had the luck to get a commission from a shipping company or shipbuilding firm they might be much bigger. Some old-established firms are full of large, dull paintings of 19th-century steamships.

Right: Model of a ceremonial vessel from Thailand, 19th century, Bu.
Page 174: a, Stem figure from the Asmat region, New Guinea, Rv; b, c, Stem figures from large dugouts, Sepik River, New Guinea, Rv.
Page 175: a, Stem figure from the Asmat region, New Guinea, Rv; b, c, Stem decorations from dugouts, Northern New Guinea, Ld.
Page 176: a, Stern decoration of a communal vessel, Tanimbar, Indonesia, Rv; b, Stem decoration of a dugout, Geelvin Bay, New Guinea; c, Stem decoration of a Borneo river boat, Ld; d, e, Stem and stern decorations of a Maori sea-going vessel, Au.

A number of painters, though they achieved a certain importance as marine artists and won local fame, remained essentially ship portraitists and never tried to seek their fortune in London, which was the only place where an artist with talent and ambition could reach the top of his profession. The doyen of the English ship portraitists was William John Huggins (1781–1845), who enjoyed a rather higher reputation during his lifetime than his talents merited, but who set the pattern for 19th-century ship portraiture and had many imitators, notably John Lynn. In the third quarter of the century the best remembered ship portraitist in London was F. Tudgay, who also worked for Richard Green, the shipbuilder at Blackwall, decorating the interiors of the ships.

a

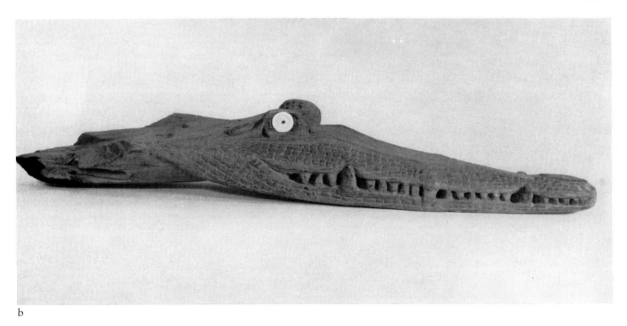

b

c

a

b

c

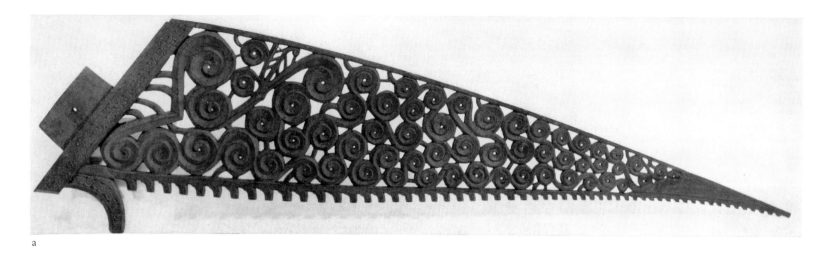

a

b

c

d

e

a

b

a

b

a

b

c

d

e

f

218e; 228f

214a, c

Venice, 18th century

214b

218b

197

Page 177: Figure from stem of a sea-going vessel, Rubiana, Solomon Islands, Ld.
Page 178: Votive tablets from Madonna dell'Arco in Naples; a, 1592, Vn; b, 1608, Vn.
Page 179: a, Detail of picture 178b; b, Stem decoration of a Venetian trabaccolo, wood carving, about 1900, Vn. Left: Votive tablets from Madonna dell'Arco in Naples, 17th century, Vn.

181

In the provinces the most fruitful port was Liverpool, where a considerable business in ship portraits was done for the sailors, mainly British and American. The principal painter there was Samuel Walters (1811–1882), who became a general marine painter but accepted many commissions for ship portraits, so that our knowledge of mid-19th-century ships that used the port mainly comes from his brush, and that of his son George. This activity combined well with the family frame-making business. Other Liverpool artists we know of were D. McFarlane and G. Nelson.

A more interesting marine school grew up at Hull, led by John Ward (1798–1849), who did many portraits of whalers and other craft. He was self-taught, which was a pity since his style is in many ways most finished, and yet one feels that his control was precarious. He did in fact work with William Anderson, the Scottish marine painter, who lived in Hull for a time. Other notable Hull ship portraitists working during Ward's lifetime were Thomas Binks (1799–1852) and Henry Redmore (1820–1887). The fourth great port in England to be a centre for ship portraiture was Bristol, but the only painter of note there was Joseph Walter (1783–1856), who painted Huggins-style portraits, but with a pleasing grey palette.

In Scotland the Clyde and the port of Glasgow offered further opportunities for the ship portraitists, but the only well-known one was William Clark (1804/5–1883), who lived at Greenock. Another Glaswegian who signed himself George Napier was working in the 1860's.

The most profitable aspect of the ship portrait was the sale of prints of those paintings that were engraved, for there was a public interest in them as decorations beyond the immediate interest of the captains or owners. Of course, only the better painters had their pictures engraved. Huggins had many of his paintings aquatinted, but by far the most prolific was a slightly later man, Thomas Goldsworthy Dutton (1820–1891), who produced beautiful lithographs from the 1840's through the third quarter of the century. Unlike Huggins and Walters he does not seem to have painted in oils but merely made water colours for the engravings. He often published them himself, but Ackerman and Foster and others also published his work. He lived in Clapham, but for all his industry only left £60.

On the naval side a number of the personnel were amateur marine painters who also did ship portraits, but as they were nearly all officers, even admirals, perhaps they fall outside what is intended by the term 'sailors' art'. The rank and file seem to have preferred to work in wood rather than paint. There was one man, however, W. F. Mitchell, who had an arrangement with a shop on the Hard outside Portsmouth Dockyard gates, where he took orders for portraits of the naval ships mostly from the naval officers. As these pictures were mainly for hanging in small cabins they tended to be on the small side and in water colours.

Ship portraits that originated in Danish ports and which can be seen today in museums, private collections and even in sailors' homes in harbours and coastal towns are no different in character from works of painters in other countries. They are often called *kadrejerbilleder* (literally, this word means 'bumboat pictures'). In Denmark, *kadrejer* (Dutch *kadraaier)* means a trader who came alongside passing or moored ships in a small boat to sell or exchange goods. Most of these paintings were made for the captain, mate or owner of a ship by local artists with a knowledge of the sea, who came on board to offer their services. Sometimes several copies were made at once. The delivery time was very short and the price modest. As a rule they were painted in water colours, less frequently in oils. The value of these pictures, for which collectors today pay high prices, lies in the fact that they portray in detail certain named vessels of which no other pictorial record exists. They are rarely of high artistic quality, but their naivety and subject matter can make them extremely attractive ornaments. The sailing ships are depicted from an angle which shows them off to advantage, mostly broadside on running before the wind, with their sails full and drawing, flying oversize *Danebrog* flags. Often the artist has not been satisfied with showing the ship once in the picture but has painted it again in the background, this time from the stern. The sky is full of big white clouds and the sea is slightly ruffled. Very seldom is a ship depicted in a storm or in distress. The waves are rather stereotyped and lifeless. Every artist had his own characteristic way of painting them so that it is not usually difficult to identify unsigned pictures by their waves. A popular background is Kronborg Castle, at the narrowest point of the Øresund, which at that time, that is prior to the building of the Kiel Canal, was the most important link with the Baltic. The bay of Copenhagen, the island of Bornholm, Cape Skagen with the old lighthouse and Heligoland are other popular background subjects.

Doubt has often been expressed as to whether these representations of ships are technically accurate. The argument has been put forward that the artist was satisfied with a few outline facts concerning the type, rig, colour and ornamentation of the ship he was about to paint, that he even painted the ships in his studio without ever having set eyes on them. This may occasionally have happened, but on the whole, considering that in many cases the artists had themselves been to sea, the paintings can be relied upon as being authentic. Besides, had there been serious errors in them the customers would certainly have objected.

Most of the pictures bear an inscription giving the type and name of the ship, her home port, the name of her captain and the year. They were usually signed by the artist, to serve as a kind of advertisement, and were frequently delivered already framed.

In common with the lack of information on the subject in other countries, no research has been made into the history of ship portraits and their painters in Denmark. Art historians have ignored them. The following survey is therefore based on the paintings themselves, which are preserved largely in museums, and on rare scraps of information which have been handed down to us. Very often we know neither when nor where the artist lived. In the following list of the most important names dates have only been given where they can be corroborated.

In Denmark, too, the ship portrait as a type of painting goes back to about the middle of the 18th century. The oldest known examples are three gouaches from about 1765 one signed by Clement Mogensen Clementsen (at Copenhagen) and two of Danish East Indiamen which are unsigned, as well as four gouaches of West Indiamen painted about 1780 by a Copenhagen artist whose name was probably Fr. Wessel Munck (all four are at Helsingör). Just before 1800 we come across three very prolific painters: the former seaman, T. E. Lønning (1762–1823), whose works fall into the period from about 1791 to 1805; C. Butty, who painted from about 1797 to 1810; and a naval lieutenant called Conrad Chr. Parnemann (born 1774), of whose work between the years 1792 to 1820 we have record. The period from about 1810 to 1870 can be called the heyday of the ship portrait. The leading painter until the middle of the century was Jacob Petersen (1774–1855) born at Flensburg. He was first a captain in the navy and then came into contact with C. W. Eckersberg, professor at the Copenhagen Academy, who taught him to paint. In his turn he assisted Eckersberg, who was working on his large seascapes, to solve some technical problems concerning hulls and rigs. Jacob Petersen drew and painted hundreds of ships, and with very few exceptions his pictures are far superior to the works of his contemporaries.

Amongst the other painters, we might mention Captain Jörgen Peter Olsen from Rønne on the island of Bornholm (died 1869; known works from the period from 1824 to 1869); C. Clausen from Helsingör (worked in the years between 1838 and 1846); the painter Carl Olsen (1818–1878), who is known to have painted ship portraits between 1851 and 1864; and the cooper Per N. Foss from Dragør, who painted from 1860 to 1882.

During the last decades of the 19th century photography more and more took the place of painting. Instead of painters it was now photographers who came on board to offer pictures of the ship. Parts of them, like the water, funnel markings and flags, were often coloured. But strangely enough the old trade has not died out completely even today. There are still artists at work drawing ships: the pilot F. Landt (since about 1927), O. Stoltenberg from Kalundberg and H. Schøsler-Petersen (both since about 1930).

Some Danish artists worked abroad, like J. Dahl, who for some time was a pilot at

Venice, 18th century

Drawing of a fluyt by H. W. Sellmer, from the account books of the merchants and shipping guild of Stade, 1749/50, St.

183

Dungeness (1872–1889), Alfred Jensen (1859–1935; painted from 1889), a former seaman, 220a, b; 226e who later became a professor in Hamburg, and Antonio Jacobsen, born in Copenhagen in 1850, who after receiving an art training at Copenhagen Academy, emigrated to America and painted a large number of ships in New York (mostly steamships) from about 1875 till his death in 1921. He bought a horse to get more quickly from one end of the harbour to the other, and is reputed to have had a constant supply of half-finished pictures with the sea and sky already painted in so that he only had to add the ship. In fact, all his pictures are uniform and stereotyped and scarcely betray the fact that he was a student of the famous Copenhagen Academy. There has, nevertheless, been a surprisingly lively interest in his paintings in the United States recently.

Apart from these 'artistic craftsmen' there were several excellent marine artists in Denmark in the 19th century. Their pictures of ships are, of course, far superior to the simple works we have so far considered, but even they were sometimes painted to order. The most outstanding representative of this school was the said professor C. W. Eckersberg (1783–1853) whose reputation as the father of Danish painting is perhaps not quite justified. We have seen that he learnt a lot from the experienced ship portraitist Jacob Petersen. We must also mention Vilhelm Arnesen (1865–1948), who started painting ordinary ship portraits when he was twelve; Carl Bille (1815–1898); C. Blache (1838–1920); F. Th. Kloss (1802–1876); Carl Locher (1851–1915); the brothers Anton Melbye (1818 — 1875) and Vilhelm Melbye (1824–1882), who also became well-known abroad; C. Mölsted (1862–1930); Carl Neumann (1833–1891); C. Benjamin Olsen (1873–1935); and C. F. Sörensen (1818–1879). Even the Danish poet Holger Drachmann (1846–1908) painted pictures of ships before he decided on a literary career.

Like other German seaports, Schleswig-Holstein, which till 1864 belonged to the Danish monarchy and had a prosperous merchant navy, had a number of gifted ship portraitists whose works were frequently known under the name of 'captains' pictures'. Most of them lived in Altona and found abundant scope for their work in the nearby international port of Hamburg. Among them were F. T. Albinus, Altona, who was 208e, f; 226d active as a painter between about 1827 and 1846; Jacob Böttger, Altona (about 1806–1841); B. H. Hansen, Altona (about 1827–1846); and H. C. Hansen, Altona (about 1838–1847), who must have been related to each other, their works being almost indistinguishable; Heinrich von Minden, 'navigator' from Kiel (about 1826–1835); Heinrich Reimers, pilot at Kiel (about 1826–1835); M. Truelsen, Altona (about 1850–1870); Nils Nissen Truelsen, Altona (about 1839–1849); and finally the marine artists H. Petersen, P. Holm and L. Petersen, who individually as well as jointly painted many ship portraits (authenticated between 1841 and 1877).

Following the founding of Bremerhaven in 1827 shipping to and from Bremen increased

Right: a, b, c, d, Votive tablets from Madonna dell'Arco in Naples, 17th century, Vn; e, Votive tablets from Madonna del Carmine, Torre del Greco, Naples, about 1800, Vn.
Page 186: Votive tablets from Madonna dell'Arco, Naples; a, About 1600, Vn; b, 1600, Vn.

a

b

c

d

e

a

b

Combattimento Accaduto al Paren Mavore Simene a Punta Deira en a Ensena Nom. ti S. Martin

a

HAIELAURENSEN   D. GUDE HOOP

b

a

b

c

d

e

f

tremendously. These were the great days of ship portraiture in the Weser estuary. The existing shipyards in Bremen and Vegesack and between Elsfleth and Brake on the Oldenburg bank of the Weser were joined in quick succession by six large yards in Bremerhaven and another nearby port, Geestemünde in Hanover, founded in 1845. The ever increasing activity in shipping and shipbuilding provided the painters with wealthy customers from among yard and shipowners (many of them combining both functions) and the captains of ships. The most important of these painters was Carl Justus Harmen Fedeler (1799–1858) from Bremen, who also produced copper engravings and lithographs. From the time he settled in Bremen in 1831 until his death he was attracted over and over again by the roadstead of Bremerhaven with its many ships as a subject for painting. In the 1830's and 1840's he painted many excellent seascapes of Bremerhaven, which are of high artistic quality. They reflect the development of shipping there. Today several of his pictures are in the possession of the Focke Museum in Bremen. In 1850 he produced a monumental painting of Vegesack and its shipyards and different types of ships, which now hangs in the town clerk's office at Vegesack. His best-known work is the lithograph of the arrival of the first American mail steamer *Washington* in Bremerhaven on 19 June 1847. Typical examples of his mastery of painting sailing ships are his oil paintings of the fully rigged ship *Humboldt* (1852) and the ships of the shipowner Wencke (1857), now to be found in the Morgenstern Museum in Bremerhaven.

His son, Carl Fedeler (1837–1897), followed in his father's footsteps. He worked almost exclusively in Bremerhaven and produced some very expressive paintings, among them that of the two sealers *Bienenkorb* and *Albert* from Geestemünde on their Polar expedition in the Arctic Sea (1867, now in the Morgenstern Museum) and the paintings of pilot schooners on the Weser (1892, now in the Maritime Museum at Brake). He became acquainted with life at sea by making a voyage in a sailing ship to the East Indies. Many of the steamships of the North German Lloyd, founded in 1857, were painted by Carl Fedeler and found a large market as printed reproductions. Several of his drawings were reproduced as woodcuts in the popular Leipzig *Illustrierte Zeitung* (Illustrated News) to illustrate shipping news from the Weser estuary, for instance on the departure of the two ships *Germania* and *Hansa* for the second German Arctic Expedition on 15 June 1869.

Addig Jaburg (1819–1875), a painter from Vegesack, specialized in portraits of captains and their families. A sizeable collection of his works can be seen in the local history museum in Vegesack. His younger brother, Oltmann Jaburg (1830–1908), confined himself to pure ship portraits, as his oil paintings in collections in Vegesack, Bremen, Brake and Bremerhaven show. For the shipowner C. J. Borgstede, for example, he painted an excellent portrait of the emigrant ship of the same name (1858), and for the *Wurster Schiffahrtsverein* (Wurst Associated Shipowners), which was owned by wealthy

205; 228d

Venice, 1794

226a

226c; 228e

Page 187: a, Coloured drawing of a landing, about 1800, Vp; b, 'De Gude Hopp', Riga, Captain Haie Laurensen from the island of Hooge, about 1790, Wh.
Left: Votive pictures from Madonna del Carmine, Torre del Greco, Naples, 19th century, Vn.

fenland farmers, he portrayed one of their largest ships, the *Wursata*, showing her once beam on and once over the quarter (1857). It is interesting to note that towards the end of the 19th century, Oltmann Jaburg turned more and more to photography, as it was increasingly taking the place of ship portraiture.

In Norway there were several painters trained in academies, like the professors I. C. Dahl, Hans Gude and C. Krogh, whose fine seascapes included some very accurately depicted ships. This is equally true of Barth, Benetter, Skari, Haaland and several others. But here again we are chiefly interested in the ordinary painters of ship portraits who worked in the ports and who all share a preoccupation with accurate detail. Typical parts of the ship, such as the rigging, have often been painted with almost exaggerated care, although in most cases the accuracy of the dimensions of parts of the ship is questionable. For instance, the flags were usually painted stretched out stiff in order to make them more easily legible, and even pointed into the wind. What is more serious is that the ships are often painted to a pattern. We know of cases where the painter used stencils with small holes with which he determined the main points in the drawing and then completed the masts and rigging by simply joining them up.

The earliest Norwegian ship portraitist to be mentioned is Ole Johnsen Selbøy, who worked for some years in Bergen. His water colours are dated from 1800 to 1842. H. P. Dahm, who painted some rather good water colours from the second quarter of the 19th century, examples of which still exist, also deserves our attention. The works of A. Halvorsen, who chose more unusual motifs, fall into the same period. He portrayed sailing ships in peril, but they were always particular ships, and his style is the same as that found in ordinary ship portraits. Perhaps he was influenced in his work by the Romantic style of painting.

The painter Halvor Mikkelsen, who was born in Stavanger in 1842, worked between 1877 and 1899 and might have been the pupil of T. L. Gabrielsen, who was his senior and also worked in Stavanger as a ship portraitist. Another productive painter was Frederik Martin Sørvig from Bergen (1820–1892), who also worked as a scene-painter for the Norwegian National Theatre. His numerous ship portraits were mostly painted in gouache; only the last of his paintings are in oils. Some of his pictures were published as lithographs.

Another painter of ship portraits was Andreas Lind, who worked in Drontheim until 1860. After that he seems to have lived in London, where he painted until shortly after 1890. Some of his pictures are in gouache, others in oils. He is said to have made rough sketches of ships as they were towed up the Thames and then taken them home to his studio and turned them into paintings so quickly that they were ready for delivery on board the ship before she had finished discharging.

At the beginning of the 20th century Norwegian ports, too, witnessed a disappearance of sailing ships. It is significant that most of the ship painters disappeared at the same time, and apparently it was not only the increasing competition of photography that ousted them. The ship portraitist and the photographer could work perfectly well in one and the same port without interfering with each other as was proved by several examples in the 19th century. This development must, therefore, have had something to do with a change in mentality: the men in steamships were no longer the same as those in sailing ships. There were steamship painters in Norway: Olaf Gulbrandsen for example, who worked in Oslo, then called Christiania, but his social status was far below that of the painters of sailing ships and the prices he got for his paintings were low. This may be one of the reasons why the quality of ship portraits declined more and more in the years to follow.

200

In Sweden the 19th-century ship portraits show characteristics very similar to those from Norway. Amongst many others P. W. Cedergren, who worked in the 1830's, deserves to be mentioned, as well as D. H. Hansen, who worked in Gävle ten to thirty years later. In the 1860's there were A. Björkman and J. Hägg, who was known chiefly

234d

for paintings of steamships, in Stockholm. L. P. Sjöström, most of whose portraits of vessels built by the busy Gothenburg shipyards are in the Sjöfartsmuseet in Gothenburg, worked there from the 1870's to the end of the century.

There were ship portraitists at work on the other side of the Baltic Sea, too, in ports like Stettin, Danzig, Königsberg, the coastal towns of the Baltic countries and in what was then St. Petersburg. But their paintings are not easily accessible today, so that accurate details of them cannot be given.

It is different in Holland, the home of classical marine paintings. A large number of ship portraits have been preserved in private collections and in large and small museums there, many of them tucked away in store rooms. Among them are paintings of canal boats and coastal vessels which are striking in their naïvety (most of them can be found in smaller places like Groningen, Hoorn, Sneek, Leeuwarden and the nearby German ports of Emden and Papenburg on the river Ems), as well as the usual big portraits of large sea-going ships, painted chiefly in the large ports of Amsterdam and Rotterdam. It will suffice to mention as an example of the first category the scene of a whaling fleet

193

in the Arctic Ocean painted by J. Moog in 1805 in strikingly bright colours, which has

see Notes

some even more attractive counterparts in earlier paintings of a similar scene in the

228c

museum in Wyk on the island of Föhr. They were painted between 1776 and 1778 and obviously go back to the same original painting. In the second category we might mention the pictures by D. A. Seupken and J. Spin of Amsterdam, who were the leading

ship portraitists in Holland in the 1830's and 1840's, and the works of P. Vermaas, who worked in Rotterdam in the last third of the 19th century and by whom many paintings of steamers are preserved.

A late phenomenon was the American John Henry Mohrmann, born of German parents in San Francisco in 1857, whose interesting career is recorded in a work by van Beylen. He went to sea as a cabin boy when he was thirteen and during the fourteen years he plied the oceans painted regularly in his spare time. He decorated cigar boxes for his shipmates, painted murals in a church in Kassel together with an Italian friend, and restored paintings in England. He is also said to have been a student at the Antwerp Academy. His ship portraits date back to 1881. The most productive period in his career was from 1890 to 1913 when, after a restless life at sea, he had settled in Antwerp. In 1913 he emigrated to Canada and died there three years later. We are told that in 1908 he was paid the equivalent of £5 for one of his portraits, which was half the monthly pay a first officer on a merchantman received in those days. Together with the Danish painter Antonio Jacobsen mentioned earlier, who lived in New York and whose fame was contemporary with that of Mohrmann, he was a typical representative of the closing phase in the art of ship portraiture. He developed a considerable activity in one of the busiest ports of the world, and many of his paintings are preserved in both Europe and America.

Jacobsen, who came from a Copenhagen family of violin-makers, emigrated to New York in 1871 when he was twenty-one. Music and painting were his hobbies. An employee of the Old Dominion Line saw his pictures and persuaded him to take up ship portraiture. Thus began the career of a ship portraitist whose financial success, next to that of Antoine Roux and his sons, must have been the most remarkable. Jacobsen mainly painted steamers, in particular those of the Fall River Line, and later the revolutionary new vessels of the White Star Line, the *Oceanic*, *Celtic* and *Baltic*. He died in New York in 1921. His pictures are spread all over the world, but a considerable number of them, dated from 1875 to 1919, are in the Peabody Museum in Salem, in the Mariner's Museum in Newport News and in the museum of the Historical Society in New York.

In North America, too, mainly in the New England ports on the east coast, ship portraits came on the market as early as 1800 or thereabouts. In keeping with the cosmopolitan character of this type of painting they are not distinguished by any peculiarities from contemporary portraits of European origin. Some early American portraits like, for example, those of the *Ceres* built in Boston in 1805 and of the *America* built in Newbury in 1830, both in the Mariner's Museum at Newport News, follow the contemporary custom of depicting the ship a second time in the background, smaller and from a different angle. This particularity has already been mentioned in connection with the earliest Danish portraits.

228 b

Drawing from a log book, 19th century, Nb.

234 c

Right: Whaling scene, probably off Spitzbergen, copy of an original in the Altonaer Museum dated 1776, Wh.
Page 194: Ship portraits; a, 'Sint Johannis', about 1765, Os; b, 'Catrina Sclave', 1783, Wh; c, Venetian galleass, second half 18th century, Vn; d, 'Mette Catrina', about 1780, St; e, 'Anders de Bruce', 1783, Go; f, 'De Hoffnung', water colour by Guiseppe Fedi, Ancona, 1792, Ap.
Page 195: Ship portraits; a, 'Catarine & Sophia', Livorno, 1800, Ap; b, 'Haabet', Livorno, 1800, Ap; c, 'Venere', Livorno, water colour by Guiseppe Fedi, 1817, Ap; d, 'Hoffnung', Naples, 1795, He; e, 'Prinzessin Friederike', Naples, 1864, Wh; f, Roadstead of Naples, about 1870, Bk.
Page 196: a, Frigate 'Fredensborg Slot', Copenhagen, about 1765, He; b, Frigate 'Dronning Sophie Magdalene', Copenhagen, about 1765, He; c, Danish warship painted in tempera by Clement Mogensen Clementsen, about 1760, Co; d, Brig 'Industria', Apenrade, 1799, Ap.

192

a

b

c

d

e

f

a

b

c

d

e

f

a

b

c

d

a

b

c

a

b

c

Bergantin Goleta "Costa Brava" Capt.ⁿ J. Serrat

d

Drawing from a ship's journal, 19th century, Nb.

238b

225; 227

Page 197: Warship 'Edinburgh', water colour by Captain Bay, about 1812, Mh. Page 198: Ships off Venice; a, 'Familie' from Blankenese, 1850, Ha; b, 'La Speranza' from Venice with Austrian flag, 1857, Vn; c, 'Hunze' from Groningen, 1865, Gr.
Page 199: a, Brig 'Solide', water colour by Antoine Roux, Marseilles, 1802, Pm; b, Warship 'La Ville de Marseille' from Toulon (1812), water colour by François Roux, Marseilles, 1876, Pm; c, Warship 'Luisa', oil painting by F. Hernandez, first half 19th century, Mn; d, Hermaphrodite brig 'Costa Brava', water colour by Barneda, Barcelona, 1887, Mh.
Left: 'Fredericia', oil painting by D. H. Hansen, Gävle, 1852, Ga.

There are two types of ship portraits which are really unique to America: those of the famous large clippers, which from 1850 gained widespread popularity as coloured lithographs, many of them based on oil paintings by N. Currier, and those depicting aspects of the American whaling trade, which at the time held a dominating position in the world. Museums in Mystic, New Bedford, Newport News, Nantucket, Salem and Sag Harbor possess numerous contemporary pictures of whalers and whaling scenes from the heyday of this trade, which had previously looked to Holland, the leading nation until 1800, for its pictorial recorders. Whaling scenes were also painted on long panoramic scrolls which were unrolled and exhibited to the audience in public showings. The sea, sky and horizon run continuously over the whole length of the scroll, while the various stages of a whaling expedition are shown side by side. There are extremely dramatic situations which appear amusing by the naïvety of their presentation, and in between there are the whalers themselves, painted in the usual style of the ship portraits. One such panorama, painted in the 1830's, is in the Peabody Museum in Salem; another, whose history is known in detail, is in the Whaling Museum in New Bedford. It was painted by two men, Purrington and Benjamin Russell, in 1848. The latter came from a New Bedford family of well-to-do whaling-fleet owners and had himself been round the world in a whaler between 1841 and 1843. After his return he and Purrington painted this monumental panorama, about 7 ft. high and over 650 ft. long, which describes the episodes of this whaling expedition. It presents a contemporary and authentic picture and describes scenes which recur in Melville's famous novel *Moby Dick*. Melville, who himself went whaling from New Bedford, may have known it and been inspired by it. Russell remained the foremost painter of American whalers until his death in 1885. Apart from Russell and Purrington, C. S. Raleigh, whose works were done in approximately the same period, ought to be mentioned.

The portraits of American steamers already mentioned are by Charles B. Lawrence, who painted the paddle steamers *Phoenix* and *Philadelphia* in 1815. Early paintings of steamers include water colours by J. F. Huge of Bridgeport, who worked between 1840 and 1860. But by far the best known of American ship portraitists in those days were the brothers James and John Bard. They produced hundreds of oil paintings, water colours and pencil drawings, mainly of steamers on the Hudson River and in New York harbour. Their first known picture is dated 1830, the last, by James, who lived to a ripe old age, dates from 1890.

Ship portraits are known from many other ports throughout the world, Spanish, Portuguese, South American and Australian. In Spain, for example, we have portraits by F. Hernandez from the first and Barneda from the second half of the 19th century, both known by their signatures only. Then there are those portraits which originated in Far

Eastern ports and were painted to suit Western tastes. A few examples of this very special *199c, d* category are preserved in maritime museums in Europe and America. They are characterized by the obvious desire of the Chinese or Japanese artist to adapt his style to the criterion of the Western customer, and yet they possess the undeniable delicacy which is so typical of Eastern art.

In conclusion we might mention those drawings of ships which are occasionally found in old log books, private diaries of ships' officers and account books of shipping guilds.

42, 43, 172, 183, 192, 201, 223, 231

Much of what is said in the following chapter by van Beylen about ship paintings on glass applies in general to the history of ship portraiture as it has been sketched here, especially with regard to the iconographic aspects. Thanks to van Beylen's research, much detailed and reliable information is now available on the subject of glass painting and it is hoped that one day we will have an equally thorough knowledge of the complex aspects of ship portraiture in general. In summing up, though, it can be said that we have here a very special type of painting which cannot be described as high art, except possibly in isolated cases, but which, on the other hand, lacks an important characteristic of so-called folk art by being entirely cosmopolitan. As a rule the exponents of this art were not professional artists, but they all possessed a thorough knowledge of ships and ports and many of them had been to sea, for which there is ample documentary evidence. A number of them could certainly be called 'Sunday painter' amateurs. This is best demonstrated by two specific paintings whose appeal lies in the naïve originality of the painters' perception and the strikingly carefree manner of execution: the view of the New England port of Marblehead in the possession of the New York Historical Society, and a painting of building activities at the Rickmerswerft (Rickmers Shipyard) in Bremer- *217d* haven (about 1860). Pictures like this, of varying quality, can be found in their thousands in ports all over the world, even the smallest. Many of them are family possessions, Though usually less refined, they have much of the irresistible charm of the 'primitive masters' whom Wilhelm Uhde discovered in Paris: Vivin, Bombois, Bauchant and the customs official Henry Rousseau, the first of these 'classical primitives'. Rousseau's self portrait in the Prague museum is very interesting in this connection: in the background we can see a dressed ship moored along the Seine quay. In the way it is painted it might have been done by any of the anonymous mariners who dabbled in painting at that times.

Until now the primitive marine painters have scarcely been noted, let alone given their due, although the works of the Paris customs official who, drawing on his imagination and on existing illustrated works, spent his leisure hours committing his fanciful visions to canvas, and those of the sailor who spent his free time recording his visual experience in an equally naïve way, have obviously much in common.

Glass Paintings of Ships

Origin, Technique, Antwerp as a Centre of the Craft

see Notes

We have no conclusive knowledge about the origin of glass painting. Some sources claim that the art of painting on the back of glass was well-known in antiquity, others attribute its first appearance to the 4th century A.D. Its birthplace may have been Byzantium, whence it spread to Italy and from there into Central Europe. Apart from the 'hot' process used in making stained-glass windows, the technique of painting on glass with cold lacquer was employed at quite an early date. A number of very attractive German pictures from the 14th century were made in this way. In the 16th century painting on

see Notes

glass spread to Switzerlann, Holland and many other countries. In Italy these paintings were even mass produced. Their themes were primarily religious and allegorical.

Around 1700, painting on glass began to be introduced into the arts and crafts, particularly in the centres of the glass industry in Bohemia and Silesia. Amongst the paintings that came from there were many incorporating cut details and a mirror base. The trade experienced a particular boom in Augsburg but also flourished in the Netherlands, France, Switzerland and England, where paintings were predominantly of mundane

239a; 248a

subjects: landscapes, genre-paintings, portraits, decorative and heraldic patterns. Although the technique was hardly practised any more by the end of the 19th century, a number of painters are using it again today.

It was not until the 18th century that glass painting really became an instrument of popular art, and in the beginning it was almost exclusively confined to the production of votive pictures of the kind that can be seen in places of pilgrimage, churches and

see Notes

Catholic homes. Small religious pictures which were handed out at places of pilgrimage and sometimes used there as votive pictures have been known since the 15th century. They show events from both the New and Old Testaments or portray saints and pious deeds. People took these pictures back with them to their home towns and villages, where

local painters and talented amateurs frequently used them as models for coloured pictures on glass, altering and adapting the drawings and colours to suit their own taste. In this process many of the pictures were unwittingly given what we would describe today as expressionist or surrealist traits. In this way glass painting passed on from being a craftsman's art to becoming a folk art. In many areas it was later practised as a semi-industrialized occupation. Pedlars going from house to house sold large quantities of these pictures throughout Europe and even in America, until towards the end of the 19th century, when the art went completely out of fashion.

Folk art, as far as it has been inspired by ships and the sea, has found expression in the most varied techniques. There are model ships and ships in bottles, ships cut out of paper, ships painted on tiles, on furniture and on glass. There are obviously quite a number of inferior products among them, but not infrequently we come across extremely skilfully and carefully executed pieces which stand in sharp contrast to the tasteless and primitive creations which some people see as the sole embodiment of the term 'folk art'.

Amateur painters who sought their themes in the maritime sphere painted mainly sea-going ships. Fishing boats and inland water vessels seem to have been less favoured. Sea-going ships stimulated their imagination and they depicted them mainly in two forms: in portraits and in narrative paintings which, nevertheless, present a clear portrait of the ship as the centre-piece of storms, sea battles, shipwrecks and harbour scenes.

Paintings of this kind are generally classed as folk art because of the way in which they are painted. But it is not only the technique which decides whether a painting belongs to the category of folk art, but the manner in which the theme is rendered, the composition, colouring and spiritual background. Maritime glass paintings must not, therefore, be compared to the widely popular general glass paintings of the 18th and 19th centuries. Their origin and content belong to another order and their value lies in another sphere. They are more akin to the amateur painting which flourished in the towns during those centuries, while their origin is rooted in a nautical custom of that time.

The introduction of maritime glass painting was not the result of a religious impulse but of a profane custom among seamen which arose in the second half of the 18th century and lasted until the beginning of this century. It was probably spread by the initiative of local amateur and professional painters who painted ships in the harbours, employing all manner of techniques. Foreign seamen who could afford it bought or ordered these portraits of ships with the harbour in the background as a souvenir of their stay. Captains, too, acquired them in their home ports and hung them up at home so that their families would have a reminder of them during their long absences. Every time a captain was given a new command, he ordered a picture of the ship to express his pride in his new assignment. It is not surprising, therefore, that the same ship was painted several times with the names of different captains on it, or that the name of

see Notes

Right: Whaler 'Bremen' in the South Seas, by C. J. H. Fedeler, 1843, Br.
Page 206: a, Venetian Brig, second quarter 19th century, Vn; b, Whaler 'Atlas' from Nantucket, early 19th century, Na.

a

b

a

b

a

b

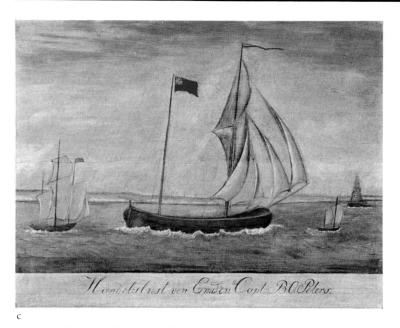

Handelslust von Emden Capt. B. O. Peters

c

Schooner Liemen Capt H. Schumacher Neapel Janu. 1865.

d

e

f

the same captain is to be found on pictures of several different ships. Shipowners and builders also ordered portraits of ships. They decorated their offices with them to demonstrate the importance of their firms – publicity we would call it today.

Towards the end of the 19th century the custom lost importance and all but disappeared in the first years of the 20th century. Its end coincided with the disappearance of sailing ships from the oceans of the world. At the turn of the century quite a number of portraits of steamships were still painted, but as the painters in this genre died so did the genre itself. Amongst a number of social and economic reasons, the main one was probably the competition of the camera. Another cause was the fact that steamers spent shorter and shorter times in port so that it became more difficult to place orders for pictures, especially since the painter needed a certain time in which to paint them. A change in the mentality of seamen must have been a further contributary factor. It seems that the captains of sailing ships were more receptive to the romantic art of ship portraiture than the more technically minded commanders of steam and motor ships.

Ship portraits were painted in their thousands in European as well as foreign ports. Their quality varied from poor or mediocre pieces to paintings with real artistic merit. These ship portraits provide all seafaring nations with a very important iconographic source. Very often they are the only clue to the maritime history of a certain region and the last remaining evidence of ships of bygone days. Without these portraits we would have but a very vague picture of the history of navigation in some countries and ports. At the same time they illustrate very well the written sources of information. Their documentary value is, for the most part, incontestable and can be verified in written and printed records, like Lloyd's Register of Shipping or the Registre Veritas. In very many cases their documentary value exceeds that of classical marine paintings which are of far superior quality artistically. In fact, the painters of ship portraits hardly ever presented personal interpretations, yet each one had a more or less individual way of expressing himself. The nature of their themes left little scope for the imagination since the type and name of the ship as well as the name of the captain were always indicated in some way in the painting or at the bottom of it.

Ship portraitists always endeavoured to reproduce as true a likeness of a ship as possible, a portrait that would satisfy the customer who had ordered it and who, since he was a captain or shipowner, would be an expert on ships. As there were no photographs at that time, this accuracy of detail is of priceless value. Indeed, some of the ships were painted with almost photographic accuracy, a little stiff and sober but without exception 'ship-shape', correct in outline and proportions, technically reliable. No-one looking at these pictures could say that the painters merely painted pretty, decorative ships and gave them a few masts and sails to make them look like sea-going

see Notes

Page 207: a, Merchant brig 'Bernstorff' off Marseilles, water colour by Antoine Roux, Marseilles, 1804, Ap; b, English ship of the line on the roadstead of Malta, about 1800, At.
Left: a, 'Venus', Bremen, water colour, 1852, Bm; b, 'Admiral', water colour by J. Gaun, 1850, Bm; c, 'Handelslust', Emden, water colour, first half 19th century, Bk; d, 'Lienen', tempera, Naples, 1865, Bk; e, 'Ida', Hamburg, oil painting by L. Petersen and P. Holm, about 1860, Bm; f, 'Archimedes', Hamburg, oil painting by L. Petersen and P. Holm, 1859, Hh.

vessels. The painters obviously knew exactly what they were about, and they must have had a sound knowledge of contemporary ships. Naturally they lived in the ports, some even had been to sea themselves so that they had ample opportunity to get a clear picture of the apparently confusing muddle of a ship's rigging.

When depicting particular events the painter had to be familiar with the attendant circumstances. In the majority of cases he did not personally witness the event to be painted, or at least not from close to. So he had to get his inspiration mostly from other sources unless he was to paint entirely from imagination. These sources might be contemporary engravings or lithographs, illustrations in newspapers or books and even eye-witness descriptions. It was quite customary in folk art for paintings to be based on small, printed pictures—and vice versa—and it is safe to assume that painters on glass followed the same method. They may also have borrowed from popular prints of sea battles and naval operations which were in widespread circulation. Other paintings suggest, by the way in which the theme is presented, that the artist must have had verbal or written accounts to fall back on. Of course, it is difficult to determine to what degree any of these paintings can be relied upon as a faithful reproduction of reality without knowing exactly from what sources the painter drew his information. With the exception of pictures painted after prints it seems as good as impossible. Nevertheless, these painters cannot be denied the merit of artistic initiative, even if it applies only to the composition and colouring of their works.

Many different techniques and materials were used for painting on glass. In the genuine *eglomisé* technique a drawing is engraved in a layer of wet or dry paint spread on glass and the lines are then filled in with gold or silver foil or with another paint or colour. The ordinary kind of glass painting is done with only paint, which can be any one of several basic types: ordinary lacquer, tempera, water colour mixed with gum arabic, casein paint, oil paint mixed with varnish and ordinary oil paint.   *see Notes*

The painting itself is done on the back of a sheet of glass but in such a way that the completed picture can be looked at from the front. The unsuspecting viewer thinks that he is looking at a picture framed behind glass and does not notice at once that the glass itself is the 'canvas'. In comparison with the usual methods of painting the work is done in reverse order. What is painted last in normal paintings is usually painted first in glass paintings. This means that there is a very definite order in which every part of the picture has to be built up. If a small detail is missed out at one stage it cannot be painted in afterwards. The correction can only be made by removing all the subsequent layers of paint. The *eglomisé* technique is used for texts or for decorations on stem- and stern-posts and rudder heads and other gilded ornaments.

Unlike the ordinary glass painter working inland, the painter of ship portraits did   **210** not actually copy any existing picture except his own working drawing, which he had to prepare for every portrait beforehand. This was probably a line drawing with the colours indicated on it and it was a reflected image of the finished painting. If the ship was seen from starboard in the working drawing then it would be seen from the port side in the painting. A tower which was to be on the left in the finished work would be on the right in the working drawing. Any writing which was to be normally legible in the finished painting had to be drawn in reverse in the working sketch. In some cases this peculiarity shows up very well. Several painters of ship portraits on glass also did oil paintings on canvas, and these are always reflected images of the glass paintings.

see Notes In some instances both versions of the same ship are in existence. The working drawing had to be complete in every detail because it was from this that the painter built up his portrait. He had to be able to see where all the many lines of the rigging began and ended, whether they ran before or behind the sails, masts or superstructure, where they disappeared and where they reappeared. To start with all these lines were painted in out of context, merely copied from the working drawing. The whole picture gradually materialized as the main areas of the sails and hull, the shadows, the water and the sky were filled in. The back of the glass was initially coated with gum or varnish, and the vertical streaks, like those on a badly cleaned window, which can be seen running between the glass and the paint in many ship portraits, result from this coating having become discoloured or containing impurities. After the painter had placed his working drawing under the glass he could start work. In order to understand how the work progressed we must put ourselves in the place of the viewer of the finished picture, that is on the other side of the glass. The painter must first complete those parts which are to be found in the foreground, in other words, those lines and surfaces which are not crossed or concealed by other lines and surfaces. In a ship these are the lines of the hull, the rigging and the sails, but they may also include things in the background, like a town, a coast or another ship. As far as the hull is concerned the planks and all the parts which are seen on the outside of the ship must be painted in first: anchors, bull's-eyes, rudder pintles and so on. Only after these initial details are completed can the hull colour be painted in. Next come the parts of the rigging which can be seen in front of the sails, masts and yards. A sail is painted in the following way: first come all the seams, brails and reef points, then the shadows which appear on the sail are put in and finally the colour of the sail cloth is applied. Everything in the drawing must be copied until a complete picture results from the patient application of lines and surfaces. Without a preliminary drawing the painter could not possibly imagine how all the different parts of the picture are related. This process is repeated for all parts of the picture which lie in the frontal plane, including background details such as ships, coastlines and outlines of towns. In a later stage of the work the water is painted in. Some paintings look as though the *eglomisé* technique had been used for the bow waves. The way the wave tops lie alongside the hull is characteristic of this method. They have clearly been added by scratching away parts of the painted hull and filling the exposed space with 'foam'. In some paintings the part of the hull that was scratched away is still discernible. The waves are painted in the same way as the rest of the picture: first the white tops, then the waves themselves.

The background is filled with clouds and sky. The clouds, since they are seen in front of the open sky, are painted first. Many nuances of colour can be seen in these clouds and in parts of the sky. Clouds with light top edges have these painted in first before the cloud itself is filled in. Certain painters varied the colours from a grey high up in the sky to a pink on the horizon, the colours merging imperceptibly with each other. Behind the clouds either the open blue sky or a second layer of grey clouds is put in. Finally the whole painting is given a coat of sky blue paint that covers even the ship and fills in all the spaces between the rigging, at the same time providing a kind of protective backing for the picture. Sometimes the sky, clouds and background were not painted on the back of the glass but on a separate sheet of paper or on the front of a second pane of glass. They were then painted in the normal way, of course, not in reverse. If this separate background was placed some distance behind the picture ($^1/_2$ in to 2 ins.) it gave a definite three-dimensional effect. The majority of maritime glass paintings were provided with a text describing the picture. In the 18th-century pictures the text is always found along the upper edge, in the 19th-century ones along the lower edge. The *eglomisé* technique was used for this in all but the later 19th-century paintings. The letters were scratched out and filled with gold foil, less frequently silver foil. The painter's signature, where it appears, is also found on the lower edge. In a few paintings it is in reverse.

Unlike religious and profane folk painting, maritime glass painting did not spread all over Europe, although it was known and practised outside the European continent*. All indications point to this kind of painting having only occurred in a few isolated places. Which these places were cannot always be said with certainty, and when it comes to the few remaining 18th-century pieces their origin can hardly be established at all. Only a very few glass paintings of seascapes and harbour scenes of the period before 1800 remain today* and only seven ship portraits are known to exist from that time.* It is, of course, quite possible that a number of these pictures are still undetected in public or private collections. An example of genre-painting, an anonymous work, is preserved in the Handels- og Söfartsmuseum paa Kronborg in Helsingör, Denmark. In the same museum there are also several 18th-century scenes by unknown Chinese

247c

247f

248f

Right: Full-rigged ship 'Willy' off New York, about 1860, Bm.
Page 214: a, Ships off Liverpool, oil painting by G. Nelson, about 1850, Lg; b, Brig entering the Avon at Bristol, oil painting by Joseph Walter, 1838, Lg; c, American passenger packet 'Antarctic' off the South Stack, approaching Liverpool, oil painting by D. McFarlane, 1853, Lg.
Page 215: The 'Warrior 74' in the mouth of the Tagus, about 1815, oil by Thomas Buttersworth, Lg.
Page 216: a, Dutch ships in the Bay of Nagasaki, Japanese painting, 1825, Rm; b, Roadstead of Whampoa, Chinese painting, early 19th century, Ap.

246a, b; 248b

* see Notes

a

b

c

a

b

a

b

a

b

c

d

e

f

g

h

a

b

a

b

masters, among them a view of Venice. A number of works from this period are known in Belgium, too: one of them is of a river scene in Italian style, but with an English caption; another is a coastal landscape, probably by the same painter and also bearing an English title; a third is a harbour scene in an unknown town in the tropics. A small glass painting which turned up in the Munich antique trade and is known to have come from Belgium is similar in many ways to the English river scene. Two other harbour scenes, both of the port of Brest, are in the possession of the Peabody Museum in Salem. Curiously, both have German captions. It cannot be ascertained whether these pictures were made in Brest or elsewhere. The painter might easily have got his inspiration from the well-known 18th-century engravings. The style of the paintings certainly does not rule out this possibility.

Ship portraits from the 18th century are to be found in the following museums and collections: the museum at Apenrade (Denmark), the Sjöfartsmuseum vid Åbo akademi (Finland), the National Maritime Museum at Greenwich and the Falmouth Municipal Museum (England), the Museo Civico Navale at Genoa (Italy), the Hallands Museum, Halmstad (Sweden), the private collection of Schiffbau-Oberingenieur F. Stache, Lübeck (Germany) and the Gotland Fornsal Museum, Visby (Sweden). The oldest known work is the painting in Lübeck. Dated 1757, it shows the whaler *D:Stadts Welvaert* from Altona and is one of those rare pictures which is taller than it is wide. The method of presentation is also unusual: the ship is shown in three-quarter view. So is the whaler in the painting at Apenrade, while the portraits at Åbo, Falmouth, Genoa and Halmstad show the ships broadside on. A critical comparison of the styles leads to the conclusion that all these works came from Italy and from one and the same painter. Nothing can be said with certainty about the origin of the Visby painting. In execution it bears a remarkable similarity to the previous ones: the way the bowsprit extends over the edge of the picture, the scroll bearing the inscription at right-angles to the mast, the way the bow and stern are drawn, the long pennant flying from the main mast, the shape of the anchor, the appearance of the sails, the way the ship's name, captain's name and year are grouped on the scroll. As in the pictures at Falmouth and Halmstad there are two sailors standing in the tops. Another important clue which underlines the remarkable similarity is the picture frame. The same frame is used on the Visby picture as on the others, which strongly suggests that it has the same place of origin. But is it quite incidental that this portrait bears a later date than the others? It has obviously been painted with less care and the letters of the text are less precise. In view of the obvious similarity one is definitely tempted to ascribe the Visby picture to the same painter as the others. Perhaps he painted it when he was older, which would account for the rather more careless way in which it is painted and the comparatively late date.

248 b

246 a, b

see Notes

239 b, c, d

Page 217: a, Valparaiso harbour, possibly Chinese painting, mid 19th century, Hh; b, Rickmers shipbuilding yard at Bremerhaven, painting, about 1860, Bm.
Page 218: British ship portraits, Lg; a, 'East Indian' by Thomas Binks, 1819; b, 'Margaret Galbraith' in the Clyde, by William Clark, mid 19th century; c, 'The Tweed', Chinese artist, about 1870; d, 'Morley' off the Downs, painted in three positions, by William Adolphus Knell, 1828; e, The barque J. P. Smith near Liverpool, by Samuel Walters, about 1875; f, The clipper 'Star of the East' in the English Channel, by Joseph Heard, 1853; g, 'Barossa' in the English Channel, by F. Tudgay, 1874; h, The snow 'Mary Ann' at the mouth of the Tyne, J. Scott, 1864.
Page 219: a, Mail packet off Liverpool, by Robert Salmon, 1804, Lg; b, The East Indiaman 'Asia' off Hong Kong, William John Huggins, 1836, Lg.
Left: a, Steamer 'De Ruyter' from Antwerp, oil by Antonio Jacobsen, New York, 1886, At; b, New York pilot schooner 'Joseph Palitzer', oil by Antonio Jacobsen, New York, 1896, At.

221

Even if many of the 18th-century glass paintings have been broken, the fact that so few remain and are known indicates that they were never produced in large numbers. This technique of painting only reached its peak in the 19th century. The oldest of the 19th-century portraits is to be found in the Handels-og Söfartsmuseum paa Kronborg in Helsingör. It is an anonymous work dated 1800 which shows a trading frigate called *Den Drag*. Compared with the glass paintings from the 18th century, of which we can assume that the majority originated in the Mediterranean, the difference in interpretation and composition is very marked. Another school has undoubtedly been at work here. The centre of maritime glass painting in the 19th century was no longer Italy, but Flanders, where initially Ostend and later Antwerp were the leading towns.

236a

Glass painting as such had certainly not been unknown in this region in earlier centuries and was still practised in the Flemish country districts in the 19th century. But maritime glass paintings were made exclusively in the ports, and their first definite traces go back to the year 1805. The Nationaal Scheepvaartmuseum in Antwerp is in possession of a glass painting signed with the initials W.W. It is of a brig of unknown nationality portrayed in three-quarter view. From several other pictures signed with a full name and from official registers it has been established that the painter was a certain Wenzeslaus Wieden. In the register of inhabitants in Ostend this Wenzeslaus Wieden is described both in 1802 and 1803 as a glass merchant. His wife was Joséphine Thérese Vermeire. It follows that the 1805 painting was almost certainly done in Ostend, because Wieden lived there until his death on 19 September 1814. How, when and why this glass merchant came to Ostend is not known. Wenzeslaus Wieden was born at 'Langemo' (which means Langenau near Görlitz in Silesia) in 1769. After the Seven Years War the Central European glass industry went through a crisis which forced many glass workers to emigrate. It is possible, therefore, that Wieden's parents looked for a promising existence elsewhere and this is how he came to Ostend as a child. His homeland was a centre of the glass making industry, and glass painting was a very widely practised trade and a branch of folk art in that area. On the other hand he may have been a travelling glass salesman who came as far afield as Ostend to sell his Silesian glass paintings. At any rate, it was probably he or his parents who brought the knowledge and skill of glass painting with them to Western Europe. The fact that he was a glass merchant is proof of his membership of the trade and leads to the assumption that he continued to buy glass wares from his home country. We might refer back in this connection to the two harbour scenes of Brest in the Peabody Museum in Salem. The captions in German point to the fact that their painter came from Central Europe. Could it be that other German-speaking glass painters besides Wenzeslaus Wieden migrated westward? Or is it conceivable that the Salem paintings come from

246d

see Notes

Drawing of a ewer by Joh. Felgenberg, from the account books of the merchant and shipping guild at Stade, 1768/69, St.

the hand of Wieden? Up to now we know of six pictures signed by him, and all are of a high standard. They reveal a certain talent for drawing and a proficient use of the brush. Two pictures are known from 1808 which are obviously intended as a matching pair. Both show a French ship in company with another vessel. The first is a picture of the French galliot *Le Dragon* from the quarter. The accompanying ship is a Dutch topsail schooner (p. 246). It may be pure chance that the caption of *Le Dragon* closely resembles that of *Den Drag* in Kronborg Castle.

The second painting of this pair shows another French ship, the galeass *Caroline*, in profile. In the background we see a three-masted lugger. A third work by Wieden dated 1808 is an unusual narrative picture of a small sea battle in the Ostend Roads on 16 May 1808 with a detailed explanatory text. An English brig had launched two armed boats with the intention of seizing a fleet of Ostend fishing boats. The French pirate lugger *Le Hazard*, armed with 14 guns, lay at anchor in the roads and succeeded in capturing the two English boats and towing them into Ostend. Apart from recording this local event, which must have caused quite some excitement in Ostend, this picture has definite value as a rare pictorial document. It clearly portrays the typical Ostend fishing boats, which could be seen along the Flemish coast until the beginning of the First World War, and is one of the oldest illustrations that exist of these boats.

Another beautiful picture by Wieden is a painting from 1812 entitled 'The Great Admiral Nelson'. It shows a fleet during manoeuvres. It is surprising that Wieden, at that

237b

time a French subject or at any rate living in a country occupied by Napoleon, should have painted a picture which obviously pays homage to Nelson. Did he perhaps cherish an admiration for the great Admiral and the English who had defeated the French

253a

at Trafalgar in 1805? In 1814, the last year of his life, Wieden painted another harbour scene entitled 'De Haven van Oostende' (Ostend Harbour). It shows a French corvette approaching Ostend mole in order to enter the harbour and being greeted by gun salutes from other ships. The ship, with her sails brailed up to reduce her speed, is beautifully painted, and the whole picture makes a very fine ship portrait. On the outer harbour wall we can recognise the lighthouse and the mast of the semaphore. Wieden has surrounded the caption of this painting with an extraordinary ornament, a kind of stage with open curtains, or it might be called a canopy. On either side of it he has painted a selection of military accoutrements which also appear in his portraits

246a, b

of *Le Dragon* and *Caroline* and, in a different grouping, in the two harbour scenes of Brest.

Wenzeslaus Wieden painted his ships in an outstanding manner, and his works, unlike those of rural folk-artists, were certainly not mass-produced. They had a decidedly individual character, and his art was that of a talented amateur who made

it into a profession. He founded 19th century Belgian maritime glass painting.

Even during Wieden's lifetime glass painting in Ostend had several pupils. One of them was a certain François Laurent Meseure. We do not know where this painter with the French-sounding name was born nor when or where he died. He was born in 1772 and lived in Ostend, where his name occurs in the town registers of 1803 and 1806. His wife, Isabella Claire Vergauwe, was obviously Flemish. We only know of one painting by François Meseure, signed and dated 1808. It shows two French ships of the line, *Le Gaulois* and *Le Mont clao* (which means 'Mont Blanc'). The ships lie at anchor in a bay off a fortress which, according to the caption inscribed at the foot of the walls, is meant to represent Fort Dauphin at San Domingo. A text in faulty French pays homage to the French Vice-Admiral Charles Magon, who was killed in the Battle of Trafalgar in 1805. The spelling mistakes suggest that Meseure had a poor command of French and was probably Flemish. The question is, where did he get his details? Was the painting commissioned by a Frenchman who had himself fought at Trafalgar and was now serving in the French fleet at Ostend? Is the painting an original work or is it a copy of some other picture, maybe by Wieden? The small number of surviving works by Wieden and the single one by Meseure do not permit a decisive Comparison to be made. In a small town such as Ostend then was, Meseure must have known his fellow citizen Wieden. Who knows if he did not perhaps buy his glass from him? Was he a pupil of Wieden, his friend or his competitor? A comparison of Meseure's painting of 1808 and Wieden's one of Ostend Harbour of 1814 reveals that the captions in both paintings are decorated in a similar way. As far as we can tell from Wieden's known works he repeatedly used military accoutrements as ornamentation. But was this his own invention, which Meseure copied, or was it the other way round? The only surviving work by Meseure tells us that he was no beginner and that he must certainly have done other paintings. Nevertheless, Wieden seems to have had more experience as a painter. If we consider Wieden's origin and the important role glass painting played in his home country, we can safely assume that the Silesian was the protagonist of glass painting in Ostend and Meseure his pupil. No-one knows how long Meseure worked in Ostend. One thing is certain, though: both his and Wieden's portraits of ships must have satisfied the taste of their customers and they found followers. The first known successor was Petrus Weyts, who may be regarded as the most prominent of Flemish glass painters.

Petrus Cornelius Weyts was born on 4 January 1799 at Gistel, about six miles from Ostend. He married in Ostend in 1824 and his occupation on his marriage licence describes him as 'painter'. Although the Dutch word for painter can also mean 'house painter' or 'decorator', it is fairly certain that here it stands for 'artist'. It is, of course, conceivable that he was a house painter by trade and that he did glass painting as an amateur. His earliest dated painting is from 1824 and is entitled 'De Haven van Ostende'.

237a

237a

253a

Right: Whaler 'Wanderer', by C. S. Raleigh, 1879, Nb.
Page 226: a, Barque, 'C. J. Borgstede', by Carl Fedeler, about 1860, Bm; b, Oldenburg barque in China, Chinese artist, mid 19th century, Bk; c, Full-rigged ship 'Andromeda', by O. Jaburg, about 1880, Bv; d, Barque 'Mathilde', by L. Petersen and P. Holm, 1861, Wh; e, Barque 'Nereus', by Antonio Jacobsen, 1878, Rm; f, Frigate 'Garibaldi', by A. Gallizioli, about 1860, Vn.

a

b

c

d

e

f

a

b

c

d

e

f

One glance at the picture is sufficient to establish who inspired him: Wenzeslaus Wieden. Weyts clearly must have known Wieden's harbour scene, if not actually had it to hand, in order to be able to paint his picture. True, there are several differences. Wieden's French corvette (of Napoleonic times) has become the merchant frigate *Flora de Gaend*. The ship is sailing under the Dutch flag (this is the time of the United Netherlands under William I, 1815–1830). The frigate is not entering the harbour but leaving it. The semaphore has disappeared from the harbour wall, but otherwise the picture is

247c

identical. The caption is surrounded by the same decoration, though the military accoutrements are missing. If any doubt remains about the connection between Wieden and Weyts then there is a second harbour scene of Ostend which confirms it. This is a picture entitled 'Vue du port d'Ostende', neither signed nor dated, which is an almost identical copy of Wieden's harbour scene. The style, and above all the use of colour, can be recognized as Weyts' handiwork. The corvette in the picture flies the Dutch flag so that the work must have been done before 1830. There is yet a third harbour scene of Ostend, also in the Nationaal Scheepvaart Museum in Antwerp, in which the ship is the English paddle steamer *Talbot*. It dates from the same time as the others.

Petrus Weyts also owes tribute to F. Meseure. It is possible that he knew Meseure. When Weyts painted his scene of Ostend harbour in 1824 Meseure was fifty-two years old. Was Weyts Meseure's pupil? The 1808 picture by Meseure was repeatedly copied by Petrus Weyts and in such accurate detail that we must assume that Meseure's work was in his possession. His first copy is almost a perfect reflected image of Meseure's painting, apart from a few unimportant details. The caption has been taken over word

247a

for word, except for the spelling mistakes, only '*Mont clao*' has been changed to '*Mont*

247b

Blanc'. In another, similar picture, Weyts has borrowed from both Wieden and Meseure. It is entitled 'Le Fort St. Marie près Cadiz' and is signed and dated 1831. This 'Fort

237a

St. Marie' is an enlarged copy of Meseure's 'Fort Dauphin à S. Dominique'. The white

237b

French flag has been replaced by a Spanish one. The ships sailing in the roads have

247d

clearly been taken from Wieden's 'The Great Admiral Nelson'. Without a doubt the picture refers to the bombardment of Cadiz in 1800 by an English fleet under the command of Nelson. This scene, too, was painted several times. Although by now Petrus Weyts showed considerable proficiency, he still seems to have continued to draw on the works of his predecessors.

In 1831, however, he produced a picture which is extremely unusual in its conception and execution. It is a diptych illustrating an event from the 18th century, and Weyts must have followed very precise instructions in painting it. The left half shows a ship, which 'sailing in latitude 22° 22' south and longitude 34° 48' was overtaken by a fearful hurricane in the month of March 1787'. The three-masted vessel, struck by lightning,

Page 227: Whale attacking a whaling boat, painting by C. S. Raleigh, 1879, Nb. Left: a, Whaler 'Niger' off New Bedford, about 1850, Nb; b, Merchant ship 'Joseph Willem' on the Maas, by J. Vermaas, 1864, Rm; c, Frigate by J. Spin, 1839, Rm; d, Full-rigged ship 'Humboldt', by C. J. H. Fedeler, 1852, Bm; e, Full-rigged ship 'Bremerhaven', by O. Jaburg, about 1850, Bv; f, American full-rigged ship 'Aurora', by S. Walters, about 1870, Nb.

229

is being tossed about by the waves like a plaything. The rigging has almost all been swept away and the ship is on the point of sinking. Obviously this did not happen in the end, since the second half of the picture shows it 'sailing with jury masts to Mauritius in March 1787'.

It is very likely that Petrus Weyts painted further pictures in Ostend. But Ostend was only a small port with a limited amount of maritime traffic. Naturally Weyts' circle of customers could not have been excessively big. Following the Revolution of 1830 traffic in the port of Antwerp expanded considerably, and this does not seem to have escaped Weyts. A large harbour like Antwerp obviously offered a professional artist specializing solely in pictures of ships much greater opportunity. So in 1838 Petrus Weyts decided to move and to settle in Antwerp with his family and brother.

But this did not mean that glass painting in Ostend died out. Pictures bearing the initials P.N., an artist about whom absolutely nothing is known, are clearly the work of an Ostender. The three pictures which have so far come to light (two of them are in the Nationaal Scheepvaart Museum in Antwerp) are all connected with Ostend ships. The first work, painted in 1836, is known only through literature. It shows the see Notes schooner *Le Bien Venu* from Ostend being shipwrecked in the Danzig Roads. The whereabouts of this picture is not known. The second picture is dated 1839 and shows the English schooner *Gilblas* from London aground on the Flemish Banks with a broken mainmast, in the vicinity of Ostend and Nieuwport, in danger of sinking. The crew of the Ostend pilot cutter *Lotsen 2* has taken the crew off and is towing the ship into Ostend. This happened in September 1839. What connection the painter P.N. had 254a with his colleague Weyts no one knows. His way of putting the caption under a canopy might suggest a link. The background in this painting is novel: the Flemish coast can be made out on the horizon, on the left is Ostend, on the right Nieuwport. The same coast appears in the third picture by P.N., a straightforward ship portrait. It pictures the Ostend barque *Aigle*. The year of origin must be 1841, since the caption names see Notes her captain of that year. P.N.'s presentation differs from the usual pattern of ship portraits on glass by showing the ship from the starboard instead of the port side. 254b

P.N. was not the only one who continued to paint on glass after Weyts and his family had moved. There was also a certain E. Devriese, whose name cannot be found on the register of inhabitants of Ostend. It is almost certain that he was not a professional artist. If he was not an Ostender, then he certainly did not live far away and had close connections with the Ostend fishermen. The only known painting by him shows a collision between two fishing boats from Ostend which occurred on 23 January 1852. The picture dates from the same year. It was probably commissioned by Leonardus Demey, the captain of the ship which was struck.

Right: Drawings from the ship's journal of the 'Clara Bell' by Robert E. Weir, 18th century, My; a, Harpooned whale sounding; b, Stripping off the teeth of a sperm whale

a

b

A picture from 1863 called 'Vue du port d'Ostende' is in the possession of a collector in Brussels. There is nothing to be seen of the harbour itself, so the title of the picture is rather misleading. The picture shows two fishing boats from Ostend which were entered in the official register of fishing boats of 1863. The boats are being towed by a tug which operated in Ostend harbour in those days whenever an unfavourable wind made it difficult or impossible for the fishing boats to leave harbour. The tug was known under the name *Zwarte Triene* and it was probably her captain who commissioned the picture. Everything points to the painter having lived at Ostend.

The picture of the paddle-wheel steamer *Leopold Premier* might be by the same painter. In certain details, such as the positioning of the caption, the dark streak of water in the foreground and the general colouring, this ship portrait shows a remarkable similarity to the previous painting. The *Leopold Premier* was built for the Ostend-Dover Line in 1869 and the picture must have been painted in that year or one of the following. She is one of the few steam ships which were painted on glass. It is interesting to note that the ships in these two pictures are shown from the starboard side, just as in those by P.N. P.N.'s pictures show the same dark streak of water in the foreground. Are all these pictures by the same painter, or did one painter copy the other?

248g

No further information about glass painters working in Ostend has so far come to light. It seems that the art died out there around 1870. Judging from the number of paintings still in existence the total production must have been modest. The painters were probably not professionals but amateurs, perhaps even seamen who had retired in Ostend.

From 1838, when Weyts moved there, until about 1878, Antwerp was the centre of glass painting. Ship portraits on glass became an Antwerp speciality, known on all the oceans of the world. Petrus Weyts and his family turned their occupation into a flourishing trade. He built up a kind of family business which was passed on from one member of the family to the other. Weyts arrived in Antwerp with his wife, his son Carolus Ludovicus and his brother Ignatius Jozef Johannes (born in Ostend on 17 May 1814, died in Antwerp on 19 March 1867). In Antwerp the family was increased by the birth of a son, Ignatius Jan. All the four male members of the family are described in the Antwerp register as 'artists'. Signed pictures by three of them are known. Only Petrus' brother Ignatius is missing. It is not certain whether he painted glass pictures. In all probability he worked in the workshop of his brother, as did Petrus' son Carolus Ludovicus. In fact, until Petrus Weyts' death only pictures with his signature are known, not a single one with anybody else's. Even the unsigned pictures are obviously by him. It looks as though Petrus Weyts, as the senior, ran the 'firm' and had a kind of monopoly over the signature. He came to specialize in pure ship portraits.

Right: Glass paintings; a, Battle of Trafalgar, early 19th century, Lg; b, Dutch full-rigged ship, early 19th century, Rm; c, 'Polarstern' from Tromsö, by Petrus Weyts, Antwerp, 1851, Os; d, 'Charlemagne' from Antwerp, by Petrus Weyts, Antwerp, 1852, At.
Page 234: a, Paddle steamer 'König Christian VIII', coloured drawing by Jacob Jebsen, Apenrade, 1847; b, Italian steamfrigate ship 'Governolo', oil, 1867, Vn; c, 'Helene Grisar', oil by Henry Mohrmann, Antwerp, 1899, At; d, 'Oscar Dickson' on the Yenisei, water colour by L. P. Sjöström, 1880, Go; e, 'Hollandia', water colour, Rotterdam, about 1880, Rm.
Page 235: 'Paul Rickmers', oil, 1892, Br.
Page 236: Glass paintings; a, 'Den Drag', 1800, He; b, Funeral barge conveying Nelson's body from Greenwich to Whitehall, by P. Barnaschina, 1806, Lg.

232

a

b

c

d

a

b

c

d

e

a

DEN DRAG
Commendiert durch Capt. PETER BRODERSEN, von Amrum 1800,

A Correct Representation of the Funeral Barge which conveyd the Body of the late Lord Nelson from Greenwich to Whitehall Jan.r 8.th 1806

b

a

Hommage au contre amiral charles mason, membre de la legiond'honneur
Commandant painte droite de la flotille nationale   N° 15+8 F. Maisure

THE GREAT ADMIRAL NELSON.

b

a

b

a

b

c

d

e

f

Hundreds, if not thousands, of them must have left his atelier in Antwerp and were spread all over the world on board foreign ships. Even today there are considerable numbers of them in public and private collections in Germany, Denmark, Holland, Norway, Sweden and the United States. More than half the pictures known today, however, are in Belgian collections. The Nationaal Scheepvaart Museum in Antwerp has more than sixty. It should be added that by no means all the existing examples either overseas or in Belgium are known. Judging from the ones we do know, we can say that narrative pictures were seldom painted. Petrus Weyts may have produced the odd genre picture. One of these is the 'Combat de Navarin 1827'. This picture of the famous sea battle of Navarino was obviously painted long after the event, probably in 1840. Both in style and technical approach this painting is better than Weyts' Ostend works. The characteristic way of painting which he acquired in Antwerp is quite noticeable in it.

Petrus Weyts developed a very individual, stereotyped style in Antwerp, which comes out especially in the water and the clouds. His works from the early days in Antwerp still show traces of his Ostend brush technique, but after 1840 this gave way to a more animated style. This can clearly be seen in 'Combat de Navarin'. The history of this picture is again unknown, but it can be assumed that it was commissioned. Belgians often served on foreign ships. One of them might have been present at the battle of Navarino and ordered the picture. Whether Petrus Weyts drew on any contemporary picture to help him with his work in this case we do not know. If we look at the two ships in the centre we are strongly reminded of Wenzeslaus Wieden's 'The Great Admiral Nelson'.

There is another picture which portrays a sea battle. The first thing we notice about it is its unusual colouring, which completely separates it from other paintings. In no other picture we know has Petrus Weyts used such sombre colours, and it is therefore questionable whether it actually is by him. In fact, there are very few clues which point to his style, except maybe the way the water is painted, which is similar to that in some of his early Ostend works. But there is one factor which gives rise to doubt. On closer inspection this sea battle turns out to be a simplified version of the 'Combat de Navarin', a reflected image, in fact, with many details in the foreground and background left out. The main motif, that is the two ships of the line which are to be seen in the Battle of Navarino, and the lugger and boat in the foreground, are the same, only in reverse. This gloomy sea battle must be a copy of the Navarino picture. Did Weyts once again copy one of his own works, or was it another painter? If so, it could only have been his son and successor Carolus Weyts. We cannot be sure of either. There is one small indication which warrants a supposition. It concerns the picture frame, about which more will be said later on.

see Notes

248c

253b

Page 237: Glass paintings; a, French ships of the line near San Domingo, by F. Meseure, 1808, Ak; b, British fleet with flag ship in the foreground, by W. Wieden, 1812, Bb.
Page 238: a, Brunshausen on the Elbe, lay painting by a seaman, signed A. v. G., 1848, St; b, Whalers of the 'Kutusoff' pursuing sperm whales off the west coast of Australia, from a panorama by Benjamin Russell, New Bedford, 1848, Nb.
Page 239: Glass paintings; a, Mediterranean scene, second half of 18th century, Mc; b, Yacht 'Charlotta', about 1770, Hs; c, Brig 'S. Antonio', 1768, Gn; d, Merchant ship 'Pontuncturn', 1775, Ab; e, 'Königin Juliana-Maria', about 1775, Ap; f, 'Provincien Gothland', 1785, Vi.
Left: Barque 'Land Wursten' from Dorum, by C. L. Weyts, Antwerp, 1859, Bm.

241

Petrus Weyts has also left behind a series of four related pictures, which are in the Nationaal Scheepvaart Museum in Antwerp. They tell the story of the voyage and sinking of the *Charles Quint* of Antwerp. In the first picture we see her leaving Antwerp harbour with the Cathedral of Our Lady in the background. The caption reads '*Charles Quint* d'Anvers 1840'. The second picture shows the ship near Flushing, and the caption says '*Charles Quint* setting out to sea from Flushing on 4th August 1840'. The third 254c scene with the title '*Charles Quint* d'Anvers 1840' depicts her in a storm with her sails reefed, seen from broadly over the quarter. This is an unusual view-point and one which Petrus Weyts chose for a number of other ships, all of them in a storm. Finally, the fourth picture shows the '*Charles Quint* in the Gulf of Mexico at 5 o'clock in the afternoon of 16th September 1840'. At this time the vessel was struck by lightning.

Another painting which probably originated in Antwerp but whose composition reflects Weyts' Ostend days, is a second copy of Meseure's 'Homage au Contre-admiral Charles Magon...' and is at the same time a reflected image of Weyts' first copy of this picture. The ships in this third version of the same subject are less well painted, but the water is rendered in the same manner as in other pictures Weyts painted in Antwerp.

In Antwerp the ship portrait found a new market among the seamen whose ships were at anchor there. Weyts' Ostend works occasionally suffered from faulty perspective; in Antwerp he painted nearly all his ships in profile, which lessened the risk of such errors in perspective. One has to look very closely indeed to discover any mistakes. There is also an improvement in the way waves and clouds are painted. In Ostend they were mostly made up from horizontal brush strokes. From 1831 onwards a change can be noticed as Weyts adopts the nebulous kind of cumulus clouds which are typical of all his Antwerp works. After 1838 the water becomes dark green with white crests on rather strongly stylized curving waves. The ships are portrayed both under full sail and with reduced canvas, that is with the upper topgallants, topsails and upper topsails reefed. Sometimes the ship is sailing on the port tack and the sails are seen from ahead, sometimes on the starboard tack with the sails seen from behind and all of the rigging visible. Petrus Weyts had a preference for ships sailing close-hauled, but without heeling appreciably. The flags stream out astern as they ought. They always consist of at least the national flag, which is flown from the gaff, and the pennant bearing the ship's name at the top of the mainmast. Sometimes they are joined by a house flag on the fore or mizzen masts. There is no strict rule about this. Some ships have signal flags 254d hoisted on the mizzen mast, spelling out the ship's registration numbers, and some fly a special flag such as a town flag or the flag of a seamen's association. The rigging is always depicted in detail and with great accuracy, and the hull shape is true to life, so that the type of ship is perfectly recognizable. There are always several sailors on deck wearing flat-topped hats. The captain, who is either giving commands with an outstretched arm or scanning the horizon with a telescope clapped to his eye, is seldom missing. In the background there are usually one or two other ships. One of them is a repeat of the portrayed vessel, seen from a different angle, and the other a pilot cutter. Usually there is also a town to be seen on the horizon; frequently this is Flushing, less often Ostend or another port. Flushing is always on the left of the picture, Ostend on the right. This is geographically wrong, because Flushing lies on the right bank of the river. A ship coming in from the sea to go up the Scheldt would leave Flushing to port, but on the pictures it is shown to starboard. However, the silhouette shows quite clearly that this town is Flushing, and it is also confirmed in several captions, for example 'Barque Balti of Thoaston, Alfred K. Spear Comd., passing Flushing 1844'. Ostend can be recognized by the high lighthouse tower which appears on all the paintings that show this town in the background.

Petrus Weyts always added a descriptive text to his paintings. The caption just quoted is an example of the detailed information these texts provide. It mentions the type of ship, her name, the port of registry, the name of the captain, sometimes the place depicted in the picture ('passing Flushing') and finally the date. Some portraits show a ship on the open sea, usually in a storm. The caption explains the circumstances; for

see Notes

example: 'Antonie, Capt. J. H. O. Meyer, Bey Cap Horn D 19. Sept. 1841'. On rare occasions the name of the shipping company is given. Petrus Weyts did not sign all his pictures, nor was his signature always the same. In Ostend he signed himself 'P. Weyts à Ostende', in Antwerp 'P. Weyts à Anvers', and in some cases in Dutch 'P. Weyts, Antwerpen'.

During the last months of his life several portraits of Antwerp fishing boats belonging to the same company were painted in Petrus Weyts' workshop. They are all dated

254e

1855 and four of them are obviously by Petrus Weyts, even though he has not signed them. A fifth picture, also anonymous, is clearly painted by another hand. Petrus Weyts died on 29 March 1855 and was probably unable to finish the picture. It must have been done by one of the other Weyts, possibly his brother Ignatius Jozef Johannes, but there is no way of proving this since no signed work by him has ever come to light. There is no basis, therefore, on which to compare the style. Petrus Weyts' son Carolus Ludovicus (born in Ostend on 22 February 1828, died in Antwerp on 2 May 1876) took over the father's firm. There are a few signed works by Carolus Ludovicus still in existence and thanks to these we can ascribe a number of anonymous works to him. At the same time it is possible that certain paintings were not done by him but by his

uncle Ignatius Jozef Johannes and in later years by his brother Ignatius. But without reliable norms of comparison this cannot be ascertained, for the pictures painted after Petrus Weyts' death do not nearly show the same uniformity of style and brushwork, especially in the rendering of water and clouds. The different manner of painting is immediately apparent, even in the ships themselves. At the same time it must be said that Weyts' successor was no beginner and certainly had practical experience. His pictures differ in palette and are also less stylized than those by Petrus Weyts. In the beginning Petrus Weyts' influence is still apparent, especially in the rendering of the water. The colouring and style of painting have been taken over from him. But the water is not the same in all pictures: Carolus Weyts painted confused seas with white tops as well as fairly regular, oncoming waves, sometimes with white tops, sometimes without. Later pictures with his signature show yet another kind of sea which is rather more true to life and reveals a more exacting technique. He stuck to this style, especially after 1870. Before this there is virtually no uniformity.

The rendering of the sky also changed continuously. At one time Carolus painted clouds in 'tiers', between two and five of them. In most cases two are horizontal and the others run diagonally upwards from right to left. Later he painted clouds which were evenly distributed over the sky. In general his skies are more transparent, less hazy, than those painted by Petrus Weyts. But here again there are numerous variations so that no generally valid characteristic applies. It is striking that Carolus Weyts has 254f; 255a; 248e; 255c signed relatively few pictures. Until his sixtieth year he painted the caption on a dark band at the bottom of the picture, after that in black letters on a white band. A number of his paintings have no explanatory text at all, and the ships can only be recognized from their name pennants and their house flags. These portraits were not commissioned by captains but by shipping companies or shipbuilders, sometimes even before the ships had been launched. A change in the backgrounds is also noticeable. The pilot boat is not always clearly depicted and accurately drawn. This applies also to the view of Flushing, which is occasionally substituted by another town or coastal scene. A few 254f; 255a pictures are altogether less carefully painted.

Carolus Weyts also painted a number of oil paintings of a very high standard. On these the ships are always seen from the starboard side, which means they are reflected images of the glass paintings. After 1867 a third – if not fourth – Weyts made his appearance as a painter: this was the second son of Petrus Weyts, Ignatius Jan (born in Antwerp on 24 April 1840, died in Antwerp on 10 May 1880). For a long time there was doubt as to whether he, too, had worked as a marine glass painter. One genre painting by him was known, but no portrait of a ship. Finally, however, one of these bearing his signature was found and it proved that he was the successor to his brother Carolus. But meanwhile the heyday of ship portraiture was past. In the few years which were

see Notes

Right: Brig 'Miranda' off Flushing, glass painting by C. L. Weyts, Antwerp, about 1860, Bm.
Page 246: Glass paintings; a, Brest harbour, late 18th century, Sa; b, Pair to a, Sa; c, English brig attacking Ostend fishing boats, by W. Wieden, Ostend, 1808, At; d, Brig, by W. Wieden, 1805, At; e, 'Le Dragon' and a Dutch schooner, by W. Wieden, 1808, Al.

a

b

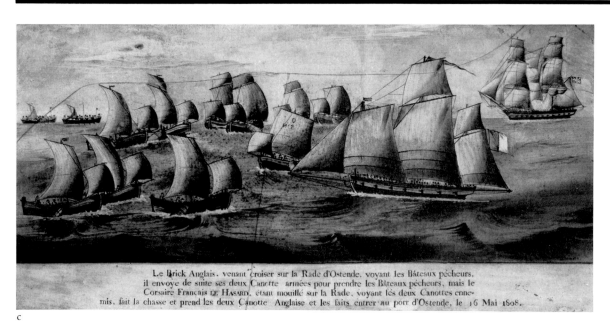

Le Brick Anglais, venant croiser sur la Rade d'Ostende, voyant les Bâteaux pêcheurs,
il envoye de suite ses deux Canotte armées pour prendre les Bâteaux pêcheurs, mais le
Corsaire Français LE HASARD, étant mouillé sur la Rade, voyant les deux Canottes enne-
mis, fait la chasse et prend les deux Canotte Anglaise et les faits entrer au port d'Ostende, le 16 Mai 1808.

c

d

e

a

b

c

d

e

f

a

b

c

d

e

f

g

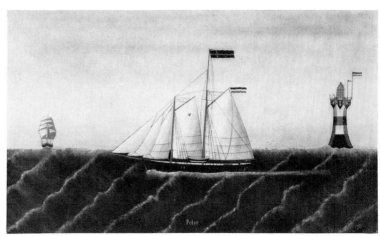

h

see Notes

255e

allowed him before his early death, Ignatius Weyts could not paint as many pictures as his predecessors. But we know that he took the trouble to obtain an exact knowledge of ships and how to portray them by attending for some time a course in shipbuilding at the Antwerp academy. Apart from the one portrait signed by Ignatius Weyts there are several anonymous works which might be by him, but there is no way of proving this. They could equally well have been painted by Johannes Franciscus Augustus (born in Antwerp on 3 September 1842, died there on 3 January 1893). By profession he was a house painter but had also been a seaman for some time. One of the ships he served on was the American full-rigged ship *P. C. Blanchard*, which he painted on glass in 1878. A second picture of this ship exists, which Augustus probably painted in the same year. In one of the two the sky is painted on a separate sheet of paper just as it is in the anonymous painting of the Norwegian barque *Gronsvaer* from the year 1878. Judging from a number of agreements in style this too, might have been painted by Augustus.

256a

255f

The last known representative of Antwerp glass painting was the marine insurance broker Frans Jan Bruloot (born in Antwerp on 16 October 1861, died there on 28 October 1917). In 1886 he painted a picture of the American passenger ship *Westernland*, which sailed under the Belgian flag. We know from one of his sons that Frans Bruloot did a whole series of similar glass paintings. He also had a mastery of the technique of oil painting. Pictures by him are in the Nationaal Scheepvaart Museum in Antwerp and in private collections. Frans Bruloot was probably the last Belgian marine glass painter. We know of no further ship portraits on glass that were done in Antwerp after this time. The technique obviously died out at the end of the last century.

see Notes

248f

Glass paintings of ships were also made in Germany, but the output of the German painters never came anywhere near that of their Antwerp colleagues. In a way it is surprising that not more of these paintings were made in Germany, for glass painting was widely practised there. The Altonaer Museum in Hamburg has a painting of the Hamburg barque *Viktoria* built in 1858. It is a beautiful piece of work, painted in the best tradition, signed by a certain E. Weissgern. He signed his name on the back of the glass so the signature appears in reverse on the front. So far it is the only known German ship portrait on glass from the 19th century. It can be assumed, though, that Weissgern painted other pictures of this kind.

After 1900 yet another German painter appeared who produced a number of entirely unsophisticated pictures. He signed himself C. H. Meyer or H. M. He must have lived somewhere on the Weser estuary and, among others, painted two Weser pilot schooners, one of them the *Peter*, in 1916. The other schooner is the *Erbgrossherzog Nicolaus*, while a third picture portrays the tjalk *Sofie*. His works are very stylized and of an almost child-like simplicity.

Page 247: Glass paintings; a, French ships of the line near Fort Dauphin, by Petrus Weyts (?), about 1830, At; b, English ships of the line near Fort St. Marie, by Petrus Weyts, 1831, At; c, Ostend harbour, by Petrus Weyts (?), about 1824, At; d, Twin pictures of a ship in two different positions, by Petrus Weyts (?), 1831, At; e, Barque 'Burlington' from Boston, by Petrus Weyts (?), 1859, Sa; f, Brig 'Olaf Kyrre' from Bergen, by Petrus Weyts, 1840, Bg.

Left: Glass paintings; a, 'The Watermill', late 18th century, Li; b, African port, late 18th century, Li; c, Battle of Navarino, by Petrus Weyts (?), 1840, At; d, Collision between two fishing boats, by E. Devriese, 1852, At; e, Clipper 'Marnix de St. Aldegonde' from Antwerp, by C. L. Weyts, 1863, At; f, Three-masted barque 'Viktoria' from Hamburg, by E. Weissgern, 1869, Ha; g, Mail steamer 'Leopold Premier', about 1869, Bb; h, Pilot schooner 'Peter' near the Rotesand Lighthouse, 1916, Bk.

With Meyer the line of glass painters comes to an end. Their work had been popular with seamen of all nations for over a century. It was an art that owed its origin to a seafaring custom and was expressed in a popular, unaffected technique. It has provided us with one of the most revealing and entertaining insights into navigation in the 19th century.

The frames of marine glass paintings deserve special attention. Judging from a large cross-section of paintings it can be said that almost every painter used his own kind of framing. Up to a point he used the frame to add to the general impression of the picture. It can be assumed that as a rule the picture and frame come from the same man, but this can seldom be proved without a doubt, and it is, of course, possible that some frames were later changed. Nevertheless, it is remarkable that some of the paintings from the 18th century which have been discussed here have identical frames, among them a number whose origin has not been ascertained. This would scarcely be so if the paintings came from different sources. Wenzeslaus Wieden used various different frames. Some of his pictures are framed in moulded gilt surrounds, others have flat frames faced with a polished walnut veneer. Petrus Weyts used similar frames of handsome, deep brown wood for some of his works. On most of them the inner and outer edges are capped by a wooden beading, the rounded profile of which projects above the surface of the frame. One or two very beautiful examples have inlays of one or more strips of lighter wood. Petrus Weyts also put some of his pictures into gold frames. These have concave profiles with a raised outer edge and are decorated with stylized flowers and leaves in the corners and the centre of each side. Carolus Weyts used similar frames, but he also worked with more modern ones with a simple profile covered with gold leaf and without any orn-amentation. A similar frame is used for the anonymous sea battle, the painter of which cannot be named with certainty, though up to now it was thought to be Petrus Weyts.

The pictures of later painters are framed in many different ways and their number is too small for any conclusion to be reached as to which type each painter preferred.

Finally, a piece of advice to the owners of glass paintings might not come amiss. The sheets of glass used in these pictures are made of thin, blown glass which is not always quite flat and can occasionally be a little distorted. A relatively light pressure will break it. It is, therefore, a wise precaution to provide these delicate objects with some kind of reinforcement. This can be done by framing the original sheet of glass behind a second one, a method particularly to be recommended for pictures which are already cracked. The back should be covered with a sheet of hardboard which can be screwed to the frame – never nailed! Since the whole picture thus becomes much heavier it must be hung very securely.

Seamen's Crafts

Scrimshaw, Wood, Paper and Rope Work, Ships in Bottles, Panoramic Models

It has already been established in connection with ship portraiture and model building that many works in these fields were done by amateurs – by seamen, in fact. But the skill of seamen was by no means confined to these industries, and it is worth taking an overall look at the whole of their artistic repertoire.

All of their products are characterized by the fact that, whilst being what is generally called folk art, they were international in their style, their subject matter and the materials from which they were made, because those who made them belonged to every seafaring nation in the world. The products of this amateur art have found an increasing number of admirers in recent times, and without doubt represent the most original and interesting collectors' pieces.

Seamen are condemned to spend a part of their life in a very restricted place of work which they cannot leave for long periods at a time. In the days of the sailing ships such a stay on board, could, depending on circumstances, last weeks, months or even years. It was hard work in bad weather and there was very little free time. Everybody was only too pleased when such a voyage was over. But in fine weather the crew of a sailing ship had enough time during the watch below to busy themselves with their hobbies. Reading was not a common occupation then because very few seamen could read. So there was nothing else to do but to pass the time with some kind of handicraft.

Some of the crew drew or painted, often with primitive materials, others carved pictures in ebony, bone, ivory, copper or whalebone. Others borrowed tools from the ship's carpenter, the 'chippie', if they did not possess their own, and made little chests, cupboards, benches and stools and other small items of furniture, either to be used on board or for their relatives back home. Sewing cases and tobacco boxes were favourite presents. All along the North Sea coast of Germany and also in Denmark richly decorated mangle boards, mostly from the 18th century, carved by seamen during their long

251

voyages and then brought back home, are very common. Other skilfully ornamented objects made by sailors included writing stands with or without ink-pots, dressing-table tops with mirrors and tools for every conceivable purpose.

A particularly favoured material were the bones or teeth of walrusses or sperm whales which were caught on the voyages to Greenland and in the South Sea fishing grounds. In particular the members of the so-called South Sea fishing expeditions (which were not fishing but whaling expeditions and took place north of the equator as well as in the South Seas) made large numbers of 'scrimshaws' from ivory, engraved with attractive patterns, whaling scenes or scenes from the Bible, occasionally even romantic scenes. They are reminiscent in their execution of man's earliest pictorial efforts, the engraved figures of animals on reindeer bones from the early Stone Age Ahrensburg culture, and at the same time of the motifs seamen had tattooed on their skin.

But these rough men also knew of subtler ways of working the ivory: many cut proper bas-reliefs and very delicate pictures from this durable material. Without the help of a lathe their large hands shaped fragile little boxes and needle-holders which were scarcely inferior to the work of an ivory turner. There were also rulers, prettily decorated, clothes pegs, fishing rods, clothes hangers, pastry cutters, paper knives, butter knives, dividers, corset stiffeners and many other useful objects. All these things are to be found in large numbers in American maritime museums, because the Americans made the longest whaling trips. The late President Kennedy collected some very fine pieces. Apart from bones and ivory the baleen whale, which was first hunted in the Arctic and later in the Antarctic, also yielded baleen, popularly called whalebone, which was ideally suited for making boxes and caskets. Elliptical hat boxes could be shaped very easily from the elastic and flexible whalebone; they were often decorated with engraved ornaments and painted into the bargain.

It is worth going into the art of scrimshaw in some detail – this most remarkable of folk arts. In the middle of the last century Herman Melville wrote in *Moby Dick*: 'Throughout the Pacific, and also in Nantucket, and New Bedford, and Sag Harbor, you will come across lively sketches of whales and whaling scenes, graven by the fishermen themselves on Sperm Whale teeth, or ladies' busks wrought out of the Right Whale bone, and other like skrimshander articles, as the whalemen call the numerous little ingenious contrivances they elaborately carve out of the rough material, in their hours of ocean leisure. Some of them have little boxes of dentistical-looking implements, specially intended for the skrimshandering business. But, in general, they toil with their jack-knives alone; and with that almost omnipotent tool of the sailor, they will turn you out anything you please, in the way of a mariner's fancy.

'Long exile from Christendom and civilisation inevitably restores a man to that con-

Right: Glass paintings; a, Ostend harbour, by W. Wieden, 1814, At; b, Sea battle, by C. L. Weyts (?), third quarter 19th century, At.
Page 254: a, Schooner 'Gilblas' being brought in by the Ostend pilot, signed P. N. 1859, At; b, Three-masted barque 'Aigle', signed P. N. 1841, At; c, Brig 'Charles Quint' from Antwerp, by Petrus Weyts (?), 1840, At; d, Barque 'Petronille' from Gent, by Petrus Weyts, 1851, At; e, Sloop 'Jonge Maria', by Petrus Weyts, 1855, At; f, Three-masted barque 'Grossfürstin Catharina' from Rostock, by C. L. Weyts, 1856, At.
Page 255: Glass paintings; a, Barque 'Berdiansk Packet', by C. L. Weyts (?), 1859, At; b, Three-masted barque 'Quimper' from Brest, about 1870, Al; c, Brig 'Haparanda', by C. L. Weyts, 1871, Ss; d, Steamer 'Julia David' from Antwerp, by C. L. Weyts, 1872, At; e, Three-masted barque 'Landbo' from Arendal, by I. J. Weyts, 1877, Ad; f, Three-masted barque 'Gronsvaer' from Grimstad, 1878, At.
Page 256: Glass paintings; a, Full-rigged ship 'P. C. Blanchard' from Yarmouth (Maine), by J. F. Augustus, 1878, At; b, Brig 'De Ruyter', by C. L. Weyts (?), 1862, At.

252

a

DE HAVEN VAN OOSTENDE.

b

a

b

c

d

e

f

a

b

c

d

e

f

a

b

a

b

c

d

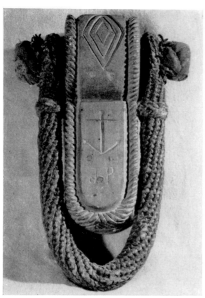

e

f

a

b

Das Fregat Ocean und die Brig Maria Im durch Seglen von die Englische Canaal
Capertit durch ein 14 Canon Schif mit Olderny und die Kiskasten insgesig.

c

d

e

a

CAMILLA · CATHARINA · CHRISTINA · Com.d & Capt. · S · F · KÜLLMAN · I·A·SEEL

b

c

d

Stamp in a whaling journal, 18th century, Na.

dition in which God placed him, i.e. what is called savagery. Your true whale-hunter is as much a savage as an Iroquois. I myself am a savage, owing no allegiance but to the King of the Cannibals; and ready at any moment to rebel against him. Now, one of the peculiar characteristics of the savage in his domestic hours, is his wonderful patience of industry. An ancient Hawaiian war-club or spear-paddle, in its full multiplicity and elaboration of carving, is as great a trophy of human perseverance as a Latin lexicon. For, with but a bit of broken sea-shell or a shark's tooth, that miraculous intricacy of wooden network has been achieved; and it has cost steady years of steady application. As with the Hawaiian savage, so with the white sailor-savage. With the same marvellous patience, and with the same single shark's tooth, or his one poor jack-knife, he will carve you a bit of bone sculpture, not quite as workmanlike, but as close packed in its maziness of design, as the Greek savage, Achilles's shield; and full of barbaric spirit and suggestiveness, as the prints of that fine old Dutch savage, Albert Dürer.'

The art of scrimshaw has been considered the only important indigenous folk art, except that of the Indians, which has ever developed in America. At the same time it has, of course, always been international. The term once applied to all forms of carving or decorating of whales' teeth, walrus' tusks, or bone, but nowadays usually refers specifically to the teeth engraved by the whalemen. The subject has been given scant notice by literate whalemen and the historians of whaling, except for Herman Melville. In recent years, however, an increase in antique collecting has focussed attention on these miracles of whale ivory sculpture achieved with the crude, scanty tools available to the sailor of the whaling era.

The origin of the word 'scrimshaw' is obscure. Several dictionaries attempt to derive it from the surname 'Scrimshaw'. This is doubtless in error, since Scrimshaw is the more recent of the several forms of the name. Others, tracing the word to Nantucket, surmise it to be of Indian origin. Another theory, advanced on the basis of 'skimshander' or 'skrimshander' offers a possible analogy between these forms and the words 'skimp' and 'scrimp', meaning 'scant', or, in verb form, 'to economize'. There was always a dearth of good material, for large pieces of whale ivory were rare. Thus the nature of the material commonly made scrimping necessary. However, considering the term 'scrimshant', an early form, others believe that scrimshaw comes from an old word 'scrimshander' or 'scrimshanker', an idle, worthless fellow. Gradually the term may have come to mean the artistic results of a sailor's idle hours at sea. This would seem to be the most satisfactory derivation, but it is no more conclusive.

The earliest reference to the art of scrimshaw, by name, occurs in the logbook of the brig *By Chance* of Dartmouth, Massachusetts, preserved in the collection of the New Bedford Whaling Museum. Under the date, 20 May 1826, it reads: 'All these 24 hours small breezes and thick foggy weather, made no sale (sic). So ends this day, all hands employed Scrimshanting.' However, the true beginnings of the art must be found in the 18th century.

Soon after Nantucket's first sperm whaling venture in 1712, longer voyages left considerable time at the disposal of the whalemen. To Nantucketers indoctrinated with the belief that idleness was a 'most heinous sin' and trained in the cooper's trade whatever their future occupation might be, wood-carving was second nature. St. John de Crevecoeur, visiting the island during the latter part of the century, observed:

'I must confess that I have never seen more ingenuity in the use of the knife; thus the many idle moments of their lives become usefully employed. In the many hours of leisure which their long cruises afford them, they cut and carve a variety of boxes and pretty toys, in wood, adapted to different uses which they bring home as testimonies of remembrance to their wives and sweethearts. They have showed me a variety of little bowls and other implements executed cooper-wise, with the greatest neatness and elegance ... almost every man in this island has always two knives in his pocket, one much larger than the other; and though they hold everything that is called *fashion* in the utmost contempt, yet they are as difficult to please, and as extravagant in the choice and price of their knives, as any young buck in Boston would be about his hat, buckles or coat.'

Although at first wood was used more than ivory, whalemen must soon have discovered the choicer material. Certainly, despite its lack of publicity, the art of scrimshaw played a major role in the everyday life of the whalemen. On some ships every man from captain to cabin boy had an article of scrimshaw under way. Men swapped tobacco– the universal currency aboard whalers–washed clothes or did other menial tasks in order to gain coveted pieces of ivory. New Bedford owners once fiercely debated whether the engrossing interest of the whaleman in his scrimshaw was not seriously detrimental to the success of voyages. Men had even been known to sight whales and then fail to report them rather than interrupt some particularly fascinating stage of their artistry. For captains to forbid scrimshaw altogether was unusual but not unknown. On some vessels scrimshaw was limited to the forecastle and was subject to confiscation if brought on deck. Scrimshaw was so widespread that it may be said to have become universal.

Clifford Ashley, a foremost student of the technique, summarized the requirements of the ambitious fashioner of scrimshaw as including proficiency alike in joinery, turning, carving, inlay, coopering and engraving. That the sailor's tools in no way met the most meagre requirements of any of these trades is further tribute to his artistry. We have already quoted Melville on the tools used. Sometimes sail knives were used instead of jack-knives. Improvized files, converted chisels and gimlets fashioned from nails were

262

also employed. Green whalebone was soft enough to be planed or otherwise worked, but the harder whale tooth required sharp cutting tools.

Some ships had jigsaws or home-made turning lathes–most often owned by mates in their more spacious quarters–to attain lace-like effects in the pieces of more intricate design. However, the majority of the examples of fine turning and execution resembling scroll-saw work were actually produced by the use of makeshift files. For the American whaleman pioneered a form of art which required that he must first fashion the very tools he would use.

The sailor's needle was the most versatile element in the paraphernalia of scrimshaw. From it were contrived a variety of files, fine saws, and the piercing and boring instruments used in executing the openwork patterns found in rings, bracelets, brooches, needle cases, etc. These awl-like tools were also used to trace the outline of a future design by a series of pricked or punched holes. Ivory or bone parts entered into a large proportion of the hand-made implements. Bone handles were standard. It would seem that the tools themselves could be placed in the category of scrimshaw.

The polishing process has been given credit for much of the mastery of the pioneers. This is due no less to the preliminary grinding, filing, smoothing, or sandpapering necessary to reduce the ribbed whale's tooth to a more workable surface than to the finishing done with wood ash and laborious hand polishing. The more skilful, on occasion, even used the skin of the shark, in lieu of sandpaper, as a smoothing agent. Ash, pumice and whiting were usually employed for conditioning the whale teeth. In this, as in every other stage of scrimshaw evolution, patience was the price of perfection. Whalemen put the fresh teeth in brine to soften them, for, as they grew older, the teeth became harder and correspondingly more difficult to work. Even so, it was possible by the use of hot water to get a surface that would respond to their tools.

The scrimshaw creators were cautioned by the knowledge that a slip of the knife, or a cut too deep with the bodkin, would force them to discard a literal labour of love which had occupied months or even years. Some of the men became very expert in carving and decorating the teeth and produced marvellously delicate and beautiful handiwork despite the crudeness of their tools. The inking or colouring of these scrimshaw etchings or engravings was a detail that is in no small degree responsible for the elusive characteristics of old scrimshaw. Indeed, it is the inability of most of the present practitioners of the art to simulate this subtle quality which has been responsible for the criticism that contemporary pieces look 'too new'. The supposition has been that India ink alone was used to emphasize the engraved designs, while in actuality ink was not always as available as paint, tar, or even soot from the try-works. In most cases black pigment was depended upon to obtain contrast for the incised lines. Occasionally red

263

was introduced in conjunction with the black. In rare instances other colours, notably green, blue or orange, were used in combination. By this laborious and crude method results equalling the finest steel engravings were often produced, although the majority of scrimshaw teeth show little evidence of artistic talent.

There is little reminiscent of other arts in scrimshaw. Despite attempts of writers to seek its origins in the primitive art of the Eskimo or of the South-Sea islander, it is well established that the sources of inspiration were to be found in the environment of the whaleman – either in the home surroundings he had left or in his life at sea. Certainly a trophy of the whale hunt, the symbol of the whalemen's success – a huge tooth taken from the gigantic sea mammal whose capture held his life in constant danger – was a most natural gift to a distant friend or loved one: a gift made even more meaningful by its carefully etched pictures of the ship under full sail, incidents of the chase and capture of whales or other maritime scenes.

In his choice of scrimshaw designs the sailor expressed great individuality, although, on occasion, a man of artistic talent might influence the output of a whole ship. Life around him constituted his dictionary of ornament – the knots in the rigging; the stars in the heavens above him; the figure-head and the stern board of his ship; the fish of the sea; whales, birds, sails, boats, casks, bells; the wheel, the anchor and similar symbols. Some of the best and most elaborate work was traced or transferred from books, magazines or illustrated papers, which found their way into the forecastle of the whaling ship. Pictures of women were frankly copied, primarily from *Godey's Book*. In all the seaman's work, however, there is a marked and sturdy originality in selection.

The earliest dated piece of scrimshaw in the collection of the Nantucket Historical Association is a tooth decorated 'off the coast of Japan' on the first voyage of the ship *Susan* of Nantucket in 1829. On the reverse one can read the following couplet:

'Death to the Living, Long live the Killers,

Success to Sailors' Wives, and Greasy Luck to Whalers.'

There is also a whaling scene and the name of the master, Captain Frederick Swain.

Although his graphics on whale teeth were the most familiar fruit of his craft, it was in the busk, made of planed whalebone, that the whaleman etched his most inspired pictures and waxed most sentimental. To the uninformed, a busk was a flat ruler-like 'stay' about two inches wide, which milady of the 19th century thrust into an open slit at the front of her corset. It has been said, as much in truth as in jest, that any woman so fortified was bound to remain true to her sailor.

Frequently these functional ornaments bore appropriate and tender verses. One could ill afford to omit this oft-quoted tribute to the charms of a loved one and to the lure of the sea:

Incised drawing on a brick, 15th century, He.

280f

Right: Name and stern boards; a, 18th century, Wh; b, c, Three-masted schooner 'Emanuel' from Thurö, 1880, He; d, Barque 'Ceres', 1867, Os; e, Four-masted schooner 'Teie', Tönsberg, 1819, He; f, 19th century, Os; g, 18th century, At; h, 18th century, Wh; i, First half 19th century, Sn; j, 19th century, Gr.
Page 266: Sneek town hall in a bottle, work by a seaman, early 19th century, Sn.

264

a

b

c

d

e

f

g

h

i

j

a

b

a

b

c

d

e

'Accept, dear Girl, this busk from me;   Has been the Whale,

Carved by my humble hand.   In which this bone did rest,

I took it from a Sperm Whale's Jaw,   His time is past,

One thousand miles from land!   His bone at last

In many a gale,   Must now support thy breast.'

273d, e; 277a–f; 280b–e

More ambitious and skilful whalemen fashioned articles from the teeth as delicately carved, as well finished, and as intricate in design as any work of the Orient. The majority of these items were designed for human adornment; still others provided recreation after, as well as at the time of, their execution; while a few must be classified purely as objets d'art.

Among the extensive scrimshaw collection of the Nantucket Historical Association one can find numerous items which were commonly found in island kitchens–chopping knives, a corkscrew, butter stamps and butter paddles, dippers, dish mops, spoons and forks, a corn skewer, lamp picks, napkin rings, and rolling pins. More numerous than all

237b, c

such articles are the odd 'jagging wheels', elaborate implements for cutting, piercing and crimping the edges of pies. No one seems to know just why the whalemen were so fond of making these. Perhaps it was the challenge they offered in craftsmanship. Perhaps they were a natural tribute to the delicious pies baked in New England kitchens, which for years at a time were but memories of the past or expectations of the future. Whatever the reason, these carved pastry wheels, produced in vast numbers, were ingeniously constructed and most beautifully wrought. The best collection of these in existence is that of the Old Dartmouth Historical Society of New Bedford, Massachusetts. Many of the wheels were highly ornamented with inlay of mother-of-pearl or metal. Others are intricately carved. Nearly every one bears a fork at one end for piercing the pie crust, and in some instances the fork is so arranged as to fold down. Two, three or perhaps as many as five or seven wheels of varying sizes might be combined on one instrument– mute tribute to the patience and skill of the carver.

Nor did the sailor ignore the housewife's responsibilities for the family wardrobe and linen. In his leisure time he fashioned clothes pins, spool racks, thimble and needle cases. The Nantucket collection contains several swifts or reels which were used for unwinding yarn from a skein. One such reel is believed to have been made in the bark *Afton* during the 1850's. A swift box marked 'C.P.K.' was made in the ship *Java* in 1838 by Captain Randall Kelley for his wife, Charlotte (Plaskett) Kelley.

Other subjects of the whaleman's craft were door knobs, hooks, boxes, baskets, bird-cages, paper knives, yardsticks and rulers, seals and stilettos. The latter items frequently found their way into the captain's desk on board ship. Still others served practical purposes in the equipment of navigation, as in ropemaking. Handles were also made for gimlets, hammers, knives, and so on.

Page 267: Ships in bottles with scenic background, 19th century; a, At; b, Wl. Left: a, b, Compasses hung from deck-heads of ships' cabins; a, Standing compass, signed L. W. C., 18th century, He; b, Crown compass, signed Iver Iversen Borger, Copenhagen, 18th century, He; c, d, e, Ships' lanterns; c, Off an admiral's galley, late 17th century, Vo; d, Second half 17th century, Ar; e, Off the captain's galley of Francesco Morosini, 17th century, Vc.

269

Common recreational activities of the 19th century were games of cribbage, checkers, chess and dominoes. To these leisure time pursuits the craftsmanship of the sailor contributed cribbage boards of whale ivory or walrus tusks, checker and chess boards, chessmen and dominoes. Strangely enough few ship models were made. Perhaps quarters were too cramped or perhaps the whaler failed to offer the artistic inspiration of the faster clipper ship. Thus the whalebone model of the *Lagoda* in the Nantucket Whaling Museum is indeed a rarity.

Another branch of scrimshaw art includes articles made for adornment. For himself the sailor carved collar buttons, cuff links and rings; for his wife, decorative combs, beads, earrings, pins and brooches. Outstanding in this phase of scrimshaw were the handsomely wrought canes and cane heads which the whaleman treated with great individuality, selecting his designs from all areas of his nautical experience. The collection of whale bone and ivory canes in the Nantucket Whaling Museum provides ample illustration of the variety in subjects – innumerable geometric designs, clenched fists, Turk's head knots, sea bird heads, dogs, snakes, and antique editions of pin-up girls in high-buttoned boots.

280a

The sailor benefited from one great advantage: in foreign ports he could get hold of rare species of wood which were easy to work and looked most attractive. From them he usually built his sea chest, the most important piece of equipment on board besides his berth. The crew's quarters on the old sailing ships were exceedingly primitive. They often had no windows or only skylights; along the walls were bunks and in the middle a table and perhaps two benches. The seaman had to stow his private belongings in his sea chest, which often served as a seat as well. Cupboards or wardrobes were unheard of. The sea chest, called *Sviptikista*, was already known in Viking times, and literary references to it are supported by the fact that no kind of seating has ever been found in the remains of Viking ships. Sea chests with all their contents were also found in the *Vasa*. The old sea chests had sloping sides, which made their bases wider than their tops, which gave them a firm stand when the ship was rolling, even with men sitting on them. In some only the two longer sides were sloping, since this was enough to give them the necessary stability. Most chests were about 3 ft. long, 18 in. wide and 18 in. high. Chests from the last days of the sailing ships usually had straight sides and very often were made from inferior wood compared to the old chests. They were all very strongly built to withstand the rough treatment they received, and were often painted on the outside, usually brown, sometimes rust or a handsome bright green. The lid sometimes overlapped and was closed with two strong iron hinges. The sailors were unaccustomed to fitting locks; a simple hasp and staple were enough. Theft was not, and still is not, tolerated on board. The lid was covered with sailcloth and generally painted black. The

279a–g

Engraving on a poor box of the merchant and shipping guild of Stade, 18th century, St.

two rope handles, one at either end, were much easier to grip than the screwed-on iron or brass handles which were used later. These rope handles were not just simple rope, knotted on, but they were 'grafted' and decorated with Turks' heads, and their owners took great pride in them.

A sailor who could afford to went in for teak wood and got the ship's carpenter to build him a chest, which was not only extremely strong but needed no painting on the outside. The inside of the lid, however, was usually painted white and then decorated with all kinds of ornaments, flowers and garlands, flags, symbols of faith, love and hope, or at least the owner's initials adorned with countless flourishes. The most handsome chests are probably those decorated by their owners with paintings of ships; although similar to ship portraits or votive pictures they are much more primitive, because the paint on board was of inferior quality. Besides, sailors knew more about painting their own ship than they did about painting pictures. But the loving care with which a sailor built and decorated his sea chest shows how attached he was to it. It was the only piece of furniture which actually belonged to him during the voyage; everything else was the property of the shipowner. In order to provide a tidy stowage place for buttons, tapes and other small objects the chest was often fitted with small compartments, some with a folding or sliding lid. These lids were occasionally decorated with coloured inlays. All in all the various sea chests were real ornaments in the otherwise stark quarters. Bones and ivory, which we mentioned in connection with scrimshaw, were also used in building ship models because they were easy to work with file and saw. Some of the smallest models were made from bone. Another material that was popular for its workability was mahogany. It is doubtful whether planked models were ever made at sea, but whole and half models made from solid blocks of wood were extremely common. Many of them were far from perfect, but those that turned out particularly misshapen probably did so not because their makers suffered from lack of taste but because they were so awkward with their hands. Even then it is surprising how the rough, gnarled hands managed the delicate task of rigging the models and reeving thin thread through small, block-like pieces of wood. The yards usually turned out too thick, but the standing and running rigging was correct in every detail. Every stay was where it belonged and every sheet was led in exactly the same way as on the ship in which the man crossed the oceans and which he wanted to remember.

The little ships were either put into a glass case or into a wooden one with a painted background which might portray a stormy sea, the white cliffs of Dover or Naples with the smoking cone of Vesuvius. But the water with its magnificent waves had to be made from coloured putty. Sometimes a small pilot cutter would be sailing in front of the ship. Finally a glass front was put on. If the sides of the box were angled obliquely and

271

the scene was framed, as many of them were, it looked like a three-dimensional oil painting. But why build a whole ship if only one side could be seen? So in due course the seamen left out half the ship. They gave them sails, too; not of cloth or paper but of wood, which had to be very thin so that the sails could be made to belly out in the wind. They were usually close-hauled to show them in their full width, but some models had them squared off and a mirror put in as background to give the impression of a complete model. Such 'panoramic models' can be found on the coasts of all countries, frequently hanging on the wall above the door of a captain's house.

278b; 260c; 275b

Another spare-time occupation among sailors was rope work. As though there was not enough of it anyway! Part of a sailor's duties on board consisted of remaking the rope, as it came from the ropemaker, into items that were needed as part of the ship's gear and rigging. For example he had to unlay the separate strands of ends of rope and 'splice' two ends of rope together. There were also a great variety of knots to be made for different purposes, eye splices or ends of rope to be 'whipped', and rope to be 'grafted', that is covered with a weaving of thinner line.

It is obvious from nautical literature how these simple tasks gradually inspired a more and more complicated and refined technique, which is not surprising when one considers that the many idle hours aboard ship gave the sailor ample time to apply himself to imaginative work. Knots and splices were turned into new and attractive shapes which the sailor called 'fancy-work', an appropriate enough term, since most of it was unnecessary from the point of view of seamanship. This occupation, rightly classified as folk art, had its heyday in the second half of the 19th century. In recent times its products have found many collectors who have publicized it widely.

Engraving on a poor box of the merchants and shipping guild of Stade, 1663, St.

Practical seamanship in our times has no uses for fancy-work. It was based on very definite shapes in which the knot proper, either flat, or raised, or round, sometimes cube-shaped, was the starting point. We also meet with cylindrical shapes in which the strands were rove like a spiral, a turban (Turk's head) or in a herring-bone pattern. Many imaginative patterns were also used in the making of mats and in grafting.

Another thing sailors made were nets. In them, as in fishermen's nets, the efficiency and durability depended on the knots being firm and immovable. The sailor calls this type of knot a 'sheet bend'. Nets and mats were needed in places where the sails chafed against mast or ropes and could have been damaged. A more important use of nets was as a safety precaution under the bowsprit and in other places where men were in danger of falling off and might have to be caught. So this kind of rope work had a practical value. Fancy-work was also employed to adorn objects of everyday use: there were the handles of buckets, water casks and sea chests, and the D-shaped handles on duffle-bags which could be locked. Rope ends were grafted with 'nettles' to make it easier to reeve them

Right: Scrimshaw; a, Chess figure, 19th century, Pm; b, c, Pastry wheels, 19th century, Nb; d, e, Walrus tusks with incised drawings, 19th century, Bf.
Page 274: a, Ship in bottle, model of the 'Cutty Sark' under sail, late 19th century, Lg; b, Chapel with altar and pulpit in a bottle, 1844, Sn; b, Miniature ship in inverted wine glass, 19th century, Sn; c, Crucifixion in a bottle, by Edvin Johansson, about 1860, Go.
Page 275: a, Ship in bottle in wooden stand, work by a seaman, 19th century, Wh; b, Panoramic model from Sicily, 19th century, Vn.
Page 276: Scrimshaw; a, Catching sperm whale east of Australia, incised drawing on whalebone, about 1820, Na; b, Whaling scene, first half 19th century, Lg.

a

b

c

d

e

a

b

c

d

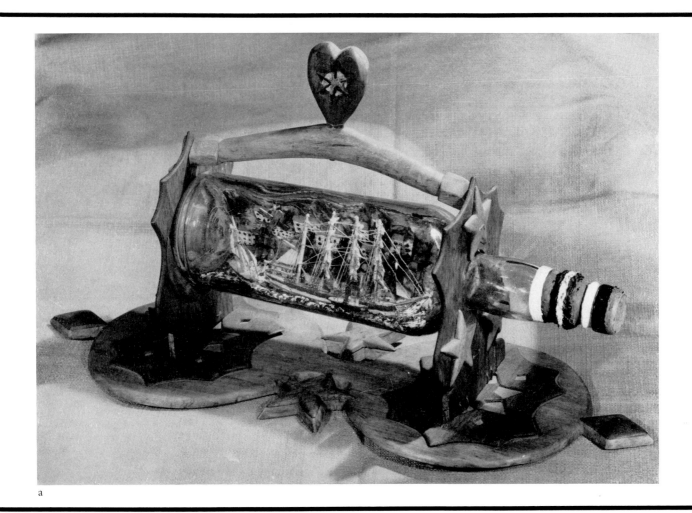

a

b

Lat 31..59..0 S.   . SPERM . WHALING .   Long . 159..0..0 E.

a

b

a   b   c

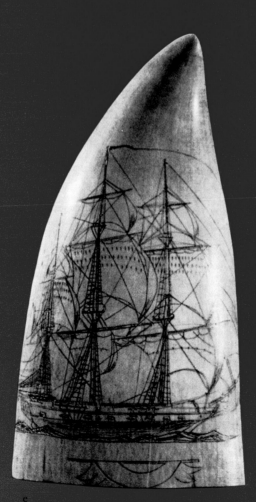

d   e   f

a

b

a

b

c

d

e

f

g

a

b

c

d

e

f

258e, f

through blocks. Turk's heads were applied to sounding poles, oars and the like. Railings were often grafted along their entire length to protect the rope. Of particularly interesting design was the weaving applied to shark harpoons. Varied and attractive designs were also found on bell ropes and on the handles of the canvas 'ditty-bags', which were the repair kits the sailors took with them when they went aloft to do repair work.

Sailors were adept at sewing and they had to be, because they spent many hours helping the sailmaker repair sails or make new ones. In their leisure hours they made overalls, shoes, ditty-bags, sea bags, and hammocks from canvas, and tobacco pouches from the webs of sea birds' feet.

258b

It follows that they did not confine their activities in these fields to making things for use on board but also made presents for their loved ones at home. They wove elaborate ladies' handbags, mats, covers and net curtains, even embroidered them. The writer knows of a flower- or fruit-basket made entirely of rope, knotted, grafted and spliced. It is not quite obvious whether the decorations depict fruit or flowers, but it makes a most impressive ornament, the manilla rope being painted in various colours. In the Second World War the crew of a submarine made a Christmas tree of rope, which shows that vestiges of this folk art survived for a long time.

267a, b; 274a; 275a; 278a

One of the best-known leisure occupations of sailors was the building of ships in bottles. Landlubbers see in this some kind of magic and always ask, 'How did this ship, complete with sails and rigging, get into the bottle?' The answer is simple: through the only opening there is, the one at the top. The most difficult part of building a ship in a bottle is the careful preparation of all the parts. The hull, all the masts and spars, the lifeboats and so on are carved with a knife and then painted. The sails are cut out of thin paper. Then the hull and rigging are assembled with the masts lowered and pointing aft. The standing rigging, that is the stays and shrouds, are made of thin thread, and the stays must be long enough for their ends to protrude from the bottle when the ship is inside. Each stay is led over the stemhead or the bowsprit. But first of all a coastal landscape with neat little houses and a lighthouse, or perhaps a patch of sea, is modelled from putty inside the bottle and painted with oils. These are the usual motifs. Then the ship, with masts lowered, is inserted into the bottle and pressed firmly into the soft putty. The masts and sails are then erected by pulling on the shrouds. The spare lengths of shrouds are best removed by burning them off with a long piece of red-hot wire. Finally the bottle is corked and sealed with sealing wax, and the little masterpiece is finished. But it is easier said than done.

The fashion of ships in bottles really started with the mass production of bottles in the middle of last century, but it probably goes back to the nativity scenes and similar miniature tableaux built in the 18th century. From before 1800 we know of depictions

Page 277: Sperm whale teeth with incised drawings, 19th century; a, b, c, Lg; d, f, Na; e, Wk.
Page 278: a, Fishing port in northern Spain, in a bottle, about 1900, Bc; b, Sea battle of Toulon, panoramic model, 1744, Mn.
Page 279: Lids of sea chests; a, 18th century, Go; b, 19th century, Gr; c, 19th century, Go; d, 1864, At; e, Complete chest to d; f, 19th century, Fb; h, 19th century, Bk.
Left: Scrimshaw; a, Cane from whalebone, 18th century, Wh; b, c, d, e, Sperm whale teeth with incised drawings, 19th century, b, c, Gr; d, e, Rm; f, Incised drawings on a busk, 19th century, Lg.

of the crucifixion, street scenes and ships built by sailors into upright carafes in a similar *266; 274b, d* way to the ships in bottles, which were all made to be laid down horizontally. Modern ships in bottles, which are now made on land in large numbers, can, of course, be made with far more care, because their makers have special materials and tools, and work in a clean and quiet room. An interesting example of a land-made ship is the one in which the ship is not firmly fixed in the putty but attached to a screw inserted through a small hole drilled into the side of the bottle. The screw passes through a spring so that the mounting is elastic, and the secret is covered up with folds of blue velvet – the sea. By pressing the screw head lightly the little ship can be made to roll in the waves.

Sailors also did embroidery, a natural follow-up on rope work. Several collections contain embroidered ship portraits, usually framed behind glass. Objects and scenes made very meticulously in paper were another speciality. As early as the beginning of the 17th century individual ships and even whole fleets were cut out of paper in delicate filigree work and placed in front of a coloured background. Since the material was so delicate, it is understandable that very few of these pieces still survive. Amongst those still in existence are a ship portrait from about 1750 at Greenwich, a fleet of several ships from 1812 and a panorama of Hamburg made most beautifully out of coloured paper by a retired sea captain at Hamburg.

Maritime Objets d'Art and Antiques

Collectors' Pieces and their Value

Many of the objects described in this book are coveted pieces among collectors of maritime art and antiques. But it is by no means easy nowadays to find such pieces for sale. Not so many years ago it was still possible on occasion to find an old sailing ship or a yacht with carved decorations, but these vessels are nearly all broken up now and their parts have become rarities. Looking round the large ports of Antwerp, Amsterdam, London or Hamburg, we find not a single clipper or paddle steamer left afloat. Only models of them survive in maritime museums.

In recent years the demand for antiques has rapidly increased, as have the prices for parts of old ships and models, ship portraits and other artistic handiwork by seamen and shipbuilders, which ten to twenty years ago sold for a comparitively moderate price at breakers' yards and antique shops.

When, as a young man, I worked in my father's art business, I picked up an old print of a sea battle in a market one day for only five guilders★. On discovering that it was a copper engraving by Romein de Hooge, I promptly re-sold it to a maritime museum for twenty-five guilders. By now that engraving is worth at least 350 guilders. (The illustrations referred to in the margin indicate the approximate type of object described, not the actual priced object itself.)

The small wooden rowing boats and sailing ships of the Egyptians (the 'ships of the dead') are very much in demand from collectors, including collectors of Egyptian art. In 1958 one such ship was sold at an antiques sale in Delft for 2500 guilders. There are some which today fetch ten times as much.

Complete models of ships from the 17th, 18th and 19th centuries have always been expensive because of the great amount of work which goes into the making of a more or less authentic model. In 1930, I acquired a five-foot model of an 18th-century French frigate for 2400 guilders, which was a very high price at the time. Today a similar ship, always

★ *10 Guilders* = £ *1 or* $ *2.80*

providing one came onto the market, would cost about 30,000 guilders. The very valuable 17th- and 18th-century votive ships are equally elusive. A 27-inch model of a Dutch warship from the 18th century was sold in 1964 for 2800 guilders, and in 1966 two very handsome, 6-inch contemporary models from about 1800 fetched 900 guilders in Holland.

Slightly more common are 19th-century models made by seamen in their leisure time from bone, wood or ivory. Similar models were also made by French and English prisoners of war during the Napoleonic era. Their value depends on how true to life they are in their details and proportions and how well the rigging is done. They may be priced from £100 to £500 or more. In 1965 a fine piece made of bone sold for 8000 francs★ in France. A 12-inch long model of a frigate from about 1860 would sell for 1000 francs. Cruder, less carefully made smaller models of sailing ships and steamers from about 1900 fetch between 500 and 700 francs. Modern models of ocean liners and other transatlantic vessels, as we see them in the offices and display windows of shipping lines, are equally valuable and seldom or never come onto the market. They are very expensive to produce because they require a great amount of careful work, which can only be done by skilled model makers. Their value depends on the quality of the detail work, which reflects the taste and the many and various skills of the old craftsmen and shipbuilding experts.

Then there are the very popular ships in bottles, which come in many different shapes and are much sought-after in all parts of the world. The more ancient ones among them, depending on size and quality, fetch between £20 and £100. A fairly simple panoramic model, on the other hand, is priced at about 400 francs by Paris art dealers. More elaborate pieces sell for twice as much. In Spain they are generally half as expensive–if one can get hold of them, that is.

In recent years rudder decorations of sailing ships, lions' heads, reclining lions, figures of dragons, heads and busts of mermaids and similar pieces, some of them grotesque in appearance, have been much in demand by collectors, especially in the United States. It would be rare to find anything in this line for under £30. The handsome mastheads, many of them masterpieces of wood-carving, were in great demand at one time, but they are probably all in the possession of museums by now.

Other decorative parts of old frigates and clippers occasionally crop up in the art trade, as does the odd figure-head. The figure-head of an Indian, presumably of American origin, was sold in Holland in 1965 for 2500 guilders. In the same year a late 19th-century

53f, 83

267a, b; 274a; 275a; 278a

260c

275b

102, 103, 104

84

167c

★ *13.8 francs = £1 or $2,80*

284

167d

127, 128b

194, 195, 196, 197, 198, 199, 200, 205,
206, 207, 208, 213, 214, 215, 216, 217,
218, 219, 220, 225, 226, 228, 234, 235

figure-head about 5 ft. high fetched 800 kroner★ in Copenhagen. In 1961 the maritime museum in Amsterdam bought a stern board for 400 guilders; today it would cost twice if not three times as much.

Ship portraits are very popular collectors' pieces. Their prices can vary tremendously according to their age, style, size and quality. Accurately painted oils and water colours from the first quarter of the 19th century, about 20 in. × 28 in. in size, invariably fetch over £100, exceptionally good 18th-century pieces twice to three times as much. In 1966 two tiny pencil sketches by Antoine Roux, about 5 in. × 7 in., with touches of water colour added, were sold for 520 francs in Paris. A typical price for a 9 in. × 15 in. water colour of a sea battle from about 1820 is 780 francs. For a good ship portrait from the middle of the century one would expect to pay about 700 francs in France, 500 DM in Germany★ and £40 in England – correspondingly more for larger formats. For example, in 1966 a Danish art dealer sold a 32 in. × 40 in. oil painting signed by H. Reimers in 1858 for a little over £100. Even paintings of inferior quality and more recent pieces, from the end of the 19th century, fetch at least £10. Some glass paintings of ships are priced by dealers at 800 guilders and more, but a genuine Van de Velde is worth its £15,000.

Sea chests with ship portraits painted on the lid are relatively scarce and are usually less than 100 years old. If they are well preserved they fetch upwards of £50. In Spain one can occasionally pick up 18th-century sea chests with votive pictures for between 3000 and 5000 pesetas★, but they are not usually in very good condition.

236, 237, 239, 240, 246, 247, 248, 253,
254, 255, 256, 257

The genuine 'maritime' collector is interested in anything connected with navigation. The field comprises more than one might initially suspect and more than can be covered in this book. For example, it extends to coins and medals depicting ships and commemorative coins, among them the magnificent medals of the sea battles led by the Dutch admirals de Ruyter and van Tromp against the English. There are various versions of these and they are valued at between 800 and 2000 guilders. Maritime coins and medals find an increasing number of bidders at coin auctions. Other objects which are in great demand are silver cups and glasses depicting generally nautical scenes, mostly from the 17th to 19th centuries. Many of the tobacco boxes carried by sailors also bear maritime pictures or inscriptions or have ship portraits engraved on them. According to whether they are brass or silver, they fetch between 80 and 300 guilders.

The ships of the various East India Companies in the 17th century brought back exotic goods from India and China, among them the very valuable Ming porcelain. At first the design was Chinese, and the monogram of the Dutch East Indies Company,

Town seal of Stralsund, 1329

★ 19.3 kroner = £ 1 or $ 2.80

11.1 DM = £ 1 or £ 2.80

167 pesetas = £ 1 or $ 2.80

V. O. C., was occasionally added. But soon the dealers and importers took to ordering European patterns, which they had made from engravings and drawings the ships' captains were asked to take with them. This so-called *chine-de-commande* is very rare today and fetches high prices. In the 17th and 18th centuries the Delft potters imitated Chinese porcelain and in many of their faiences depicted nautical scenes, one example being the famous series of plates showing the various stages of a whaling expedition. Similar plates commemorating voyages to the Polar Sea, to India or America appear on the market now and then.

'Rolling-pins' are glass containers, open at one end, in which sailors are reputed to have sent messages ashore–providing the current was such that they ever got there. Most of them came from Bristol in the 19th century and were made of blue glass or a combination of other colours. They are coveted collectors' pieces, not least because of the many inscriptions to be found on them.

Pennants and flags are extremely rare, but from time to time they come to light in old collections and fetch collectors' prices which are entirely unpredictable.

Parts of ships which can hardly be described as objets d'art but which were really purely functional fittings, such as navigation lights and stern lanterns, ships' bells, wheels (which are fairly common but nevertheless fetch upwards of £10), sextants, octants, as well as old tools used by ship's carpenters and sailmakers, find a market among collectors. So do the many types of blocks and tackles, even old rope ladders and Jacob's ladders. The copper grills from a 17th-century yacht cabin – very rare objects with whose function only very few experts are acquainted – were recently sold in Holland for 2000 guilders. Even curious objects like a piece of wood from van Speyck's cannon boat which blew up at Antwerp, or from one of Nelson's warships that was broken up at Portsmouth, find their buyers.

After all this, it is by no means impossible for a collector to walk through a flea market or into a junk shop or breaker's yard in a coastal town and pick up a really fine and valuable piece for a ridiculously low price. This is the kind of good luck every collector dreams about.

Lantern from a Venetian galley, about 1700

Illustrations are referred to in the margin alongside the text. The figure indicates the page number, the small letter the particular illustration on that page. For example, 176e means picture e on page 176. The captions list the nature and nomenclature of the object illustrated, the name of the artist, the time and place of origin and the place where it can be seen, as far as these data are known. If any of them are missing it is because they cannot be ascertained. In order to save space the following abbreviations have been adopted for the museums and private collections:

ÅBO   Finland
Ab   Sjöfartsmuseum vid Åbo Akademi

AMSTERDAM   Netherlands
As   Nederlandsch Historisch Scheepvaart
      Museum
Ar   Rijksmuseum

ANNAPOLIS   Maryland, U.S.A.
An   United States Naval Academy

ANTWERP   Belgium
At   Nationaal Scheepvaart Museum
      (Steen)
Ak   Collection H. van Kuyck
Al   Collection Lilar

APENRADE   Denmark
Ap   Aabenraa Museum

ARENDAL   Norway
Ad   Aust-Agder-Museet

AUCKLAND   New Zealand
Au   Institute and Museum

BARCELONA   Spain
Bc   Museo Maritimo

BEIRUT   Lebanon
Be   Musée de Beyrouth

BERGEN   Norway
Bg   Bergens Sjöfartsmuseum

BERLIN   Germany
Bl   Staatliche Museen

BRAKE   Germany
Bk   Schiffahrtsmuseum der Oldenburgi-
      schen Weserhäfen

BREMEN   Germany
Bf   Fokke-Museum
Bv   Heimatmuseum Vegesack
Bt   Town Hall
Bu   Übersee-Museum

BREMERHAVEN   Germany
Bm   Morgenstern-Museum
Br   Rickmers Werft

BRUSSELS   Belgium
Bb   Collection A. Berqueman

CAIRO   Egypt
Ca   Museum

COPENHAGEN   Denmark
Co   Orlogsmuseet

EMDEN   Germany
Em   Ostfriesisches Landesmuseum

	FLENSBURG Germany
Fb	Städtisches Museum
	GÄVLE Sweden
Ga	Gävle Museum
	GENOA Italy
Gn	Museo Civico Navale
	GOTHENBURG Sweden
Go	Sjöfartsmuseet
	GRONINGEN Netherlands
Gr	Noordelijk Scheepvaartmuseum
	HALMSTAD Sweden
Hs	Hallandsmuseum
	HAMBURG Germany
Ha	Altonaer Museum
Hg	Collection Dr. Klaus Grimm
Hh	Museum für Hamburg. Geschichte
	HEIDE Germany
Hd	Heider Heimatmuseum
	HELSINGÖR Denmark
He	Handels- og Söfartsmuseum paa Kronborg
	HOOGE Germany
Ho	Church
	JEVER Germany
Je	Schloss- und Heimatmuseum
	KARLSKRONA Sweden
Kk	Marinmuseet och Modellkammaren
	LA SPEZIA Italy
Ls	Museo Navale
	LEIDEN Netherlands
Ld	Rijksmuseum voor Volkenkunde
	LIEGE Belgium
Li	Collection A. Nagelmackers
	LONDON Great Britain
Lm	British Museum
Lg	National Maritime Museum, Greenwich
Lk	Science Museum, South Kensington
	LÜBECK Germany
Lb	Haus der Schiffergesellschaft
	MADRID Spain
Mn	Museo Naval
	MARSEILLE France
Ms	Musée de Marine et d'Outre-Mer

	MUNICH Germany
Ma	Antikensammlung
Md	Deutsches Museum
Mc	Galerie Carroll
Mh	Collection Hansen
	MYSTIC Connecticut, U.S.A.
My	Marine Historical Association
	NANTUCKET Massachusetts, U.S.A.
Na	Whaling Museum
	NEW BEDFORD Massachusetts, U.S.A.
Nb	Whaling Museum
	NEW YORK New York, U.S.A.
Ny	Marine Museum of the Seaman's Church Institute
	OSLO Norway
Os	Norsk Sjöfartsmuseum
Ou	Universitetets Oldsaksaming
	PARIS France
Pm	Musée de la Marine
Pl	Musée du Louvre
	ROTTERDAM Netherlands
Rm	Maritiem Museum 'Prins Hendrik'
Rv	Museum voor Land- en Volkenkunde
	SALEM Massachusetts, U.S.A.
Sa	Peabody Museum
	SNEEK Netherlands
Sn	Fries Scheepvaart Museum
	STADE Germany
St	Town archives
	STOCKHOLM Sweden
Sh	Historiska Museum
Ss	Statens Sjöhistoriska Museum, Wasavarvet
	VENICE Italy
Vo	Ca' d'Oro
Vc	Museo Civico Correr
Vn	Museo Storico Navale
Vp	Private collection
	VISBY Sweden
Vi	Gotlands Fornsal
	WASHINGTON, D.C., U.S.A.
Wk	Collection Kennedy
	WYK AUF FÖHR Germany
Wh	Häberlin-Friesen-Museum
Wl	Collection Lüden

Egyptian boat, used in shadow plays.
Perforated leather.

(Numbers refer to page numbers in this book. Where there is more than one note per page they are dealt with on separate lines.)

18 Cf. chapter on 'Art in Early Shipbuilding'.

22 Cf. pp. 82, 85, 93.

93 This information from antique sources has been doubted, perhaps rightly so. But it is safe to assume that these gigantic vessels were not very seaworthy and were probably used for ceremonial occasions and parades only.

105 Cf. chapters on 'Art in Shipbuilding Outside Western Culture' and 'Votive Pictures of Ships'.

106 Cf. chapters on 'Art in Shipbuilding Outside Western Culture' and 'Votive Pictures of Ships'.

108 Cf. p. 85.

131 Cf. pp. 69, 76, 88, 132.
Cf. p. 81 concerning the position and significance of the figure of Isis on Roman ships.
A number of illustrations can be found in Ivon A. Donnelly's book (see Bibliography).

132 Cf. W. Z. Mulder and L. Audemard (see Bibliography).
Cf. C. Nooteboom in *Trois Problèmes d'Ethnologie Maritime* (see Bibliography).

137 Cf. C. Nooteboom, op. cit. concerning the significance of the split stem-post.

150 The descriptions of customs in the Asmat region are based on G. A. Zeegward's book (see Bibliography) and on oral information by A. A. Gerbrands, who spent some time there investigating the position of art and the artist in the community.

151 Cf. chapter on 'The Architecture of the Ship'.

157 Cf. pp. 69, 76, 88, 121.

170 Cf. chapter on 'Glass Paintings of Ships'. Apart from the early portraits of Danish ships mentioned here and on p. 161, there are a number of water colours related to the paintings in Oslo and Stade. They are to be found in the museum in Wyk (a *bootschip* from about 1760; the *Catrina Sclave* from 1783; *De Gude Hoop* from about 1790) and in a private collection on the island of Hooge (*De Vrou Weneletta* from 1769; *Overweege* from 1788 and an unidentified ship from about 1780).

191 Cf. the essay by Jürgen Meyer 'Vis Vincitur Arte' (see Bibliography), who could not, however, establish beyond doubt the origin of the picture in Altona. It has since been discovered that its date, 1776, was marked on the old frame and that it originated in Midlum on the island of Föhr.

203 Cf. Ritz, Brockhaus and Vydra (see Bibliography).
Cf. Keiser (see Bibliography).
Cf. Picard, Pelgen and Vydra (see Bibliography).

204 Cf. chapter on 'Ship Portraiture'.

209 Van Beylen's essay in *Mededelingen* 1958/59, pp. 214–235 (see Bibliography), gives data drawn from these registers for more than 160 glass paintings.

210 Cf. Wessels (see Bibliography).

211 Cf. Henningsen 'Handels- og Söfartsmuseets Glasmalerier' (see Bibliography).

212 Cf. Henningsen, op. cit.
Cf. Henningsen, op. cit.
Cf. Bjerring (see Bibliography).

221 According to Dr. Nissen there are two more 18th-century glass paintings of whaling scenes in the Dithmarsche Landesmuseum in Meldorf.

222 Cf. Keiser and Zinke (see Bibliography).

230 Cf. de Schuyter (see Bibliography).
Cf. van Beylen *Mededelingen* 1958/59, p. 214 (see Bibliography).

241 Their total number today is estimated at 200.

243 Hamburg, Museum für Hamburgische Geschichte.

249 Antwerp, Nationaal Scheepvaart Museum; Stockholm, Statens Sjöhistoriska Museum.
Cf. de Schuyter, p. 108 (see Bibliography).
Collection B. Gilliot, Antwerp.

Bibliography

Aarhus: *Kunstmuseums Samlinger*, catalogue. Aarhus 1963

Anderson, R. C., 'Big ships in history', *Mariners Mirror*, vol. III, 1913

Anderson, R. C., 'Henry VIII's Great Galley', *Mariners Mirror*, vol. VI, 1920

Anderson, R. C., 'The *Prince Royal* and other ships of James I', *Mariners Mirror*, vol. III, 1913

Anderson, Romala and R. C., *The Sailing Ship, Six Thousand Years of History*, London, 1926. New edition, New York, 1947

Andersson, W., 'Galjonsbildhuggaren Johan Törnström', *Tidskrift för konstevetenskap*, 1918

Annapolis: *Catalogue of Paintings*, United States Naval Academy Museum, Annapolis, Maryland, 1961

Antwerp: *Het schip sleutel van de wereld*, exhibition catalogue, Antwerp, 1958

Audemard, L., *Les Jonques chinoises, III, Ornamentation et types*, Publicaties van het Museum voor Land- en Volkenkunde en het Maritiem Museum 'Prins Hendrik', No. 7, Rotterdam, 1960

Barnes, Clare, jr., and Bowen, Croswell, 'The Scrimshaw Collector', *American Heritage*, vol. XV, No. 6 (October). New York, 1964

Bergen: *A Brief Guide*, Bergen Maritime Museum, Bergen, 1962

Bergen: *Foreningen Bergens Sjöfartsmuseum*, Arshefte, Bergen, 1946

Bergen: *Foreningen Bergens Sjöfartsmuseum*, Arshefte, Bergen, 1953

Bergen: *Katalog over samling af skibsbilleder i Bergens skipperforening*, Bergen, 1899

Beylen, Jules van, 'Vlaamse maritieme achterglas schilderijen', *Mededelingen van de Marine Academie*, Antwerp, 1958/59

Beylen, Jules van, 'De uitbeelding en dokumentaire waarde van schepen bij enkele oude meesters', *Bulletin van de Koninklijke Musea voor Schoone Kunsten*, Brussels, 1961

Beylen, Jules van, 'Schepen op kaarten ten tijde van Gerard Mercator', *Duisburger Forschungen*, vol. 6, Duisburg, 1962

Beylen, Jules van, 'De Versiering van Jachten, Binnenschepen en Vissersvaartuigen in de Nederlanden', *Neerlands Volksleven*, Summer 1963, The Hague, 1963

Bibby, Geoffrey, *The Testimony of the Spade*, New York, 1957

Bjerring, K. B., 'Glasmalningen av fregatten Charlotta, en raritet i Hallands Museum', *Ur Halland*, Halmstad, 1965

Boreux, Charles, *Etudes de Nautique égyptienne*, Cairo, 1925

Bremische Biographie des 19. Jahrhunderts, Bremen, 1912

Brewington, M. V., *Shipcarvers of North America*, Barre, Massachusetts, 1962

Brion, K. B., *Pierre Puget*, 1930

Brockhaus, Der Grosse (encyclopaedia), vol. V, Wiesbaden, 1954

Brönsted, Johannes, *Die grosse Zeit der Wikinger*, Neumünster, 1965

Bruggen, B. E. van, 'De Ontwikkeling van het Galjoen', *Jaarverslag Nederlandsch Historisch Scheepvaart Museum*, Amsterdam, 1946–47

Buch, Ada, 'Noen skutebilder fra Vestfold og litt om dem som malte dem', *Vestfoldminne*, 1940

Busley, Carl, *Die Entwicklung des Segelschiffes, dargestellt an 16 Modellen im Deutschen Museum in München*, Berlin, 1920

Callender, G., *The Portrait of Peter Pett and the Sovereign of the Seas*, Newport, 1930

Canby, Courtlandt, *A History of Ships and Seafaring*, New York, 1963

Cannenburg, W. Voorbeitel, *Catalogus der Scheepsmodellen en scheepsbouwkundigen Teekeningen 1600 bis 1900 in het Nederlandsche Historisch Scheepvaart Museum*, Amsterdam, 1928

Carr, Frank G. G., *Maritime Greenwich*, London, 1964

Cederlöf, Olle, 'Johan Törnströms galjonsbilder', *Aktuellt frän Föreningen Marinmuseets Vänner i Karlskrona*, Karlskrona, 1965

Cederlung, C. O. and others, *Das Kriegsschiff Wasa*, Stockholm, 1965

Dragon's head from the Viking era, from Birka (Sweden).

Chapelle, Howard J., *The National Watercraft Collection*, Washington, 1960

Chapman, F. H., *Architectura Navalis Mercatoria*, Stockholm, 1768

Charnock, J., *A History of Marine Architecture*, vols. I and II, 1800 to 1802

Chatterton, E. K., *Ship Models*, London, 1923

Clowes, G. S. L., *Sailing Ships* I, London, 1930

Crone, G. C. E., 'The model of the Hollandia of 1664 to 1683', *Mariners Mirror*, vol. IV, 1914

Crone, G. C. E., *Nederlandsche Jachten, Binnenschepen, Visschersvaartuigen*, Amsterdam, 1926

Crone, G. C. E., 'Scheepskunst', *Prisma der Kunsten*, vol. II, No. 6, Zeist, 1937

Donnelly, Ivon A., *Chinese Junks and Other Native Craft*, Shanghai, 1924

Durant, John and Alice, *Pictorial History of American Ships*, New York, 1953

Engelhardt, C., *Nydam Mosefund*, Copenhagen, 1865

Enkhuizen: Exhibition catalogue, *Scheeps-Sier*, Zuiderzeemuseum, Enkhuizen, 1962

Etchinson, Bruce, *Scrimshaw*, Newport News, Virginia, no date

Farrière, C., *Navires*, Paris, 1936

Farrière, C., *Histoire de la Marine française*, Paris, 1956

Franzen, A., *Das Kriegsschiff Wasa*, Stockholm, 1966

Franzen, A., *Galionsfiguren*, Altonaer Museum, special exhibition, Hamburg, 1961

Gerbrands, A. A., *Kunst als Cultuurelement, in het bijzonder in Neger-Afrika*, Leiden, 1956. English translation 'Art as an element of culture, especially in Negro-Africa', *Mededelingen van het Rijksmuseum voor Volkenkunde*, vol. 12, Leiden, 1957

Gerbrands, A. A., *Wow Ipitsj, Eight Woodcarvers in Ammannamgai*, The Hague, 1966

Gothenburg: *The Maritime Museum and Aquarium at Gothenburg*, catalogue, Gothenburg, 1959

Groenen, L., *Illustrated Marine Encyclopaedia*, 1947

Hagedorn, Bernhard, *Die Entwicklung der wichtigsten Schiffstypen bis ins 19. Jahrhundert*, Berlin, 1914

Hagen, Anders, *Die Wikingerschiffsfunde*, Oslo, 1965

Halldin, Gustaf, 'Galjonsbilder och ornament pa svenska örlogsskepp', *Samleren*, 1936

Halldin, Gustaf (ed.), and others, *Svenskt Skeppsbyggeri, En Oversikt av Utveckling genom tiderna*, Malmö, 1963

Harrison Huster, H., 'Scrimshaw: one part whalebone, two parts nostalgia', *Antiques*, New York, 1961

Heinsius, P., *Das Schiff der hansischen Frühzeit*, Weimar, 1956

Henningsen, Henning, 'Schiffsmodelle in Kirchen in Nord- und Südschleswig', *Nordelbingen, Beiträge zur Kunst und Kunstgeschichte*, vol. 33, Heide, 1964

Henningsen, Henning, 'Handels- og Söfartsmuseets Glasmalerier', *Handels- og Söfartsmuseets Arbog*, Helsingör, 1963

Holck, P., *Den Historiske Modelsamling paa Holmen*, Copenhagen, 1939

Holmes, G.C.V., *Ancient and Modern Ships*, vols. I and II, London, 1916

Holm-Petersen, F., 'Skutebilledmaleren Frederik Martin Sörvig', *Bergens Sjöfartsmuseum, Arshefte*, Bergen, 1953

Hornell, James, 'Survivals of the use of oculi in modern boats', *Journal of Royal Anthropological Institute*, vol. LIII, London, 1923

Hornell, James, 'Boat oculi survivals', *Journal of Royal Anthropological Institute*, vol. LXVIII, London, 1938

Hornell, James, *Water Transport: origins and early evolution*, Cambridge, 1946

Hose, C., and MacDougall, W., *The Pagan Tribes of Borneo*, vol. II, London, 1912

Höver, Otto, *Deutsche Seegeschichte*, Potsdam, no date

Höver, Otto, *Von der Galion zum Fünfmaster*, Bremen, 1934

Huddleston: *Catalogue of the Henry Huddleston Rogers Collection of Ship Models*, Annapolis, Maryland, 1954

Johnsrud, Even Hebbe, 'Aust-Agder og kunsten (II), 3. Antwerpen-dynastiet Weyts og 1800-arenes skipsportrett', *Aust-Agder arv 1961–1962*

Josselin de Jong, J. P. B. de, *De Malaische Archipel als ethnologisch studieveld*, Leiden, 1935

Keiser, Herbert Wolfgang, *Die deutsche Hinterglasmalerei*, Munich, 1937

Kerkmeijer, J. C., *Catalogus der Teekeningen en Reproducties van Teekeningen in het West-Friesch Museum te Hoorn*, Hoorn, 1927

Kerkmeijer, J. C., *Catalogus der Schilderijen in het West-Friesch Museum en in het Stadhus te Hoorn*, Hoorn, 1942

Knaipp, Friedrich, 'Hinterglasbilder des 18. und 19. Jahrhunderts', *Österreichischer Volkskundeatlas*, Linz, 1959

Köster, August, *Das antike Seewesen*, Berlin, 1923

Köster, August, *Modelle alter Segelschiffe*, Berlin, 1925

Köster, August, 'Schmuck und Zier des Schiffes', *Meereskunde*, vol. XVI, 10, No. 186, Berlin, 1928

Kronborg: *Handels- og Söfartsmuseet paa Kronborg*, yearbook, Helsingör, 1964

Landström, Björn, *Skeppet*, Stockholm, 1961

Laughton, L.G.C., *Old Ship Figureheads and Sterns*, London, 1925

Lehmann, Otto, *Reederei und Schiffbau in Schleswig-Holstein, Führer durch das Altonaer Museum*, Altona, 1920

Lindquist, S., *Gotlands Bildsteine*, Stockholm, 1941

Malinowski, Bronislaw, *The Argonauts of the Western Pacific: an account of native enterprise and adventure in the archipelagoes of Melanesian New Guinea*, London, 1922

Martinez-Hidalgo y Terán, José Maria, *Catálogo General del Museo Maritimo*, Barcelona, 1965

Meissonnier, Jean, *L'Age d'Or de la Voile*, Paris, 1963

Melegari, Vezio, *Pirati Corsari e Filibustieri*, Milan, 1964

Melville, Herman, *Moby Dick*, London, 1907

Meyer, Jürgen, 'Vis Vincitur Arte. Eine Darstellung des Walfanges aus dem 18. Jahrhundert', *Altonaer Museum in Hamburg, Jahrbuch 1965*, vol. III, Hamburg, 1965

Meyer, Jürgen, 'Die Restaurierung eines russischen Schiffsmodells des 18. Jahrhunderts aus dem Eutiner Schloss im Altonaer Museum', *Altonaer Museum in Hamburg, Jahrbuch 1965*, vol. III, Hamburg, 1965

Moll, F., *Das Schiff in der bildenden Kunst*, Bonn, 1929

Mulder, W. Z., 'Het Chineesche drakenbootfeest', *Cultureel Indie*, vol. VI, Amsterdam, 1944

Munthe af Morgenstierne, Bredo von, *Dansk Sejlskibe*, Copenhagen, 1947

Munthe af Morgenstierne, Bredo von, *Orlogsmuseet Vejledning*, Copenhagen, 1964

Nance, R. Morton, *Sailing Ship Models*, London, 1949

Newport News: *The Mariner's Museum, A History and Guide*, Newport News, Virginia, 1960

Nieuwenkamp, W. O. J., 'Iets over vaartuigen in onze Oost', *Nederlandsch-Indië Oud en Nieuw*, vol. II, The Hague, 1917; 'Vaartuigen in Tropisch Nederland', *op. cit.*, vol. XI, The Hague, 1926

Nooteboom, C., *De boomstamkano in Indonesië*, Leiden, 1932

Nooteboom, C., 'Trois problèmes d'ethnologie maritime, 1. L'origine des proues bifides, 2. La signification de la proue bifide', *Publicaties van het Museum voor Land- en Volkenkunde en het Maritiem Museum 'Prins Hendrik'*, vol. I, Rotterdam, 1952

Oderwald, J., 'Scheepsfolklore in de Scheepsversiering', *Buiten*, vol. 28, Nos. 34–36, Amsterdam, 1934

Oesau, Wanda, *Die deutsche Südseefischerei auf Wale im 19. Jahrhundert*, Glückstadt, 1939

Oesau, Wanda, *Schleswig-Holsteins Grönlandfahrt auf Walfischfang und Robbenschlag*, Glückstadt, 1937

Oesau, Wanda, *Hamburgs Grönlandfahrt auf Walfischfang und Robbenschlag vom 17. bis 19. Jahrhundert*, Glückstadt, 1955

Oslo: Norsk Sjöfartsmuseum, *Skuter og kunst*, catalogue of the exhibition in the Oslo Kunstforening 2/31 May 1959, Oslo, 1959

Owen, D., 'Figureheads', *Mariners Mirror*, vol. III, 1913

Paris: *Trois Millénaires d'Art et de Marine*, catalogue of exhibition, Paris, 1965

Pâris, Edmond, *Souvenirs de Marine conservés*, Paris, 1878–1886

Pelgen, Jean, *Expressionistische Bauernmalerei*, Luxemburg, 1937

Pettersen, Lauritz, jr., 'Maleren og litografen Johan Ludvig Losting', *Bergens Sjöfartsmuseum, Arshefte*, Bergen, 1954

Picard, Max, *Expressionistische Bauernmalerei*, Munich, 1918

Ralamb, Ake Classon, *Skeps Byggeri eller adelig Öfnings*, Stockholm, 1691, re-printed 1943

Rassers, W. H., 'On the Javanese kris', *Bijdragen tot de Taal-, Land- en Volkenkunde*, vol. 99, 1940. Revised reprint: 'Panji, the culture hero, a structural study of religion in Java', *Koninklijk Instituut voor de Taal-, Land- en Volkenkunde, Translation Series*, vol. 3, The Hague, 1959

Richardson, A. E., 'Naval architecture and decoration of the past', *The Architectural Review* XL, London, 1916

Ripley Nelson, W., *The Nantucket Whaling Museum*, Nantucket Historical Association, Nantucket, Massachusetts, 1964

Ritz, Joseph Maria, *Bauernmalerei*, Leipzig, 1935

Robinson, G., 'The Great Harry', *Mariners Mirror*, vol. XX, 1934

Roërie, G., and Vivielle, J., *Navires et marines* I–II, Paris and Brussels, 1930

Roncière, Ch. de la, and Clerc-Rampal, G., *Histoire de la Marine française*, Paris, 1934

Rudloff, D., 'Eine Sammlung russischer Schiffsmodelle des 18. Jahrhunderts im Eutiner Schloss', *Schleswig-Holstein, Monatshefte für Heimat und Volkstum*, Jahrgang 12, 1960

Sass, Johannes, *Von der Schaluppe zum Klipper*, Hamburg, 1963

Schaerer, Hans, *Die Gottesidee der Ngadju-Dajak in Süd-Ost Borneo*, Leiden, 1946

Schjelderup, W. M., *Katalog over Bergens skipperforenings samling av skibs- og personbilleder*, Bergen, 1917

Schlechtriem, Gert, *Schiffahrtssammlung des Morgenstern-Museums*, Bremerhaven, 1966

Schuyter, Jan de, 'Een en ander over volkseglomisés', *Antwerpen's Oudheidkundige Kring*, Jaarboek XVI, Antwerp, 1940

Shapiro, Irwin, *The Story of Yankee Whaling*, New York, 1959

Siebs, Benno Eide, *Ein Buch von Schiffbau und Schiffahrt*, Bremerhaven, 1959

Smejens, F., and van Beylen, Jules, *The National Maritime Museum*, Antwerp, 1958

Soop, Hans, 'Regalskeppet Wasas Riksvapen', *Sjöhistorisk arsbok 1963–1964*, Stockholm, 1965

Soop, Hans, *Svenska Flottans historia* I 1, 2– II 1, 2, Malmö, 1945

Soop, Hans, *Svenskt skeppsbyggeri*, edited by G. Halldin, Malmö, 1963

Steilen, Diedrich, *Geschichte der Bremischen Hafenstadt Vegesack*, Vegesack, 1926

Steinmann, Alfred, 'Les "tissus à jonques" du Sud de Sumatra', *Revue des Arts Asiatiques*, vol. XI, Paris, 1937

Stevens, J. R., *Old Time Ships*, Toronto, 1949

Szymanski, H., *Die deutschen Segelschiffe*, no date

Thieme-Becker, *Allgemeines Lexikon der bildenden Künstler*, Leipzig, 1915 ff.

Timmermann, Gerhard, 'Die Rekonstruktion einer Heringsbuise', *Hansa*, 1955

Timmermann, Gerhard, 'Vom Einbaum zum Wikingerschiff', *Schiff und Hafen*, 1956

Timmermann, Gerhard, *Das Schiffbauhandwerk*, Führer durch die Schiffbauabteilung des Altonaer Museums, Hamburg, 1964

Timmermann, Gerhard, *Chronik der Seefahrt*, a calendar, Hamburg, 1966

Topham, J., 'A Description of an ancient Picture in Windsor Castle, representing the Embarkation of King Henry VIII at Dover, May 31, 1520', *Archaeologia*, VI, 1783

Tuastad, N. H., 'Skutemaleren Halvor Mikkelsen', *Arbok for Karmsund*, 1956–1960

Ucelli, G., *Le Nave di Nemi*, Rome, 1950

Uhde, Wilhelm, *Fünf primitive Meister*, Zurich, 1947

Urbanowisz, Witold, J., *Architectura Okretow*, Danzig, 1960

Vandier, Jacques, *Manuel d'Archéologie égyptienne*, V. Bas-Reliefs et Peintures, Paris, 1967

Varende, J. de la, *La Navigation sentimentale*, Paris, 1952

Vaughan, H. S., 'Figure-heads and beak-heads of the ships of Henry VIII', *Marniers Mirror*, vol. IV, 1914

Vocino, Michele, *La Nave nel Tempo*

Vogel, J. Ph., 'De makara in de Voor-Indische beeld-houwkunst', *Nederlandsch-Indië Oud en Nieuw*, vol. VIII, The Hague, 1923

Vogel, J. Ph., 'Le Makara dans la sculpture de l'Inde', *Revue des Arts Asiatiques*, vol. III, 1930

Voigt, Chr., *Das schöne Schiff der Barockzeit*, (special edition)

Vroklage, B. A. G., 'Das Schiff in den Megalith-Kulturen Südost-Asiens und der Südsee', *Anthropos*, vol. XXXI, St.-Gabriel-Mödling nr. Vienna, 1936

Vydra, Jozef, *Die Hinterglasmalerei*, Prague, 1957

Warner, Oliver, *Sailing Ships*, London, 1957

Warner, Oliver, *Grosse Seeschlachten*, Oldenburg and Hamburg, 1965

Wessels, Ernst, *Die Hinterglasmalerei, Anleitung zur Herstellung*, Esslingen, 1913

Weightman, Alfred Edwin, *Heraldry in the Royal Navy*, Aldershot, 1957

Winslow, Helen L., 'The folk art of the American whaleman', *Historic Nantucket*, July 1954, Nantucket, Massachusetts, 1954

Winter, Heinrich, *Die Katalanische Nao von 1450*, Berlin, 1956

Witsen, Nicolaes, *Aeloude en hededaegschen Scheepsbouw en Bestier*, Amsterdam 1671

Zeegward, Gerard A., 'Headhunting practices of the Asmat of Netherlands New Guinea', *American Anthropologist*, vol. 61, Menasha, Wisconsin, 1959

Zinke, A., 'Langenauer Glasbildmalerei', *Mitteilungen des Nordböhmischen Excursionsclub*, Leipa, 1884

Index